THE RIVER READER

THE RIVER READER

The
Nature
Conservancy®

Edited by John A. Murray

THE LYONS PRESS

for my son

Compilation copyright © 1998 by John Murray
Printed in the United States of America

Design by Sans Serif, Inc.
10 9 8 7 6 5 4 3 2

Library of Congress Cataloging-in-Publication Data

The river reader / edited by John Murray.
    p. cm.
    Includes bibliographical refrences.
    ISBN 1-55821-699-5 (cloth). — ISBN 1-55821-772-X (pbk.)
    1. Rivers. I. Murray, John A., 1954– .
  GB1203.2.R58 1998
  551.48′3—dc21   98-26020
                                        CIP

Oh, Shenandoah's my native valley,
Away, you rolling river!
Oh, Shenandoah's my native valley,
Away, we're bound to go,
'Cross the wide Missouri!

Oh, Shenandoah, it's far I wander,
Away, you rolling river!
Oh, Shenandoah, it's far I wander,
Away, we're bound to go,
'Cross the wide Missouri!

Oh, Shenandoah has rushing waters,
Away, you rolling river!
Oh, Shenandoah has rushing waters,
Away, we're bound to go,
'Cross the wide Missouri!

Oh, Shenandoah, I love your daughters,
Away, you rolling river!
Oh, Shenandoah, I love your daughters,
Away, we're bound to go,
'Cross the wide Missouri!

Oh, Shenandoah, I long to see you,
Away, you rolling river!
Oh, Shenandoah, I long to see you,
Away, we're bound to go,
'Cross the wide Missouri!

Oh, Shenandoah, I'm bound to leave you,
Away, you rolling river!
Oh, Shenandoah, I'm bound to leave you,
Away, we're bound to go,
'Cross the wide Missouri!

Oh, Shenandoah, I'll never grieve you,
Away, you rolling river!
Oh, Shenandoah, I'll never grieve you,
Away, we're bound to go,
'Cross the wide Missouri!

—"Shenandoah," Anonymous

CONTENTS

Contents

Contents

OREWORD

Rivers run like an insistent current through the history of literature, symbolic of the passage of time, the fluid nature of human experience, and the constancy of the natural world. This book, which contains two hundred years' worth of appreciations of rivers, taps deeply into that current. Indeed, for those of us enamored with rivers, from the mighty untamed Colorado of John Wesley Powell to the depths of Conrad's Congo, the selections in this seductive anthology have the power to transport us from our workaday worlds to a float trip down the streams of imagination and memory.

From my perspective, this collection serves also as a reminder of the work of The Nature Conservancy, attesting to the fact that we have not always been good about protecting our rivers. We have learned the hard lessons of rivers dammed, ecosystems degraded, and species rendered extinct. We once thought of rivers as a limitless resource, placed on Earth solely for our use. Now we do not. Through the efforts of conservationists, writers such as these, and politicians and citizens who have cared about the creek flowing through their commons, we have come to regard our flowing waters as more than commodities. We have come to see them as rivers of life.

The Nature Conservancy is joining the cause for rivers. For nearly fifty years, the Conservancy has focused its conservation work on land—on terrestrial ecosystems and species. We have had great success with this strategy, and we now own and manage the world's largest system of private nature preserves. As we have gone about our business, however, our thinking and methods have evolved, and we have recognized an ecological self-evident truth: the elemental connection between land and water. One cannot preserve both the terrestrial and aquatic life of a place without protecting the waters that run through it. Human activities upstream, miles away, even states away, affect the life of a place.

The evidence bears this out. Freshwater biodiversity is currently in serious jeopardy. Freshwater plants and animals are proportionately more imperiled than their terrestrial counterparts, with two-thirds of freshwater mussels, half of crayfish, and one-third of fishes and amphibians in dire straits. In most states, more than eighty percent of riparian ecosystems have been lost, and in this century alone, more than half of our nation's wetlands have disappeared. We have a big crisis on our hands, and it calls for a big solution.

Our part of the solution is The Freshwater Initiative, a conservation effort that targets dozens of rivers and freshwater systems rich in biodiversity and under imminent threat throughout the United States and Latin America. As always, our approach is based on good science. We are gathering and disseminating the best information we can on freshwater biological inventory. We literally have hundreds of scientists up to their shins in waters surveying the plants and animals of our aquatic systems. We need to know what is there, what should be and is not, and what is and should not be.

Take the example of the Arizona razorback sucker. A dweller of the Colorado River system, living up to sixty years, the razorback is federally listed as endangered. Decades of damming, degraded water quality, and the introduction of non-native fishes in the West has routed the razorback and others like it from their historic homes. The Arizona razorback sucker could very well join the ranks of the extinct in our lifetimes—and it is not alone. This scenario is being played out across the United States and Latin America.

The Freshwater Initiative's protection strategies include working with private and public landowners within river watersheds to reduce runoff from agriculture and cities and return more natural flow conditions to some rivers. This kind of conservation takes a collective effort and it works best at a community level. Already, we have a number of such projects underway throughout the country in which major landowners like timber companies, federal agencies, local land trusts, and conservation groups such as ours, are pulling together to figure out ways to protect a river's watershed, which can encompass thousands of square miles. It is a long-term, complex task, but a necessary one. The Conservancy has a long tradition of such large-scale conservation efforts and I'm confident we will have success here as well.

As these essays suggest, it is not enough to love rivers or lament their loss. We must also act. I hope that this collection spurs some of you to act, to become involved in any number of ways to safeguard our rivers and freshwater systems. For some of us, this is a natural thing to do. River water is in our blood.

My wife and I have canoed for years. Rivers are an intimate part of our family history, and many happy memories—with more to come—stem from our river excursions. If you are like me, in that moment when you ease the canoe from the bank into the current, you sense you are a part of something very old and very precious. It is a moment that should be guarded jealously and handed down with care.

Who knows? In another two hundred years, perhaps some enterprising anthologist will be able to collect a new *River Reader*, one that testifies to the prudence and forethought of the dedicated people who took direct action at the end of the twentieth century to conserve the running waters of the planet. I can think of no more fitting legacy to leave future generations.

John C. Sawhill
President and Chief Executive Officer
The Nature Conservancy

PREFACE

To live by a large river is to be kept in the heart of things.
—John Haines, "Moments and Journeys"

With this series the Lyons Press inaugurates a new series of nature anthologies, dedicated to bringing readers the finest nature writing from the past and present. Each book will be devoted to a single environmental subject and will alternate classic selections with contemporary writings, creating a natural rhythm that we hope will add to your reading pleasure. In this first volume we celebrate writings about rivers. Future volumes will explore writings about national parks, mountains, forests, endangered species, wetlands, lakes, coasts, deserts, grasslands, urban nature, and oceans.

As always, I am committed to featuring the work of undiscovered and emerging writers as well as the work of well-established and mature authors. If you have or know of writings on any of the above subjects, please send them to me in care of: The Lyons Press, 31 West 21 Street, New York, New York 10010. I am particularly interested in writing from the following groups: (1) writers known only locally or regionally but with potential for national acclaim, (2) writers from the Midwest, Northeast, and Deep South, and (3) women writers and writers from ethnic groups offering alternative perspectives on nature. I promise to respond to each submission. Working together—readers and editor—we can build anthologies in the future that will hold both literary excellence and thematic and stylistic diversity as the standard.

We are especially pleased to have this new series so closely associated with The Nature Conservancy, an organization that has long been dedicated to preserving critical habitat, both in the United States and abroad. In 1992 I donated the royalties of *The Great Bear* to The Nature Conservancy's Pine Butte Grizzly Bear Preserve near Choteau, Montana. Two years later, while traveling by road from Alaska to the Lower 48, I had the opportunity to visit the eighteen-thousand-acre preserve and view firsthand the extraordinarily good work The Nature Conservancy is doing for conservation. I was thoroughly impressed both by the preserve managers—Dave Carr and Dave Hanna—and the preserve itself (prehistoric bison jumps and tepee rings, a flourishing prairie wetland, the stark beauty of the Rocky Mountain Front). I would encourage each person who reads this book to join The Nature Conservancy and also to consider making direct donations toward the purchase of land for conservation purposes. It is rare in life that we can see so directly the positive (and permanent) effects of our efforts to make the world a better place as in supporting The Nature Conservancy.

I have many thanks to give. First, the writers and their publishers have been extremely cooperative in securing permissions and I thank them all; no anthology is possible without such quick and enthusiastic assistance. My editor, Lilly Golden, has been wonderfully helpful; all authors should be blessed with such warm, energetic, and perspicacious guidance. I must, too, thank my readers. Over the five years in which I edited the Sierra Club nature writing annuals, you constantly brightened my days with postcards, letters, and phone calls. Some of these contacts resulted in friendly visits which, each time, reminded me that it is for my readers that I work. Finally, I must give thanks to the Murray family for their love and support, and especially my eight-year-old son Naoki, for whom everything I do is in some way related.

—J.A.M.
Denver, Colorado

Introduction

You oughta been on this old river, well well well, 19 and-a 5
You couldn't hardly find a man alive, a man alive,
You oughta been on this old river, well well well, 19 and-a 5
You couldn't hardly find a man alive, a man alive.
—from "Ol' Hannah," traditional blues song of the
Mississippi Delta

i

*R*ivers. There are rivers on Earth and rivers in outer space, rivers of the mind and rivers of the spirit. There are rivers of lava and rivers of mud and rivers of ice. Atmospheric physicists tell us of rivers of air that continually flow around the planet, and oceanographers have long charted ocean-borne rivers such as the Gulf Stream and Japan Current. There are rivers of social and political change and rivers of people moving through the channels and backwaters of history. The first cities grew up along rivers: the Yellow, Indus, Euphrates, Jordan, and Nile. Ulysses crawled up a river from the sea and found the kindness of Nausikaa. Caesar stood on the banks of the Rubicon and declared, "If we cross this river, the die is cast." Ulysses S. Grant nearly lost his command at Shiloh when the rebels unexpectedly crossed the Tennessee River and overran his position. Marilyn Monroe rafted down a river with Robert Mitchum in *River of No Return*. Ernest Hemingway's first great short story, written in Paris one autumn when he was homesick for Michigan, was "The Big Two-Hearted River." When I think of my life I think of it as a river, with the headwaters in childhood and the culmination in that distant sea the poets call eternity. All around the world there are beautiful rivers that I will never see, but that I have come to know through the writings of those who have lived beside them and loved them.

This is a book about such rivers.

1

A home river is that rarest of friends, the one who frequently surprises you with new elements of personality without ever seeming a stranger.
—Paul Schullery, "Home River"

The selections in *The River Reader* range over three continents and two hundred years. They include essays by a frontier artist (John James Audubon), a former American President (Theodore Roosevelt), a college philosophy professor (Kathleen Dean Moore), a Canadian judge (Roderick Haig-Brown), and everything in between. The selections vary widely in length, from a handful of pages to several dozen pages each, reminding us that their sources of inspiration can, like rivers, either run short and swift (Alaska's Kenai River is less than sixty miles long) or take the slow and meandering scenic route (the four-thousand-mile-long Amazon). The styles represented in this book are as diverse as their authors, as diverse, to extend the metaphor, as the habitats found along the rivers of which they write. Hemingway adopted a laconic style reminiscent of traditional Japanese prose, from which it came (transported to him via such unlikely intermediaries as Ambrose Bierce, Stephen Crane, and Jack London). Mark Twain writes in the full-blown Victorian style, with sentences as long as paragraphs and digressions that eventually become chapters. Most of the others fall somewhere between these two literary extremes. No matter length, style, or point of view, all these essays celebrate their authors' passion for rivers. For each, though in delightfully different ways, rivers awaken wonder, inspire the imagination, and powerfully evoke the larger cycles and journey of life.

Three of the selections in *The River Reader* relate to the Colorado River. For many, myself included, the Colorado is the greatest river in the American West, the river that most evokes the spectacular range of natural landscapes and extensive tracts of public domain that characterize the region and so distinguish it from the lands to the east. Born high in the peaks of Rocky Mountain National Park, the Colorado (Spanish for "red") proceeds west through the red-rock country of the Colorado Plateau and then turns south to follow the western border of Arizona before finally emptying into the Gulf of California. It is a river with a human history that extends back at least ten or twelve thousand years, and each spring the gigantic fossils exposed by the passing snowmelt remind us of even more antique times.

John Wesley Powell was the first person, so far as we know, to successfully descend the Colorado River through the Grand Canyon. On May 10, 1869, two weeks after completion of the transcontinental railroad, Powell (who had lost an arm in the Civil War) and his entourage stepped from a Union Pacific railcar at Green River, Wyoming. There were no dams then, no reservoirs, no bridges, and no satellite photographs showing tributaries and drainage basins. Many places were quite literally blank spaces on the map. Powell's dream was to descend the Green River by boat to its confluence with the Colorado River, then follow the Colorado River through the heart of the Colorado Plateau: a total distance of some one thousand miles.

Despite grave warnings from trappers and Indians, Powell succeeded in brilliant fashion, and returned for further trips in 1870 and 1871. His 1874 book *Exploration of the Colorado River and Its Canyons*, written primarily to garner congressional support for scientific exploration in the West, is now considered a classic of exploration literature. The river book is everywhere filled with Powell's intense love for nature, which formed at least partially as a result of his Civil War experiences:

> When he who has been chained by wounds to a hospital cot until his canvas tent seems like a dungeon cell, until the groans of those who lie about tortured with probe and knife are piled up, a weight of horror on his ears that he cannot throw off, cannot forget, and until the stench of festering wounds and anesthetic drugs has filled the air with its loathsome burden,—when he at last goes out into the open field, what a world he sees! How beautiful the sky, how bright the sunshine, what "floods of delirious music" pour from the throats of birds, how sweet the fragrance of earth and tree and blossom!

Speaking of music, the group of river rafters that accompanied naturalist Barry Lopez on a trip down the Colorado River through the Grand Canyon were concerned with just that. Many members of the group carried their own instruments, and in quiet alcoves and side canyons they sought to transform the natural harmony of silence into the beautiful sounds of melody and rhythm. One can hardly imagine a more wonderful way to spend a month! Ann Zwinger, author of *Downcanyon*, an acclaimed book on the Grand Canyon, writes of the Tanner Trail in her selection. Although it carries an Anglo-Saxon name, the trail is as old as the wild animals who first made it and the

Indians to whom it was as familiar as it is to modern-day hikers. The trail begins near Lipan Point on the south rim and proceeds north and downslope through the accumulated layers of time, finally ending on a sandbar near the river, approximately one billion years away, by geological layer, from the sediments on the canyon rim.

The major river of the northern plains, called the Big Blue by early trappers, is the Missouri. At the dawn of the nineteenth century it was a veritable highway into the vast wilderness of the northern plains as American explorers followed the lead of the pioneering French *couer du bois*. The narrative of Meriwether Lewis, from the historic 1804-1806 expedition commissioned by President Jefferson, shows us the river as it was in the beginning—about as wild a country as you could imagine. Forty years later, after the brief Age of Trappers had waned and George Caitlin had come and gone, John James Audubon made a similar trek up the river. By then the Mandan Indians were extinct, the Oregon Trail was bringing homesteaders into the West, and everything had begun to change forever. The selection by Dean Krakel, a contemporary writer and photographer, shows us how dramatically the region has been altered in the years since, as Krakel floats down the Yellowstone River from its source above Bridger Lake to its confluence with the Missouri.

In *The Book of Yaak*, Rick Bass devotes an entire collection of essays to the remote Montana river valley in which he lives. The book is a prolonged meditation on place, but, more than that, it offers a graphic example of the World Wildlife Fund motto, "think globally and act locally." Bass, to his continual credit, has taken it upon himself to be the guardian spirit, the resident bard, and the tireless defender of the Yaak River and the lands through which it flows. It is a tough battle—fighting for wilderness designation in a traditionally conservative western state—but he keeps trying, remembering that in politics a small vocal minority is always more powerful than a large complacent majority. In every generation there have been those like Bass (one thinks of John Muir, Margaret and Olaus Murie, Edwin Abbey) who carried on the battle, protecting the last wild places from those who would destroy them out of greed and ignorance. The Yaak River, and the valley it supports, is the center of the world to Rick Bass, as home—wherever home is—should be to each of us.

The Klamath River in northern California inspired Idaho naturalist Louise Wagenknecht, who writes intimately of the river she came to know well during her childhood, growing up along its banks.

For Wagenknecht the Klamath Country is both a green region on a state map and a wild province of the imagination:

> I was born into the generation for whom the roads were built, the rivers dammed, the old growth cut, entire races of salmon destroyed, and ten thousand years of wealth consumed in a moment of time. Yet, in a handful of years, we will be gone, too. A few hundred more, and Iron Gate and Copco will fill with silt; and the Klamath will find its own way around or over or under, and flow on, untroubled. In a million years, when our species is dust, it will still meet the ocean, somewhere off what was once the coast of California.

Alaska is, for many, synonymous with the wildest of North American rivers. Here are rivers that flow for hundreds of miles without so much as a village along their banks (virtually any river on the North Slope) and rivers that drain glaciers the size of Rhode Island (Malsapina Glacier). Here are rivers in which sixty or seventy brown bears can be seen at one time feasting on thousands of salmon, and here are runs of salmon as plentiful as those that once filled the rivers of California, Oregon, and several of the Northeastern states. Alaska is the only state I know of where a person can actually become physically tired of catching trophy-sized fish (after a day on the Kenai River once, with several dozen thirty-pound salmon caught and released, I actually could not lift my right arm). From the fabled Forty-Ninth State we have two essays. The first, by John Hildebrand, is the concluding chapter of *Reading the River,* which records his epic journey in a small boat down the entire length of the Yukon River. It is sobering to consider that the Yukon came perilously close to being dammed in the 1960s—the infamous Rampart Dam would have flooded the Yukon Flats northeast of Fairbanks—thank God that did not happen. Because there are a few things more fatuous than a writer commenting on his or her own writing, I will only mention that the other Alaskan essay concerns the Kenai River south of Anchorage, which is the most lovely river in the world.

In many ways I know the rivers of the East better than those of the West. I spent the first seventeen years of my life growing up in a small town along the Ohio River. In the summers my friends and I would bicycle to our secret camp, which was perched on a limestone outcrop above the river, and among other things we would watch the barge traffic (firing bottle rockets, bazooka-like, at them from the tree branches). Occasionally we would spot the last of the old riverboats en route from Cincinnati to New Orleans. This was the *Delta Queen*, on which my father and uncle had worked (I guess you would call it working) as bartenders during their college days. The river was a big part of our family history. Until his dying day at the age of ninety-two, my grandfather spoke profanely of the 1937 flood that nearly swept the town of Manchester, Ohio, off the map and rather abruptly brought the Murray clan from the country to the city. Later, perhaps because of the trauma of that flood, my father became a civil engineer and devoted his life to managing rivers and eventually, once the EPA was formed, to protecting their waters from industrial civilization.

In this volume the rivers of the East are represented by selections from William Bartram, Henry David Thoreau, and Mark Twain. William Bartram—a contemporary of Washington and Jefferson—undertook the earliest known scientific survey of the southeastern United States. His book *Travels Through North and South Carolina, Georgia, East and West Florida* is now considered a classic of American nature writing. In colonial times, rivers provided one of the only means of exploring the interior of the continent, and the selection included here gives us some sense of the dangers Bartram faced:

> I was attacked on all sides, several [alligators] endeavouring to overset the canoe. My situation now became precarious to the last degree: two very large ones attacked me closely, at the same instant, rushing up with their heads and part of their bodies above the water, roaring terribly and belching floods of water on me. They struck their jaws together so close to my ears, as almost to stun me, and I expected every moment to be dragged out of the boat and instantly devoured.

Thoreau, the first American author to contribute an important work to world literature (actually two: *Walden* and the essay "Civil Disobedience"), made several excursions into the Maine Woods late in his career. Because there were no roads and few trails at that time in the vast northern wilderness, he traveled primarily by canoe on rivers and river-connected lakes. Two years after his death, in 1864, Thoreau's journal *Maine Woods* was edited and published by Ellery Channing. In reading these vivid, breathless accounts of the Allegash and East Fork, one can only wonder what the naturalist would have written had he lived longer and traveled westward to view the rivers of the Far West.

No collection on rivers would be complete without a healthy excerpt from that finest of American river books, *Life on the Mississippi*. Raised in the river town of Hannibal, Missouri, Mark Twain (born Samuel Clemens) left school at the age of twelve to seek adventure. Eventually the nascent author became a steamboat pilot on the Mississippi River, which including its main branch, the Missouri, is the longest river in the world—forty-three hundred miles. According to Twain, the Mississippi is also the only river on the planet that instead of widening toward its mouth, grows narrower and deeper (reaching a depth of one hundred thirty feet near New Orleans). Included in these pages is Twain's often hilarious description of his apprenticeship as a riverboat pilot on the Mississippi. No person has ever loved rivers more, understood them more completely, or written of them more brilliantly. In his book he describes the "awful solitude" and "deep silence and loneliness" of "the great Mississippi, the majestic, the magnificent Mississippi, rolling its mile-wide tide along, shining in the sun."

A wholly different look at the Mississippi is provided by Eddy Harris, an African-American writer who lived for many years near the banks of the Mississippi in Kirkwood, Missouri. His book *Mississippi Solo* describes an incredible adventure—a solitary canoe trip down the Mississippi from its loon-haunted origins in northern Minnesota to its alligator-infested outlet in southern Louisiana. It is one thing to pilot a large steam-powered passenger boat down the river, as Twain did. It is quite another to face the full force and fury of the Mississippi in a small canoe. Harris provides a close-up look at the Mississippi and at the fascinating and sometimes bizarre people who live and work along the river.

The rivers of three continents outside North America are represented in this book—Europe, Africa, and South America. Ernest Hemingway takes us to the first. As a young correspondent, Hemingway lived in Paris for many years and traveled widely—France, Spain, Switzerland, Germany, Italy, and Austria—with his wife Hadley and their little boy Jack (to this day an avid fisherman in Idaho). Wherever the young family went, Hemingway sought out the local rivers and streams for fishing. For Hemingway, rivers were a way of getting back into the world by leaving it. He was only twenty-three years old when he wrote these lines:

He was such a fine trout that I had to keep unwrapping him to take a look and finally the day got so hot that I sat under a pine tree on the back of the stream and unwrapped the trout entirely and ate a paper-bag full of cherries I had and read the trout-dampened *Daily Mail*. It was a hot day, but I could look out across the green, slow valley past the line of trees that marked the course of the Rhone and watch a waterfall coming down the brown face of the mountain. The fall came out of a glacier that reached down toward a little town with four grey houses and three grey churches that was planted on the side of the mountain and looked solid, the waterfall, that is, until you saw it was moving. Then it looked cool and flickering, and I wondered who lived in the four houses and who went to the three churches with the sharp stone spires.

The fabled river story of Joseph Conrad, *Heart of Darkness*, is standard reading in most English survey courses. In the spring of 1890, inspired by the travel narratives of Henry "Doctor Livingston, I presume?" Stanley, Conrad traveled to the Belgian Congo in search of wilderness and adventure. At that time the resources of the Congo Basin were being rather violently devoured by the Belgians, and Conrad's book, which is based on a three-month trip upriver, speaks to both the darkness of human nature and wild nature. In *Heart of Darkness* we are transported on a river as bleak as anything in Dante's *Inferno* to the very depths of the human experience—the mass enslavement and oppression of innocent people. The book, unfortunately, presaged many of the darker events of the twentieth century, including the war that would nearly claim the life of a nineteen-year-old lieutenant from Oak Park, Illinois, named Hemingway.

Theodore Roosevelt takes us down a very different river, the Amazon, on a very different journey. It is often said that people find what they are looking for on a trip, and this was certainly true for Roosevelt, who, having recently undertaken a successful year-long safari to East Africa, was looking for the naturalist's dream trip of a lifetime. He found it and then some in the Amazon, for on the journey he discovered and navigated a previously unknown river, encountered new tribes, and returned with thousands of specimens for the National Museum, including plants, mammals, amphibians, reptiles, birds, fish, and invertebrates (including some species previously unrecorded by science). One can sense his almost child-like excitement as the expedition began:

> We were . . . on a river which was not merely unknown but
> unguessed at, no geographer having ever suspected its existence.
> This river flowed northward toward the equator, but whither it
> would go, whether it would turn one way or another, the length
> of its course, where it would come out, the character of the
> stream itself, and the character of the dwellers along its banks—
> all these things were yet to be discovered.

After Roosevelt's death in 1919, the Brazilian government, in honor
of the ex-president's journey into the heart of the country's most remote areas, named the river the Rio Roosevelt.

For the late Harry Middleton, one of his generation's most gifted
natural history writers, rivers were an elixir, a tonic, a refuge, and a
continual inspiration. In book after book Middleton pays tribute to
his favorite rivers—in the Smokies, in Colorado, and in his native
Arkansas. No one has ever written of moving water with more lyri-
cism. Sometime in the next century, when the definitive anthology of
twentieth-century nature writing is assembled, an essay by Harry Middleton will be a necessary part. I can really offer no higher praise for
Middleton's work. That book, preserving for posterity the best of what
we sought to do, will include passages like this:

> Rivers course through my dreams, rivers cold and fast, rivers well-
> known and rivers nameless, rivers that seem like ribbons of blue
> water twisting through wide valleys, narrow rivers folded in lay-
> ers of darkening shadows, rivers that have eroded down deep into
> a mountain's belly, sculpted the land, peeled back the planet's
> history exposing the texture of time itself. Rivers and sunlight,
> mountains and fish: they are always there, rising up out of ex-
> haustion, a sudden rush of sound and motion, a Wagnerian as-
> sault of light and shadow, hissing water, pounding rapids, chilly
> mountain winds easing inexorably into a requiem of distant
> rapids, a fish's silent rise, the splash of blue-green water over the
> backs of wet black stones.

iii

You can not step into the same river twice.
—Heraclitus

As I write these lines, a miniature spacecraft about the size of my
son's toy monster truck is roaming an ancient riverbed on Mars.

Roaming is perhaps too strong a verb—the machine moves along the riverbed at the rate of one foot per hour, and does so only after receiving instructions that take ten minutes to reach it at the speed of light. But roam it does, from rock to rock, sand dune to sand dune, across a strangely familiar landscape where water flowed, once. The craft is looking for fossils, photographing horizons, testing soil chemistry, examining interesting rocks, photographing eroded hills and crater rims on the horizon. All around it are rocks—primarily volcanic (andesite), although a few are said to appear sedimentary (one rock has been named "Barnacle Bill" for its encrusted surface). A river flowed through that dead valley once, more than likely a salmon-colored river, a river without a name and with not one blinking eye to see it gloaming along beneath a pale rose sky, a river that was destined to be visited by the human race, living on that blue world in the night sky one billion years into the future.

The point is this.

There will be other worlds, other places for the human race to explore. There will be other rivers. But there is only one Earth, only one place in the universe with rivers named for the silver salmon and the Yellowstone elk, the mountain beaver and the black bear. Posterity will return to this world, tired from their travels in the cold lonely gulfs between the stars, and they will sit down on the grassy banks of the Rogue River, the Brandywine River, the Roaring Fork River. They will be grateful that people in our distant barbaric age, who lived before the birth of civilization, reached out in love to save them. The authors in this book are committed to that struggle. They know that too many of our rivers are dammed, that too many of our rivers are so only in name, and that too many of our rivers are so polluted their waters could kill a child with just one gulp. They know that words have power, that books can make a difference, and that even a small group of people working together can change the world, if only one river at a time.

There is a river greater than any river on Earth, greater than any river in Hell or Heaven, greater than any river in any book of poetry written or yet to be written, and that is the river of time. We are all flowing down that stream, rather too quickly for most of us, and we have each been flowing with it in one form or another since the beginning of time. Here we stand now, in midstream, as everyone who came before us stood, composed of river clay and a hundred contradictions, and yet blessed with the grace of a canyon waterfall and given the light of a distant star. Pick a river, any river. If you sit beside it long enough you will hear many things, and most of them are worth waiting for. After a while you will hear a voice out on the waters whispering, saying, in a tone as soft and low as a mother singing to her restless child, that each of us is flowing, flowing like a river, and that one day we will all, from gossamers to galaxies, flow out of time into something even greater than a river.

Gone Back Into the Earth

Barry Lopez

I am up to my waist in a basin of cool, acid-clear water, at the head of a box canyon some 600 feet above the Colorado River. I place my outstretched hands flat against a terminal wall of dark limestone which rises more than a hundred feet above me, and down which a sheet of water falls—the thin creek in whose pooled waters I now stand. The water splits at my fingertips into wild threads; higher up, a warm canyon wind lifts water off the limestone in a fine spray; these droplets intercept and shatter sunlight. Down, down another four waterfalls and fern-shrouded pools below, the water spills into an eddy of the Colorado River, in the shadow of a huge boulder. Our boat is tied there.

This lush crease in the surface of the earth is a cleft in the precipitous desert walls of Arizona's Grand Canyon. Its smooth outcrops of purple-tinged travertine stone, its heavy air rolled in the languid perfume of columbine, struck by the sharp notes of a water ouzel, the trill of a disturbed black phoebe—all this has a name: Elves Chasm.

A few feet to my right, a preacher from Maryland is staring straight up at a blue sky, straining to see what flowers those are that nod at the top of the falls. To my left a freelance automobile mechanic from Colorado sits with an impish smile by helleborine orchids. Behind, another man, a builder and sometime record producer from New

13

York, who comes as often as he can to camp and hike in the South-west, stands immobile at the pool's edge.

Sprawled shirtless on a rock is our boatman. He has led twelve or fifteen of us on the climb up from the river. The Colorado entrances him. He has a well-honed sense of the ridiculous, brought on, one be-lieves, by so much time in the extreme remove of this canyon.

In our descent we meet others in our group who stopped climb-ing at one of the lower pools. At the second to the last waterfall, a young woman with short hair and dazzling blue eyes walks with me back into the canyon's narrowing V. We wade into a still pool, swim a few strokes to its head, climb over a boulder, swim across a second pool and then stand together, giddy, in the press of limestone, beneath the deafening cascade—filled with euphoria.

One at a time we bolt and glide, fishlike, back across the pool, grounding in fine white gravel. We wade the second pool and con-tinue our descent, stopping to marvel at the strategy of a barrel cactus and at the pale shading of color in the ledges to which we cling. We share few words. We know hardly anything of each other. We share the country.

The group of us who have made this morning climb are in the middle of a ten-day trip down the Colorado River. Each day we are upended, if not by some element of the landscape itself then by what the landscape does, visibly, to each of us. It has snapped us like fresh-laundered sheets.

After lunch, we reboard three large rubber rafts and enter the Col-orado's quick, high flow. The river has not been this high or fast since Glen Canyon Dam—135 miles above Elves Chasm, 17 miles above our starting point at Lee's Ferry—was closed in 1963. Jumping out ahead of us, with its single oarsman and three passengers, is our fourth craft, a twelve-foot rubber boat, like a water strider with a steel frame. In Sockdolager Rapid the day before, one of its welds burst and the steel pieces were bent apart. (Sockdolager: a nineteenth-century col-loquialism for knockout punch.)

Such groups as ours, the members all but unknown to each other on the first day, almost always grow close, solicitous of each other, dur-ing their time together. They develop a humor that informs similar journeys everywhere, a humor founded in tomfoolery, in punning, in a continuous parody of the life-in-civilization all have so recently (and gleefully) left. Such humor depends on context, on an accretion of small, shared events; it seems silly to those who are not there. It is not, of course. Any more than that moment of fumbling awe one feels on seeing the Brahma schist at the dead bottom of the canyon's Inner Gorge. Your fingertips graze the 1.9-billion-year-old stone as the boat drifts slowly past.

With the loss of self-consciousness, the landscape opens.

There are forty-one of us, counting a crew of six. An actor from Florida, now living in Los Angeles. A medical student and his wife. A supervisor from Virginia's Department of Motor Vehicles. A health-store owner from Chicago. An editor from New York and his young son.

That kind of diversity seems normal in groups that seek such vacations—to trek in the Himalaya, to dive in the Sea of Cortez, to go birding in the Arctic. We are together for two reasons: to run the Colorado River, and to participate with jazz musician Paul Winter, who initiated the trip, in a music workshop.

Winter is an innovator and a listener. He had thought for years about coming to the Grand Canyon, about creating music here in response to this particular landscape—collared lizards and prickly pear cactus, Anasazi Indian ruins and stifling heat. But most especially he wanted music evoked by the river and the walls that flew up from its banks—Coconino sandstone on top of Hermit shale on top of the Supai formations, stone exposed to sunlight, a bloom of photons that lifted colors—saffron and ochre, apricot, madder orange, pearl and gray green, copper reds, umber and terra-cotta browns—and left them floating in the air.

Winter was searching for a reintegration of music, landscape and people. For resonance. Three or four times during the trip he would find it for sustained periods: drifting on a quiet stretch of water below Bass Rapids with oboist Nancy Rumbel and cellist David Darling; in a natural amphitheater high in the Muav limestone of Matkatameba Canyon; on the night of a full June moon with euphonium player Larry Roark in Blacktail Canyon.

Winter's energy and passion, and the strains of solo and ensemble music, were sewn into the trip like prevailing winds, like the canyon wren's clear, whistled, descending notes, his glissando—seemingly present, close by or at a distance, whenever someone stopped to listen.

But we came and went, too, like the swallows and swifts that flicked over the water ahead of the boats, intent on private thoughts.

❦

On the second day of the trip we stopped at Redwall Cavern, an undercut recess that spans a beach of fine sand, perhaps 500 feet wide by 150 feet deep. Winter intends to record here, but the sand absorbs too much sound. Unfazed, the others toss a Frisbee, practice Tai-chi, jog, meditate, play recorders, and read novels.

No other animal but the human would bring to bear so many activities, from so many different cultures and levels of society, with so much energy, so suddenly in a new place. And no other animal, the individuals so entirely unknown to each other, would chance together something so unknown as this river journey. In this frenetic activity and difference seems a suggestion of human evolution and genuine adventure. We are not the first down this river, but in the slooshing of human hands at the water's edge, the swanlike notes of an oboe, the occasional hugs among those most afraid of the rapids, there *is* exploration.

Each day we see or hear something that astounds us. The thousand-year-old remains of an Anasazi footbridge, hanging in twilight shadow high in the canyon wall above Harding Rapid. Deer Creek Falls, where we stand knee-deep in turquoise water encircled by a rainbow. Havasu Canyon, wild with grapevines, cottonwoods and velvet ash, speckled dace and mule deer, wild grasses and crimson monkey flowers. Each evening we enjoy a vespers, cicadas and crickets, mourning doves, vermilion flycatchers. And the wind, for which chimes are hung in a salt cedar. These notes leap above the splash and rattle, the grinding of water and the roar of rapids.

The narrow, damp, hidden worlds of the side canyons, with their scattered shards of Indian pottery and ghost imprints of 400-million-year-old nautiloids, open onto the larger world of the Colorado River itself; but nothing conveys to us how far into the earth's surface we have come. Occasionally we glimpse the South Rim, four or five thousand feet above. From the rims the canyon seems oceanic; at the surface of the river the feeling is intimate. To someone up there with binoculars we seem utterly remote down here. It is this known dimension of distance and time and the perplexing question posed by the canyon itself—What is consequential? (in one's life, in the life of human beings, in the life of a planet)—that reverberate constantly, and make the human inclination to judge (another person, another kind of thought) seem so eerie.

Two kinds of time pass here: sitting at the edge of a sun-warmed pool watching blue dragonflies and black tadpoles. And the rapids: down the glassy-smooth tongue into a yawing trench, climb a ten-foot wall of standing water and fall into boiling, ferocious hydraulics, sucking whirlpools, drowned voices, stopped hearts. Rapids can fold and shatter boats and take lives if the boatman enters at the wrong point or at the wrong angle.

Some rapids, like one called Hermit, seem more dangerous than they are and give us great roller-coaster rides. Others—Hance, Crystal, Upset—seem less spectacular, but are technically difficult. At Crystal, our boat screeches and twists against its frame. Its nose crumples like cardboard in the trough; our boatman makes the critical move to the right with split-second timing and we are over a standing wave and into the haystacks of white water, safely into the tail waves. The boatman's eyes cease to blaze.

The first few rapids—Badger Creek and Soap Creek—do not overwhelm us. When we hit the Inner Gorge—Granite Falls, Unkar Rapid, Horn Creek Rapid—some grip the boat, rigid and silent. (On the ninth day, when we are about to run perhaps the most formidable rapid, Lava Falls, the one among us who has had the greatest fear is calm, almost serene. In the last days, it is hard to overestimate what the river and the music and the unvoiced concern for each other have washed out.)

There are threats to this separate world of the Inner Gorge. Down inside it one struggles to maintain a sense of what they are, how they impinge.

In 1963, Glen Canyon Dam cut off the canyon's natural flow of water. Spring runoffs of more than two hundred thousand cubic feet per second ceased to roar through the gorge, clearing the main channel of rock and stones washed down from the side canyons. Fed now from the bottom of Lake Powell backed up behind the dam, the river is no longer a warm, silt-laden habitat for Colorado squawfish, razor-back sucker and several kinds of chub, but a cold, clear habitat for trout. With no annual scouring and a subsequent deposition of fresh sand, the beaches show the evidence of continuous human use: they are eroding. The postflood eddies where squawfish bred have disappeared. Tamarisk (salt cedar) and camel thorn, both exotic plants formerly washed out with the spring floods, have gained an apparently

17

permanent foothold. At the old high-water mark, catclaw acacia, mesquite and Apache plume are no longer watered and are dying out.

On the rim, far removed above, such evidence of human tampering seems, and perhaps is, pernicious. From the river, another change is more wrenching. It floods the system with a kind of panic that in other animals induces nausea and the sudden evacuation of the bowels: it is the descent of helicopters. Their sudden arrival in the canyon evokes not jeers but staring. The violence is brutal, an intrusion as criminal and as random as rape. When the helicopter departs, its rotorwind walloping against the stone walls, I want to wash the sound off my skin.

The canyon finally absorbs the intrusion. I focus quietly each day on the stone, the breathing of time locked up here, back to the Proterozoic, before there were seashells. Look up to wisps of high cirrus overhead, the hint of a mare's tail sky. Close my eyes: tappet of water against the boat, sound of an Anasazi's six-hole flute. And I watch the bank for beaver tracks, for any movement.

The canyon seems like a grandfather.

One evening, Winter and perhaps half the group carry instruments and recording gear back into Blacktail Canyon to a spot sound engineer Mickey Houlihan says is good for recording.

Winter likes to quote from Thoreau: "The woods would be very silent if no birds sang except those that sing best." The remark seems not only to underscore the ephemeral nature of human evolution but the necessity in evaluating any phenomenon—a canyon, a life, a song—of providing for change.

After several improvisations dominated by a cappella voice and percussion, Winter asks Larry Roark to try something on the euphonium; he and Rumbel and Darling will then come up around him. Roark is silent. Moonlight glows on the canyon's lips. There is the sound of gurgling water. After a word of encouragement, feeling shrouded in anonymous darkness like the rest of us, Larry puts his mouth to the horn.

For a while he is alone. God knows what visions of waterfalls or wrens, of boats in the rapids, of Bach or Mozart, are in his head, in his fingers, to send forth notes. The whine of the soprano sax finds him. And the flutter of the oboe. And the rumbling of the choral cello. The exchange lasts perhaps twenty minutes. Furious and sweet, anx-

18

ious, rolling, delicate and raw. The last six or eight hanging notes are Larry's. Then there is a long silence. Winter finally says, "My God."

I feel, sitting in the wet dark in bathing suit and sneakers and T-shirt, that my fingers have brushed one of life's deep, coursing threads. Like so much else in the canyon, it is left alone. Speak, even notice it, and it would disappear.

I had come to the canyon with expectations. I had wanted to see snowy egrets flying against the black schist at dusk; I saw blue-winged teal against the deep green waters at dawn. I had wanted to hear thunder rolling in the thousand-foot depths; I heard Winter's soprano sax resonating in Matkatameba Canyon, with the guttural caws of four ravens which circled above him. I had wanted to watch rattlesnakes; I saw in an abandoned copper mine, in the beam of my flashlight, a wall of copper sulphate that looked like a wall of turquoise. I rose each morning at dawn and washed in the cold river. I went to sleep each night listening to the cicadas, the pencil-ticking sound of some other insect, the soughing of river waves in tamarisk roots, and watching bats plunge and turn, looking like leaves blown around against the sky. What any of us had come to see or do fell away. We found ourselves at each turn with what we had not imagined.

The last evening it rained. We had left the canyon and been carried far out onto Lake Mead by the river's current. But we stood staring backward, at the point where the canyon had so obviously and abruptly ended.

A thought that stayed with me was that I had entered a private place in the earth. I had seen exposed nearly its oldest part. I had lost my sense of urgency, rekindled a sense of what people were, clambering to gain access to high waterfalls where we washed our hair together; and a sense of our endless struggle as a species to understand time and to estimate the consequences of our acts.

It rained the last evening. But before it did, Nancy Rumbel moved to the highest point on Scorpion Island in Lake Mead and played her oboe before a storm we could see hanging over Nevada. Sterling Smyth, who would return to programming computers in twenty-four hours, created a twelve-string imitation of the canyon wren, a long guitar solo. David Darling, revealed suddenly stark, again and then again, against a white-lightning sky, bowed furious homage to the now overhanging cumulonimbus.

19

In the morning we touched the far shore of Lake Mead, boarded a bus and headed for the Las Vegas airport. We were still wrapped in the journey, as though it were a Navajo blanket. We departed on various planes and arrived home in various cities and towns and at some point the world entered again and the hardest thing, the translation of what we had touched, began.

I sat in the airport in San Francisco, waiting for a connecting flight to Oregon, dwelling on one image. At the mouth of Nankoweap Canyon, the river makes a broad turn, and it is possible to see high in the orange rock what seem to be four small windows. They are entrances to granaries, built by the Anasazi who dwelled in the canyon a thousand years ago. This was provision against famine, to ensure the people would survive.

I do not know, really, how we will survive without places like the Inner Gorge of the Grand Canyon to visit. Once in a lifetime, even, is enough. To feel the stripping down, an ebb of the press of conventional time, a radical change of proportion, an unspoken respect for others that elicits keen emotional pleasure, a quick, intimate pounding of the heart.

Some parts of the trip will emerge one day on an album. Others will be found in a gesture of friendship to some stranger in an airport, in a letter of outrage to a planner of dams, in a note of gratitude to nameless faces in the Park Service, in wondering at the relatives of the ubiquitous wren, in the belief, passed on in whatever fashion—a photograph, a chord, a sketch—that nature can heal.

The living of life, any life, involves great and private pain, much of which we share with no one. In such places as the Inner Gorge the pain trails away from us. It is not so quiet there or so removed that you can hear yourself think, that you would even wish to; that comes later. You can hear your heart beat. That comes first.

FROM *Life on the Mississippi*

Mark Twain

PERPLEXING LESSONS

At the end of what seemed a tedious while, I had managed to pack my head full of islands, towns, bars, "points," and bends; and a curiously inanimate mass of lumber it was, too. However, inasmuch as I could shut my eyes and reel off a good long string of these names without leaving out more than ten miles of river in every fifty, I began to feel that I could take a boat down to New Orleans if I could make her skip those little gaps. But of course my complacency could hardly get start enough to lift my nose a trifle into the air, before Mr. Bixby would think of something to fetch it down again. One day he turned on me suddenly with this settler:

"What is the shape of Walnut Bend?"

He might as well have asked me my grandmother's opinion of protoplasm. I reflected respectfully, and then said I didn't know it had any particular shape. My gun-powdery chief went off with a bang, of course, and then went on loading and firing until he was out of adjectives.

I had learned long ago that he only carried just so many rounds of ammunition, and was sure to subside into a very placable and even remorseful old smooth-bore as soon as they were all gone. That word "old" is merely affectionate; he was not more than thirty-four. I waited. By and by he said:

"My boy, you've got to know the *shape* of the river perfectly. It is all there is left to steer by on a very dark night. Everything else is blotted out and gone. But mind you, it hasn't the same shape in the night that it has in the daytime."

"How on earth am I ever going to learn it, then?"

"How do you follow a hall at home in the dark? Because you know the shape of it. You can't see it."

"Do you mean to say that I've got to know all the million trifling variations of shape in the banks of this interminable river as well as I know the shape of the front hall at home?"

"On my honor, you've got to know them *better* than any man ever did know the shapes of the halls in his own house."

"I wish I was dead!"

"Now I don't want to discourage you, but—"

"Well, pile it on me; I might as well have it now as another time."

"You see, this has got to be learned; there isn't any getting around it. A clear starlight night throws such heavy shadows that, if you didn't know the shape of a shore perfectly, you would claw away from every bunch of timber, because you would take the black shadow of it for a solid cape; and you see you would be getting scared to death every fifteen minutes by the watch. You would be fifty yards from shore all the time when you ought to be within fifty feet of it. You can't see a snag in one of those shadows, but you know exactly where it is, and the shape of the river tells you when you are coming to it. Then there's your pitch-dark night; the river is a very different shape on a pitch-dark night from what it is on a star-light night. All shores seem to be straight lines, then, and mighty dim ones, too; and you'd *run* them for straight lines, only you know better. You boldly drive your boat right into what seems to be a solid, straight wall (you knowing very well that in reality there is a curve there), and that wall falls back and makes way for you. Then there's your gray mist. You take a night when there's one of these grisly, drizzly, gray mists, and then there isn't *any* particular shape to a shore. A gray mist would tangle the head of the oldest man that ever lived. Well, then, different kinds of *moonlight* change the shape of the river in different ways. You see—"

"Oh, don't say any more, please! Have I got to learn the shape of the river according to all these five hundred thousand different ways?

If I tried to carry all that cargo in my head it would make me stoop-shouldered."

"*No!* you only learn *the* shape of the river; and you learn it with such absolute certainty that you can always steer by the shape that's *in your head*, and never mind the one that's before your eyes."

"Very well, I'll try it; but, after I have learned it, can I depend on it? Will it keep the same form and not go fooling around?"

Before Mr. Bixby could answer, Mr. W. came in to take the watch, and he said:

"Bixby, you'll have to look out for President's Island, and all that country clear away up above the Old Hen and Chickens. The banks are caving and the shape of the shores changing like everything. Why, you wouldn't know the point above 40. You can go up inside the old sycamore snag, now."[1]

So that question was answered. Here were leagues of shore changing shape. My spirits were down in the mud again. Two things seemed pretty apparent to me. One was, that in order to be a pilot a man had got to learn more than any one man ought to be allowed to know; and the other was, that he must learn it all over again in a different way every twenty-four hours.

That night we had the watch until twelve. Now it was an ancient river custom for the two pilots to chat a bit when the watch changed. While the relieving pilot put on his gloves and lit his cigar, his partner, the retiring pilot, would say something like this:

"I judge the upper bar is making down a little at Hale's Point; had quarter twain with the lower lead and mark twain[2] with the other."

"Yes, I thought it was making down a little, last trip. Meet any boats?"

"Met one abreast the head of 21, but she was away over hugging the bar, and I couldn't make her out entirely. I took her for the *Sunny South*—hadn't any skylights forward of the chimneys."

And so on. And as the relieving pilot took the wheel his partner[3] would mention that we were in such-and-such a bend, and say

---

[1]It may not be necessary, but still it can do no harm to explain that "inside" means between the snag and the shore.—M. T.

[2]Two fathoms. Quarter twain is 2¼ fathoms, 13½ feet. Mark three is three fathoms.

[3]"Partner" is technical for "the other pilot."

we were abreast of such-and-such a man's woodyard or plantation. This was courtesy; I supposed it was *necessity*. But Mr. W. came on watch full twelve minutes late on this particular night—a tremendous breach of etiquette; in fact, it is the unpardonable sin among pilots. So Mr. Bixby gave him no greeting whatever, but simply surrendered the wheel and marched out of the pilot-house without a word. I was appalled; it was a villainous night for blackness, we were in a particularly wide and blind part of the river, where there was no shape or substance to anything, and it seemed incredible that Mr. Bixby should have left that poor fellow to kill the boat, trying to find out where he was. But I resolved that I would stand by him anyway. He should find that he was not wholly friendless. So I stood around, and waited to be asked where we were. But Mr. W. plunged on serenely through the solid firmament of black cats that stood for an atmosphere, and never opened his mouth. "Here is a proud devil!" thought I; "here is a limb of Satan that would rather send us all to destruction than put himself under obligations to me, because I am not yet one of the salt of the earth and privileged to snub captains and lord it over everything dead and alive in a steamboat." I presently climbed up on the bench; I did not think it was safe to go to sleep while this lunatic was on watch.

However, I must have gone to sleep in the course of time, because the next thing I was aware of was the fact that day was breaking. Mr. W. gone, and Mr. Bixby at the wheel again. So it was four o'clock and all well—but me; I felt like a skinful of dry bones, and all of them trying to ache at once.

Mr. Bixby asked me what I had stayed up there for. I confessed that it was to do Mr. W. a benevolence—tell him where he was. It took five minutes for the entire preposterousness of the thing to filter into Mr. Bixby's system, and then I judge it filled him nearly up to the chin; because he paid me a compliment—and not much of a one either. He said:

"Well, taking you by and large you do seem to be more different kinds of an ass than any creature I ever saw before. What did you suppose he wanted to know for?"

I said I thought it might be a convenience to him.

"Convenience! D——nation! Didn't I tell you that a man's got to know the river in the night the same as he'd know his own front hall?"

"Well, I can follow the front hall in the dark if I know it *is* the front hall; but suppose you set me down in the middle of it in the dark and not tell me which hall it is; how am *I* to know?"

"Well, you've *got* to, on the river!"

"All right. Then I'm glad I never said anything to Mr. W."

"I should say so! Why, he'd have slammed you through the window and utterly ruined a hundred dollars' worth of window-sash and stuff."

I was glad this damage had been saved, for it would have made me unpopular with the owners. They always hated anybody who had the name of being careless and injuring things.

I went to work now to learn the shape of the river; and of all the eluding and ungraspable objects that ever I tried to get mind or hands on, that was the chief. I would fasten my eyes upon a sharp, wooded point that projected far into the river some miles ahead of me, and go to laboriously photographing its shape upon my brain; and just as I was beginning to succeed to my satisfaction, we would draw up toward it and the exasperating thing would begin to melt away and fold back into the bank! If there had been a conspicuous dead tree standing upon the very point of the cape, I would find that tree inconspicuously merged into the general forest, and occupying the middle of a straight shore, when I got abreast of it! No prominent hill would stick to its shape long enough for me to make up my mind what its form really was, but it was as dissolving and changeful as if it had been a mountain of butter in the hottest corner of the tropics. Nothing ever had the same shape when I was coming down-stream that it had borne when I went up. I mentioned these little difficulties to Mr. Bixby. He said:

"That's the very main virtue of the thing. If the shapes didn't change every three seconds they wouldn't be of any use. Take this place where we are now, for instance. As long as that hill over yonder is only one hill, I can boom right along the way I'm going; but the moment it splits at the top and forms a V, I know I've got to scratch to starboard in a hurry, or I'll bang this boat's brains out against a rock; and then the moment one of the prongs of the V swings behind the other, I've got to waltz to larboard again, or I'll have a misunderstanding with a snag that would snatch the keelson out of this steamboat as neatly as if it were a sliver in your hand. If that hill didn't change its shape on bad nights there would be an awful steamboat graveyard around here inside of a year."

It was plain that I had got to learn the shape of the river in all the different ways that could be thought of—upside down, wrong end first, inside out, fore-and-aft, and "thort-ships"—and then know what to do on gray nights when it hadn't any shape at all. So I set about it. In the course of time I began to get the best of this knotty lesson, and my self-complacency moved to the front once more. Mr. Bixby was all fixed, and ready to start it to the rear again. He opened on me after this fashion:

"How much water did we have in the middle crossing at Hole-in-the-Wall, trip before last?"

I considered this an outrage. I said:

"Every trip, down and up, the leadsmen are singing through that tangled place for three-quarters of an hour on a stretch. How do you reckon I can remember such a mess as that?"

"My boy, you've got to remember it. You've got to remember the exact spot and the exact marks the boat lay in when we had the shoalest water, in every one of the five hundred shoal places between St. Louis and New Orleans; and you mustn't get the shoal soundings and marks of one trip mixed up with the shoal soundings and marks of another, either, for they're not often twice alike. You must keep them separate."

When I came to myself again, I said:

"When I get so that I can do that, I'll be able to raise the dead, and then I won't have to pilot a steamboat to make a living. I want to retire from this business. I want a slush-bucket and a brush; I'm only fit for a roustabout. I haven't got brains enough to be a pilot; and if I had I wouldn't have strength enough to carry them around, unless I went on crutches."

"Now drop that! When I say I'll learn[4] a man the river, I mean it. And you can depend on it, I'll learn him or kill him."

CONTINUED PERPLEXITIES

There was no use in arguing with a person like this. I promptly put such a strain on my memory that by and by even the shoal water and the countless crossing-marks began to stay with me. But the result was

---

[4]"Teach" is not in the river vocabulary.

just the same. I never could more than get one knotty thing learned before another presented itself. Now I had often seen pilots gazing at the water and pretending to read it as if it were a book; but it was a book that told me nothing. A time came at last, however, when Mr. Bixby seemed to think me far enough advanced to bear a lesson on water-reading. So he began:

"Do you see that long, slanting line on the face of the water? Now, that's a reef. Moreover, it's a bluff reef. There is a solid sand-bar under it that is nearly as straight up and down as the side of a house. There is plenty of water close up to it, but mighty little on top of it. If you were to hit it you would knock the boat's brains out. Do you see where the line fringes out at the upper end and begins to fade away?"

"Yes, sir."

"Well, that is a low place; that is the head of the reef. You can climb over there, and not hurt anything. Cross over, now, and follow along close under the reef—easy water there—not much current."

I followed the reef along till I approached the fringed end. Then Mr. Bixby said:

"Now get ready. Wait till I give the word. She won't want to mount the reef; a boat hates shoal water. Stand by—wait—*wait*—keep her well in hand. *Now* cramp her down! Snatch her! Snatch her!"

He seized the other side of the wheel and helped to spin it around until it was hard down, and then we held it so. The boat resisted, and refused to answer for a while, and next she came surging to starboard, mounted the reef, and sent a long, angry ridge of water foaming away from her bows.

"Now watch her; watch her like a cat, or she'll get away from you. When she fights strong and the tiller slips a little, in a jerky, greasy sort of way, let up on her a trifle; it is the way she tells you at night that the water is too shoal; but keep edging her up, little by little, toward the point. You are well up on the bar now; there is a bar under every point, because the water that comes down around it forms an eddy and allows the sediment to sink. Do you see those fine lines on the face of the water that branch out like the ribs of a fan? Well, those are little reefs; you want to just miss the ends of them, but run them pretty close. Now look out—look out! Don't you crowd that slick, greasy-looking place; there ain't nine feet there; she won't stand it. She begins to smell it; look sharp, I tell you! Oh, blazes, there you go! Stop the starboard wheel! Quick! Ship up to back! Set her back!"

The engine bells jingled and the engines answered promptly, shooting white columns of steam far aloft out of the 'scape-pipes, but it was too late. The boat had "smelt" the bar in good earnest; the foamy ridges that radiated from her bows suddenly disappeared, a great dead swell came rolling forward, and swept ahead of her, she careened far over to larboard, and went tearing away toward the shore as if she were about scared to death. We were a good mile from where we ought to have been when we finally got the upper hand of her again.

During the afternoon watch the next day, Mr. Bixby asked me if I knew how to run the next few miles. I said:

"Go inside the first snag above the point, outside the next one, start out from the lower end of Higgins's woodyard, make a square crossing, and—"

"That's all right. I'll be back before you close up on the next point."

But he wasn't. He was still below when I rounded it and entered upon a piece of the river which I had some misgivings about. I did not know that he was hiding behind a chimney to see how I would perform. I went gaily along, getting prouder and prouder, for he had never left the boat in my sole charge such a length of time before. I even got to "setting" her and letting the wheel go entirely, while I vaingloriously turned my back and inspected the stern marks and hummed a tune, a sort of easy indifference which I had prodigiously admired in Bixby and other great pilots. Once I inspected rather long, and when I faced to the front again my heart flew into my mouth so suddenly that if I hadn't clapped my teeth together I should have lost it. One of those frightful bluff reefs was stretching its deadly length right across our bows! My head was gone in a moment; I did not know which end I stood on; I gasped and could not get my breath; I spun the wheel down with such rapidity that it wove itself together like a spider's web; the boat answered and turned square away from the reef, but the reef followed her! I fled, but still it followed, still it kept—right across my bows! I never looked to see where I was going, I only fled. The awful crash was imminent. Why didn't that villain come? If I committed the crime of ringing a bell I might get thrown overboard. But better that than kill the boat. So in blind desperation, I started such a rattling "shivaree" down below as never had astounded an engineer in this world before, I fancy. Amidst the frenzy of the bells the engines began to back and fill in a curious way, and my reason forsook its throne— we were about to crash into the woods on the other side of the river.

Just then Mr. Bixby stepped calmly into view on the hurricane-deck. My soul went out to him in gratitude. My distress vanished; I would have felt safe on the brink of Niagara with Mr. Bixby on the hurricane-deck. He blandly and sweetly took his toothpick out of his mouth between his fingers, as if it were a cigar—we were just in the act of climbing an overhanging big tree, and the passengers were scudding astern like rats—and lifted up these commands to me ever so gently:

"Stop the starboard! Stop the larboard! Set her back on both!"

The boat hesitated, halted, pressed her nose among the boughs a critical instant, then reluctantly began to back away.

"Stop the larboard! Come ahead on it! Stop the starboard! Come ahead on it! Point her for the bar!"

I sailed away as serenely as a summer's morning. Mr. Bixby came in and said, with mock simplicity:

"When you have a hail, my boy, you ought to tap the big bell three times before you land, so that the engineers can get ready."

I blushed under the sarcasm, and said I hadn't had any hail.

"Ah! Then it was for wood, I suppose. The officer of the watch will tell you when he wants to wood up."

I went on consuming, and said I wasn't after wood.

"Indeed? Why, what could you want over here in the bend, then? Did you ever know of a boat following a bend up-stream at this stage of the river?"

"No, sir—and I wasn't trying to follow it. I was getting away from a bluff reef."

"No, it wasn't a bluff reef; there isn't one within three miles of where you were."

"But I saw it. It was as bluff as that one yonder."

"Just about. Run over it!"

"Do you give it as an order?"

"Yes. Run over it!"

"If I don't, I wish I may die."

"All right; I am taking the responsibility."

I was just as anxious to kill the boat, now, as I had been to save it before. I impressed my orders upon my memory, to be used at the inquest, and made a straight break for the reef. As it disappeared under our bows I held my breath; but we slid over it like oil.

"Now, don't you see the difference? It wasn't anything but a *wind* reef. The wind does that."

"So I see. But it is exactly like a bluff reef. How am I ever going to tell them apart?"

"I can't tell you. It is an instinct. By and by you will just naturally *know* one from the other, but you never will be able to explain why or how you know them apart."

It turned out to be true. The face of the water, in time, became a wonderful book—a book that was a dead language to the uneducated passenger, but which told its mind to me without reserve, delivering its most cherished secrets as clearly as if it uttered them with a voice. And it was not a book to be read once and thrown aside, for it had a new story to tell every day. Throughout the long twelve hundred miles there was never a page that was void of interest, never one that you could leave unread without loss, never one that you would want to skip, thinking you could find higher enjoyment in some other thing. There never was so wonderful a book written by man; never one whose interest was so absorbing, so unflagging, so sparklingly renewed with every reperusal. The passenger who could not read it was charmed with a peculiar sort of faint dimple on its surface (on the rare occasions when he did not overlook it altogether); but to the pilot that was an *italicized* passage; indeed, it was more than that, it was a legend of the largest capitals, with a string of shouting exclamation-points at the end of it, for it meant that a wreck or a rock was buried there that could tear the life out of the strongest vessel that ever floated. It is the faintest and simplest expression the water ever makes, and the most hideous to a pilot's eye. In truth, the passenger who could not read this book saw nothing but all manner of pretty pictures in it, painted by the sun and shaded by the clouds, whereas to the trained eye these were not pictures at all, but the grimmest and most dead-earnest of reading-matter.

Now when I had mastered the language of this water, and had come to know every trifling feature that bordered the great river as familiarly as I knew the letters of the alphabet, I had made a valuable acquisition. But I had lost something, too. I had lost something which could never be restored to me while I lived. All the grace, the beauty, the poetry, had gone out of the majestic river! I still kept in mind a certain wonderful sunset which I witnessed when steamboating was new to me. A broad expanse of the river was turned to blood; in the middle distance the red hue brightened into gold, through which a solitary log came floating, black and conspicuous; in one place a long, slanting mark lay sparkling upon the water; in another the surface was broken by boiling, tumbling rings, that were as many-tinted as an opal; where the ruddy flush was faintest, was a smooth spot that was covered with graceful circles and radiating lines, ever so delicately traced; the shore on our left was densely wooded, and the somber shadow that fell from this forest was broken in one place by a long, ruffled trail that shone like silver; and high above the forest wall a clean-stemmed dead tree waved a single leafy bough that glowed like a flame in the unobstructed splendor that was flowing from the sun. There were graceful curves, reflected images, woody heights, soft distances; and over the whole scene, far and near, the dissolving lights drifted steadily, enriching it every passing moment with new marvels of coloring.

I stood like one bewitched. I drank it in, in a speechless rapture. The world was new to me, and I had never seen anything like this at home. But as I have said, a day came when I began to cease from noting the glories and the charms which the moon and the sun and the twilight wrought upon the river's face; another day came when I ceased altogether to note them. Then, if that sunset scene had been repeated, I should have looked upon it without rapture, and should have commented upon it, inwardly, after this fashion: "This sun means that we are going to have wind to-morrow; that floating log means that the river is rising, small thanks to it; that slanting mark on the water refers to a bluff reef which is going to kill somebody's steamboat one of these nights, if it keeps on stretching out like that; those tumbling 'boils' show a dissolving bar and a changing channel there; the lines and circles in the slick water over yonder are a warning that that troublesome place is shoaling up dangerously; that silver streak in the shadow of the forest is the 'break' from a new snag, and he has located himself in the very best place he could have found to fish for steamboats; that tall dead tree, with a single living branch, is not going to last long, and then how is a body ever going to get through this blind place at night without the friendly old landmark?"

No, the romance and beauty were all gone from the river. All the value any feature of it had for me now was the amount of usefulness it could furnish toward compassing the safe piloting of a steamboat. Since those days, I have pitied doctors from my heart. What does the lovely flush in a beauty's cheek mean to a doctor but a "break" that ripples above some deadly disease? Are not all her visible charms sown thick with what are to him the signs and symbols of hidden decay? Does he ever see her beauty at all, or doesn't he simply view her professionally, and comment upon her unwholesome condition all to himself? And doesn't he sometimes wonder whether he has gained most or lost most by learning his trade?

COMPLETING MY EDUCATION

Whosoever has done me the courtesy to read my chapters which have preceded this may possibly wonder that I deal so minutely with piloting as a science. It was the prime purpose of those chapters; and I am not quite done yet. I wish to show, in the most patient and painstaking way, what a wonderful science it is. Ship-channels are buoyed and lighted, and therefore it is a comparatively easy undertaking to learn to run them; clear-water rivers with gravel bottoms, change their channels very gradually, and therefore one needs to learn them but once; but piloting becomes another matter when you apply it to vast streams like the Mississippi and the Missouri, whose alluvial banks cave and change constantly, whose snags are always hunting up new quarters, whose sand-bars are never at rest, whose channels are forever dodging and shirking, and whose obstructions must be confronted in all nights and all weathers without the aid of a single lighthouse or a single buoy; for there is neither light nor buoy to be found anywhere in all this three or four thousand miles of villainous river.[1] I feel justified in enlarging upon this great science for the reason that I feel sure no one has ever yet written a paragraph about it who had piloted a steamboat himself, and so had a practical knowledge of the subject. If the theme was hackneyed, I should be obliged to deal gently with the reader; but since it is wholly new, I have felt at liberty to take up a considerable degree of room with it.

When I had learned the name and position of every visible feature of the river; when I had so mastered its shape that I could shut my eyes and trace it from St. Louis to New Orleans; when I had learned to read the face of the water as one would cull the news from the morning paper; and finally, when I had trained my dull memory to treasure up an endless array of soundings and crossing-marks, and keep fast hold of them, I judged that my education was complete; so I got to tilting my cap to the side of my head, and wearing a toothpick in my mouth at the wheel. Mr. Bixby had his eye on these airs. One day he said:

---

[1] True at the time referred to; not true now (1882).

"What is the height of that bank yonder, at Burgess's?"

"How can I tell, sir? It is three-quarters of a mile away."

"Very poor eye—very poor. Take the glass."

I took the glass and presently said:

"I can't tell. I suppose that that bank is about a foot and a half high."

"Foot and a half! That's a six-foot bank. How high was the bank along here last trip?"

"I don't know; I never noticed."

"You didn't? Well, you must always do it hereafter."

"Why?"

"Because you'll have to know a good many things that it tells you. For one thing, it tells you the stage of the river—tells you whether there's more water or less in the river along here than there was last trip."

"The leads tell me that." I rather thought I had the advantage of him there.

"Yes, but suppose the leads lie? The bank would tell you so, and then you would stir those leadsmen up a bit. There was a ten-foot bank here last trip, and there is only a six-foot bank now. What does that signify?"

"That the river is four feet higher than it was last trip."

"Very good. Is the river rising or falling?"

"Rising."

"No, it ain't."

"I guess I am right, sir. Yonder is some driftwood floating down the stream."

"A rise *starts* the driftwood, but then it keeps on floating awhile after the river is done rising. Now the bank will tell you about this. Wait till you come to a place where it shelves a little. Now here: do you see this narrow belt of fine sediment? That was deposited while the water was higher. You see the driftwood begins to strand, too. The bank helps in other ways. Do you see that stump on the false point?"

"Ay, ay, sir."

"Well, the water is just up to the roots of it. You must make a note of that."

"Why?"

"Because that means that there's seven feet in the chute of 103."

"But 103 is a long way up the river yet."

"That's where the benefit of the bank comes in. There is water enough in 103 *now*, yet there may not be by the time we get there, but the bank will keep us posted all along. You don't run close chutes on a falling river, up-stream, and there are precious few of them that you are allowed to run at all against it. The river may be rising by the time we get to 103, and in that case we'll run it. We are drawing—how much?"

"Six feet aft—six and a half forward."

"Well, you do seem to know something."

"But what I particularly want to know is, if I have got to keep up an everlasting measuring of the banks of this river, twelve hundred miles, month in and month out?"

"Of course!"

My emotions were too deep for words for a while. Presently I said:

"And how about these chutes? Are there many of them?"

"I should say so! I fancy we sha'n't run any of the river this trip as you've ever seen it run before—so to speak. If the river begins to rise again, we'll go up behind bars that you've always seen standing out of the river, high and dry, like a roof of a house; we'll cut across low places that you've never noticed at all, right through the middle of bars that cover three hundred acres of river; we'll creep through cracks where you've always thought was solid land; we'll dart through the woods and leave twenty-five miles of river off to one side; we'll see the hind side of every island between New Orleans and Cairo."

"Then I've got to go to work and learn just as much more river as I already know."

"Just about twice as much more, as near as you can come at it."

"Well, one lives to find out. I think I was a fool when I went into this business."

"Yes, that is true. And you are yet. But you'll not be when you've learned it."

"Ah, I never can learn it!"

"I will see that you *do*."

By and by I ventured again:

"Have I got to learn all this thing just as I know the rest of the river—shapes and all—and so I can run it at night?"

"Yes. And you've got to have good fair marks from one end of the river to the other, that will help the bank tell you when there is water enough in each of these countless places—like that stump, you know. When the river first begins to rise, you can run half a dozen of the deepest of them; when it rises a foot more you can run another dozen; the next foot will add a couple of dozen, and so on; so you see you have to know your banks and marks to a dead moral certainty and never get them mixed; for when you start through one of those cracks, there's no backing out again, as there is in the big river; you've got to go through, or stay there six months if you get caught on a falling river. There are about fifty of these cracks which you can't run at all except when the river is brimful and over the banks."

"This new lesson is a cheerful prospect."

"Cheerful enough. And mind what I've just told you; when you start into one of those places you've got to go through. They are too narrow to turn around in, too crooked to back out of, and the shoal water is always *up at the head*; never elsewhere. And the head of them is always likely to be filling up, little by little, so that the marks you reckon their depth by, this season, may not answer for next."

"Learn a new set, then, every year?"

"Exactly. Cramp her up to the bar! What are you standing up through the middle of the river for?"

The next few months showed me strange things. On the same day that we held the conversation above narrated we met a great rise coming down the river. The whole vast face of the stream was black with drifting dead logs, broken boughs, and great trees that had caved in and been washed away. It required the nicest steering to pick one's way through this rushing raft, even in the daytime, when crossing from point to point; and at night the difficulty was mightily increased; every now and then a huge log, lying deep in the water, would suddenly appear right under our bows, coming head-on; no use to try to avoid it then; we could only stop the engines, and one wheel would walk over that log from one end to the other, keeping up a thundering racket and careening the boat in a way that was very uncomfortable to passengers. Now and then we would hit one of these sunken logs a rattling bang, dead in the center, with a full head of steam, and it would stun the boat as if she had hit a continent. Sometimes this log would lodge and stay right across our nose, and back the Mississippi up before it; we would have to do a little crawfishing, then, to get away from the obstruction. We often hit *white* logs in the dark, for we could not see them until we were right on them, but a black log is a pretty distinct object at night. A white snag is an ugly customer when the daylight is gone.

Of course, on the great rise, down came a swarm of prodigious timber-rafts from the headwaters of the Mississippi, coal-barges from Pittsburg, little trading-scows from everywhere, and broadhorns from "Posey County," Indiana, freighted with "fruit and furniture"—the usual term for describing it, though in plain English the freight thus aggrandized was hoop-poles and pumpkins. Pilots bore a mortal hatred to these craft, and it was returned with usury. The law required all such helpless traders to keep a light burning, but it was a law that was often broken. All of a sudden, on a murky night, a light would hop up, right under our bows, almost, and an agonized voice, with the backwoods "whang" to it, would wail out:

"Whar'n the —— you goin' to! Cain't you see nothin', you dash-dashed aig-suckin', sheep-stealin', one-eyed son of a stuffed monkey!"

Then for an instant, as we whistled by, the red glare from our furnace would reveal the scow and the form of the gesticulating orator, as if under a lightning flash, and in that instant our firemen and deckhands would send and receive a tempest of missiles and profanity, one of our wheels would walk off with the crashing fragments of a steering-oar, and down the dead blackness would shut again. And that flat-boatman would be sure to go into New Orleans and sue our boat, swearing stoutly that he had a light burning all the time, when in truth his gang had the lantern down below to sing and lie and drink and gamble by, and no watch on deck. Once at night, in one of those forest-bordered crevices (behind an island) which steamboatmen intensely describe with the phrase "as dark as the inside of a cow," we should have eaten up a Posey County family, fruit, furniture, and all, but that they happened to be fiddling down below and we just caught the sound of the music in time to sheer off, doing no serious damage, unfortunately, but coming so near it that we had good hopes for a moment. These people brought up their lantern, then, of course; and as we backed and filled to get away, the precious family stood in the light of it—both sexes and various ages—and cursed us till everything turned blue. Once a coal-boatman sent a bullet through our pilot-house when we borrowed a steering-oar of him in a very narrow place.

THE RIVER RISES

During this big rise these small-fry craft were an intolerable nuisance. We were running chute after chute—a new world to me—and if there was a particularly cramped place in a chute, we would be pretty sure to meet a broadhorn there; and if he failed to be there, we would find him in a still worse locality, namely, the head of the chute, on the shoal water. And then there would be no end of profane cordialities exchanged.

Sometimes, in the big river, when we would be feeling our way cautiously along through a fog, the deep hush would suddenly be broken by yells and a clamor of tin pans, and all in an instant a log raft would appear vaguely through the webby veil, close upon us; and then we did not wait to swap knives, but snatched our engine-bells out by the roots and piled on all the steam we had, to scramble out of the way! One doesn't hit a rock or a solid log raft with a steamboat when he can get excused.

You will hardly believe it, but many steamboat clerks always carried a large assortment of religious tracts with them in those old departed steamboating days. Indeed they did! Twenty times a day we would be cramping up around a bar, while a string of these small-fry rascals were drifting down into the head of the bend away above and beyond us a couple of miles. Now a skiff would dart away from one of them, and come fighting its laborious way across the desert of water. It would "ease all" in the shadow of our forecastle, and the panting oarsmen would shout, "Gimme a pa-a-per!" as the skiff drifted swiftly astern. The clerk would throw over a file of New Orleans journals. If these were picked up *without comment*, you might notice that now a dozen other skiffs had been drifting down upon us without saying anything. You understand, they had been waiting to see how No. 1 was going to fare. No. 1 making no comment, all the rest would bend to their oars and come on, now; and as fast as they came the clerk would heave over neat bundles of religious tracks, tied to shingles. The amount of hard swearing which twelve packages of religious literature will command when impartially divided up among twelve raftsmen's crews, who have pulled a heavy skiff two miles on a hot day to get them, is simply incredible.

As I have said, the big rise brought a new world under my vision. By the time the river was over its banks we had forsaken our old paths and were hourly climbing over bars that had stood ten feet out of water before; we were shaving stumpy shores, like that at the foot of Madrid Bend, which I had always seen avoided before; we were clattering through chutes like that of 82, where the opening at the foot was an unbroken wall of timber till our nose was almost at the very spot. Some of these chutes were utter solitudes. The dense, untouched forest overhung both banks of the crooked little crack, and one could believe that human creatures had never intruded there before. The swinging grape-vines, the grassy nooks and vistas glimpsed as we swept by, the flowering creepers waving their red blossoms from the tops of dead trunks, and all the spendthrift richness of the forest foliage, were wasted and thrown away there. The chutes were lovely places to steer in; they were deep, except at the head; the current was gentle; under the "points" the water was absolutely dead, and the invisible banks so bluff that where the tender willow thickets projected you could bury your boat's broadside in them as you tore along, and then you seemed fairly to fly.

Behind other islands we found wretched little farms, and wretcheder little log cabins; there were crazy rail fences sticking a foot or two above the water, with one or two jeans-clad, chills-racked, yellow-faced male miserables roosting on the top rail, elbows on knees, jaws in hands, grinding tobacco and discharging the result at floating chips through crevices left by lost teeth; while the rest of the family and the few farm animals were huddled together in an empty wood-flat riding at her moorings close at hand. In this flatboat the family would have to cook and eat and sleep for a lesser or greater number of days (or possibly weeks), until the river should fall two or three feet and let them get back to their log cabins and their chills again—chills being a merciful provision of an all-wise Providence to enable them to take exercise without exertion. And this sort of watery camping out was a thing which these people were rather liable to be treated to a couple of times a year; by the December rise out of the Ohio, and the June rise out of the Mississippi. And yet these were kindly dispensations, for they at least enabled the poor things to rise from the dead now and then, and look upon life when a steamboat went by. They appreciated the blessing, too, for they spread their mouths and eyes wide open and made the most of these occasions. Now what *could* these banished creatures find to do to keep from dying of the blues during the low-water season!

Once, in one of these lovely island chutes, we found our course completely bridged by a great fallen tree. This will serve to show how narrow some of the chutes were. The passengers had an hour's recreation in a virgin wilderness, while the boat-hands chopped the bridge away; for there was no such thing as turning back, you comprehend.

From Cairo to Baton Rouge, when the river is over its banks, you have no particular trouble in the night; for the thousand-mile wall of dense forest that guards the two banks all the way is only gapped with a farm or woodyard opening at intervals, and so you can't "get out of the river" much easier than you could get out of a fenced lane; but from Baton Rouge to New Orleans it is a different matter. The river is more than a mile wide, and very deep—as much as two hundred feet, in places. Both banks, for a good deal over a hundred miles, are shorn of their timber and bordered by continuous sugar-plantations, with only here and there a scattering sapling or row of ornamental China trees. The timber is shown off clear to the rear of the plantations, from two to four miles. When the first frost threatens to come, the planters snatch off their corps in a hurry. When they have finished grinding the cane, they form the refuse of the stalks (which they call *bagasse*) into great piles and set fire to them, though in other sugar countries the bagasse is used for fuel in the furnaces of the sugar-mills. Now the piles of damp bagasse burn slowly, and smoke like Satan's own kitchen.

An embankment ten or fifteen feet high guards both banks of the Mississippi all the way down that lower end of the river, and this embankment is set back from the edge of the shore from ten to perhaps a hundred feet, according to circumstances; say thirty or forty feet, as a general thing. Fill that whole region with an impenetrable gloom of smoke from a hundred miles of burning bagasse piles, when the river is over the banks, and turn a steamboat loose along there at midnight and see how she will feel. And see how you will feel, too! You find yourself away out in the midst of a vague, dim sea that is shoreless, that fades out and loses itself in the murky distances; for you cannot discern the thin rib of embankment, and you are always imagining you see a straggling tree when you don't. The plantations themselves are transformed by the smoke, and look like a part of the sea. All through your watch you are tortured with the exquisite misery of uncertainty. You hope you are keeping in the river, but you do not know. All that you are sure about is that you are likely to be within six feet of the bank *and* destruction, when you think you are a good half-mile from shore. And you are sure, also, that if you chance suddenly to fetch up against the embankment and topple your chimneys overboard, you will have the small comfort of knowing that it is about what you were expecting to do. One of the great Vicksburg packets darted out into a sugar-plantation one night, at such a time, and had to stay there a week. But there was no novelty about it; it had often been done before.

I thought I had finished this chapter, but I wish to add a curious thing, while it is in my mind. It is only relevant in that it is connected with piloting. There used to be an excellent pilot on the river, a Mr. X, who was a somnambulist. It was said that if his mind was troubled about a bad piece of river, he was pretty sure to get up and walk in his sleep and do strange things. He was once fellow-pilot for a trip or two with George Ealer, on a great New Orleans passenger-packet. During a considerable part of the first trip George was uneasy, but got over it by and by, as X seemed content to stay in his bed when asleep. Late one night the boat was approaching Helena, Ark.; the water was low, and the crossing above the town in a very blind and tangled condition. X had seen the crossing since Ealer had, and as the night was particularly drizzly, sullen, and dark, Ealer was considering whether he had not better have X called to assist in running the place, when the door opened and X walked in. Now, on very dark nights, light is a deadly enemy to piloting; you are aware that if you stand in a lighted room, on such a night, you cannot see things in the street to any purpose; but if you put out the lights and stand in the gloom you can make out objects in the street pretty well. So, on very dark nights, pilots do not smoke; they allow no fire in the pilot-house stove, if there is a crack which can allow the least ray to escape; they order the furnaces to be curtained with huge tarpaulins and the skylights to be closely blinded. Then no light whatever issues from the boat. The undefinable shape that now entered the pilot-house had Mr. X's voice. This said:

"Let me take her, George; I've seen this place since you have, and it is so crooked that I reckon I can run it myself easier than I could tell you how to do it."

"It is kind of you, and I swear *I* am willing. I haven't got another drop of perspiration left in me. I have been spinning around and around the wheel like a squirrel. It is so dark I can't tell which way she is swinging till she is coming around like a whirligig."

So Ealer took a seat on the bench, panting and breathless. The black phantom assumed the wheel without saying anything, steadied the waltzing steamer with a turn or two, and then stood at ease, coaxing her a little to this side and then to that, as gently and as sweetly as if the time had been noon-day. When Ealer observed this marvel of steering, he wished he had not confessed! He stared, and wondered, and finally said:

"Well, I thought I knew how to steer a steamboat, but that was another mistake of mine."

X said nothing, but went serenely on with his work. He rang for the leads; he rang to slow down the steam; he worked the boat carefully and neatly into invisible marks, then stood at the center of the wheel and peered blandly out into the blackness, fore and aft, to verify his position; as the leads shoaled more and more, he stopped the engines entirely, and the dead silence and suspense of "drifting" followed; when the shoalest water was struck, he cracked on the steam, carried her handsomely over, and then began to work her warily into the next system of shoal-marks; the same patient, heedful use of leads and engines followed, the boat slipped through without touching bottom, and entered upon the third and last intricacy of the crossing; imperceptibly she moved through the gloom, crept by inches into her marks, drifted tediously till the shoalest water was cried, and then, under a tremendous head of steam, went swinging over the reef and away into deep water and safety!

Ealer let his long-pent breath pour in a great relieving sigh, and said:

"That's the sweetest piece of piloting that was ever done on the Mississippi River! I wouldn't believe it could be done, if I hadn't seen it."

There was no reply, and he added:

"Just hold her five minutes longer, partner, and let me run down and get a cup of coffee."

A minute later Ealer was biting into a pie, down in the "texas," and comforting himself with coffee. Just then the night watchman happened in, and was about to happen out again, when he noticed Ealer and exclaimed:

"Who is at the wheel, sir?"

"X."

"Dart for the pilot-house, quicker than lightning!"

The next moment both men were flying up the pilot-house companionway, three steps at a jump! Nobody there! The great steamer was whistling down the middle of the river at her own sweet will! The watchman shot out of the place again; Ealer seized the wheel, set an engine back with power, and held his breath while the boat reluctantly swung away from a "towhead," which she was about to knock into the middle of the Gulf of Mexico!

By and by the watchman came back and said:

"Didn't that lunatic tell you he was asleep, when he first came up here?"

"No."

"Well, he was. I found him walking along on top of the railings, just as unconcerned as another man would walk a pavement; and I put him to bed; now just this minute there he was again, away astern, going through that sort of tight-rope devilry the same as before."

"Well, I think I'll stay by next time he has one of those fits. But I hope he'll have them often. You just ought to have seen him take this boat through Helena crossing. *I* never saw anything so gaudy before. And if he can do such gold-leaf, kid-glove, diamond-breastpin piloting when he is sound asleep, what *couldn't* he do if he was dead!"

$\mathscr{T}$HIS $\mathscr{S}$AVAGE $\mathscr{L}$AND

Rick Bass

$\mathscr{Y}$ou can see the guys from the city getting a bit funny-eyed, when Tim and I walk down to the put-in carrying a chain saw. It's raining hard, pouring off the brims of our caps, and they think it's a practical joke—the four-weight fly rod in one hand and the Stihl 034 Super (with extended bar) chain saw in the other. They're so polite, these guys from the East—famous writers, famous fishermen and world travelers—that they don't know whether they're being had or not, but they don't want to risk hurting our feelings so they just huddle in the rain and puff cheerily on their cigars and stare through the drizzle at the damp woods pressing in from that riverside wall of green. Mist is rising from the river. Even the name itself sounds somehow terrible and sharp, *Yaak*, like the sound a hatchet might make, cleaving flesh and then bone, and perhaps they think, well, why not a chain saw?

I am not a fisherman, but the guide, Tim, my friend, has invited me along. The fishermen are dressed elegantly, ready for a bit of sport. I am wearing my old, stained overalls, ragged steel-toed boots, and I'm acutely aware of being half a foot shorter than any of these lanky, graceful gents—Tim, Tom, Charles, Dan and Chris. Actually, Chris is from Utah, Dan is from South Dakota, and Tom is from Jackson Hole, Wyoming—but from a Yaak standpoint, this qualifies them as easterners. Charles is from Nova Scotia. We have two drift boats and a raft with us and when I climb into one of the boats with my chain saw, I think they are also acutely aware of my stumpiness, and with the saw, and climbing in awkwardly—not knowing much about boats—I do not feel like a fellow fly-fisherman, but like a pirate.

Rick Bass

How gentlemanly are they? Dan hunts gyrfalcons in Saudi Arabia with princes. Charles and Tom and Chris own more bird dogs than I have empty aluminum cans in the plastic bag behind my barn. They hunt red deer in Mongolia, wild boar in Europe, and now they've come to the Yaak to fish in the rain for tadpole-sized brook trout while some troll rides along with them scouting for firewood.

"Got enough gas?" Tim asks me. "Got your saw tool?"

I nod, Tim goes over to the fishermen and asks them what kind of flies they have, and what size. Charles, Dan and Chris answer him dutifully; only Tom thinks to question authority. "Does it really matter?" he asks, and Tim looks surprised, then says, "No, they'll probably hit anything."

There is so much about fly-fishing that I do not understand, but I know enough to recognize that Tim is a great guide, so great that he does not have to be a snob. The river doesn't get too much traffic, due to the multitude of tiny unsophisticated fish that will never be anything other than tiny. Then there's the matter of the long winding flat stretches of river, and, as the gentlemen visitors are beginning to see, there is throughout the valley the vague and uncomfortable sense that the locals—us—may be watching from behind the bushes. The locals have some other-ness that is not easily defined, and which is not relaxing to visitors.

We didn't move up here to be around crowds, which may bring up the question of why I am then mentioning this river in the first place, this slow-moving water of dull-witted fingerlings. (I am tempted to tell you that Yaak is the Kootenai word for carp, or leech, or "place of certain diarrhea." It truthfully means *arrow*, but could also double to mean *rain*.)

Tim and I spend a good amount of time at other periods of the year hiking in the mountains, looking for antlers, looking for bear dens, looking for huckleberries, and in the winter, rattling deer and chasing elk—and then after that, grouse again, in the snow, in December, with our beautiful, talented dogs, and after that, ducks. . . .

On these trips, year in and year out, Tim and I go round and round in our anguish: do we keep silent about this hard-logged valley, or do we pipe up plaintively, make little cheepings, like killdeer skittering along the shore? We really don't care for the tourist hordes to come gawk at the clearcuts, or come feel the blue wet winds—to eat a cheeseburger at either of the local bars, to stand in the parking lot and marvel at the menagerie of woods-hermits-come-to-town-on-Satur-

44

day, as if a circus is parading past: gentle hippies, savage government-loathers, angry misanthropes, romantic anarchists, and a few normal people who in their normalcy appear somehow odd. Surely they are masking some great aberration. And those are the ones who come to town—who venture out into the light of day! The rest of us like to hide.

There is a certain duct-tape mentality that pervades this place. I'm not sure why, unless it's simply that things break a lot. It hasn't infected Tim yet and I guess after seven years if it were going to, it would have. He's neat and precise and does his job, finding fish and wild game, in an orderly, calculated fashion. But many of the rest of us tie socks over our broken windshield wipers, for instance, rather than venturing into town to get new wiper blades. We try to keep three of everything; one that runs, one for parts and one for a backup, if there's not time to switch our parts. But usually there's time.

We get our food, our meat and berries, from the land, and our produce from our gardens: root crops, which can stand the eternal cold. Blue smoke rises from chimneys year-round. The scent carries far in the humidity, in the drizzle.

The grizzlies aren't any problem up here; what will get you are the leeches, blackflies, mosquito hordes, and eight species of horseflies (including one the size of the head of a railroad spike whose bite is like being nipped by a fencing tool.)

I don't mean to be falling over myself so much, rolling out the welcome mat. The logging trucks keep coming and going. They drive hard and fast, and they will run your tourist-ass off the cliffs in a minute, then laugh about it.

Tim's livelihood depends, more or less, on bringing people into the valley. But like most of us, he thinks it would be nice to keep Yaak the way it is, or even better, to have it somehow reappear as it was five or ten or twenty years ago. (Twenty-eight years ago, there was only one road through the valley. Now there are over a thousand miles of road, and counting. And still not one acre of protected wilderness.)

Relax. I'm not going to lay the enviro-eco-rap on you. Or will try not to. I'm trying to kind of place you in Tim's position.

In order to keep living here he needs people to ride in his boat and cast flies, just as some must keep building roads, or cutting trees, to keep living here. But when there are no fish, and no more trees, and when every last mountain has a road onto it . . . then what? Do we learn semiconductor manufacturing in the evenings?

Tim has, among other guides, a funny reputation in some respects, as he doesn't always seem like he wants to be a guide. There's
very little telephone service or electricity in the Yaak, and it's a long
damn way to any airport—more than three hours to Kalispell, four to
Spokane, five to Missoula. Phone service and electricity are erratic up
here. Tim's answering machine has some electronic glitch—some
pulse of the wild, perhaps, that it has picked up from the soil itself, as
the coils and cables snake just beneath the skin of the earth—which
causes it to shut off on the incoming message after your first six words,
so you'd better choose them well.

Other guides joke (though I get the sense they really believe it,
too) that it's something Tim does on purpose—that not so deep down,
he doesn't want new clients. Or that maybe he wants them, but then
feels guilty about wanting them. The way I feel guilty, about writing
about this wet buggy valley.

So Tim gambles that the people he introduces to the slow snag-
infested water will fall in love with the valley and work to keep it from
being further abused, and I make the same gamble, continuing to
write about it.

We intend on this trip to use the chain saw for snags. It's a little
river, and trees fall across it regularly, blocking your passage. In other
places, the deep river suddenly splits into four braids, each only a few
inches deep, so that you may have to portage if you don't pick the
right one. Also, there is a guy up here who lives along the river and
hunts with a blowgun. He likes to hide in the bushes and shoot
tourists. At first you think it's just another horsefly. But then you develop a headache, and then you grow sleepy. You put the oars down
and lie back in the boat for a minute, just to nap, you think. . . .

If you did come all the way up to this last tiny river, it could be
deadly to not use Tim for a guide. And if you did come, there'd be that
vow of undying commitment we'd ask you to sign: to fight forever,
hard and passionately for this wet people-less place, on behalf of all
wildness—to fight to keep it as it is, at least.

Of course, we're asking you to take that vow anyway, whether
you come or not. For the grizzlies, wolves, woodland caribou, elk, and
wolverines that live back in what remains of the wet jungle, and
which you would never see anyway, if you were to come up here, as
they've all become almost totally nocturnal. And for those eight
species of horseflies, which have not.

∽

I guess you're waiting to hear about the river, and about fish, and here I am yowling about the wilderness. But it seems so simple. We have only three congressmen for the whole state. There is no designated, protected wilderness in the valley. If everyone who liked or favored clean water and the notion of a dark secret place, with feisty little fish and moose and great blue heron rookeries and dense spruce jungles— if everyone who liked these things would begin a correspondence with the three congressmen concerning the Yaak, I think they would finally come to understand that, timber budget or not, the remaining roadless acres in the Yaak should be protected.

Back to the gents. It's an honor to be in their company. They don't care if they catch fish or not. They just enjoy being out-of-doors, and in a new land. Since childhood they've probably caught seven million fish, cumulatively. Every fish mouth in the world is sore from their hooks. Today they're enjoying just being alive. They're standing in the rain.

When we set off, I'm in Tom's raft. Dan and Charles are in their own boat, and Tim's ranging ahead of them in his boat, with Chris, like a bird dog. The guys stop at the first gravel bar and get out and wade near the line where some fast water meets some slow water, and begin casting pretty casts into the line.

But nothing. Tim rows on, as if knowing there aren't any fish there. Tom watches Tim disappear around the bend and starts to say something, but doesn't. We lean back and watch Charles and Dan cast. If they catch something, maybe we'll rig up. Charles, Dan, Chris and Tom have been on a road trip across Montana—they've fished nine rivers in nine days. This is the tenth, and Charles (from Nova Scotia) is raving about what a beautiful, perfect little trout stream it is: how it reminds him of when he was a child, and was first learning to fish on brook trout rivers.

He's tired of all the muscle rivers of the past nine days and, believe it or not, of all the muscle-fish. He's content to cast and let his line drift and smoke his cigar in the rain.

The Yaak is a tiny river, but an important one, especially with the loss of the upper Kootenai River (and the now-extinct Ural Valley) to the wretched dam that formed Lake Koocanusa, in order to send more juice to California. The Yaak flows from four forks down into what remains of the Kootenai, a river that reminds one of the Mississippi. And the Kootenai then flows, Yaak-laden, into the Columbia, where it becomes fragmented by dams—lakes where salmon once ran wild.

It boggles my mind to stand in one of the cedar forests high in the mountains of Yaak and watch a creek—say, Fix Creek—go trickling down through the forest, a foot wide and a foot deep—and to picture it being received by the Yaak, and then by the Kootenai, and then by the Columbia, and then by the ocean.

This is my home.

I know that in writing about a river, you're supposed to concentrate on the fish—and then, narrowing the focus further, upon the catching of them.

Tim's a good guide, a great guide. He can find you a big deer. It's not real good elk country—too many roads, not enough security areas, according to biologists—but he can give it the best shot of anybody. His maniacal sense of sportsmanship has altered me. We shoot only about every tenth grouse. *Too slow!* we'll cry to each other when a bird crosses the other's path, or *Young bird!* or *Old bird! Let 'er go!*—year by year increasing our ridiculous standards, out of our love for this savage place, until a grouse just about has to be going 90 mph downhill through doghair lodgepole in the rain for us to get the green light.

I wonder sometimes if I in turn influence Tim with my duct-tape-ness. We often forget to be hard-core hunters. While hunting with him, I carry plastic Ziploc bags and collect bear scat to give to the biologists for DNA testing of genetic vigor. While drifting the Yaak we stop and search for pretty river rocks. We collect water samples. When we're out together on the water, we do just about everything but fish. Tim tells me the names of the insects, teaches me to cast, but time and time again I skew the subject, and talk about baseball or football—about his moribund, erratic Patriots or my choke-bound Oilers.

If it's spring, we discuss the autumn; if it's fall, we discuss the spring. In the summer and fall, when it rains, we talk about how nice it is to be dry.

I jabber a mile a minute, and never about fishing, and rarely about hunting, but always, it seems, about the valley.

Tim rows in closer to shore to examine the skeleton of a bull moose that has drowned in one of the deep holes, and tells me about the time he caught an eight-inch rainbow by dragging a nymph through the moose's algae-hued skeleton ten feet down—the fish rising from the pelvis to take the nymph and then trying to turn back to the sanctuary of the vertebrae, but no luck. Tim reeled the fish in, though after a moment he gently released him.

I know you're not going to travel this far to catch an eight-inch rainbow. But maybe you can travel over to your desk and pick up a pen. Sort through the papers until you find a stray postcard and write the three congressmen.

The five gentlemen and I drift. It's a pleasure to watch them cast. The word Tim uses to describe the river is "intimate." The Kootenai is where he makes his money (as much as any guide ever makes, which is to say, not much), and the Yaak is what he saves for a few special lazy days of the year.

It's still raining, but slants of light beam through the foglike clouds along the river; the fog hangs in the tops of the giant spruce and cedar and fir trees. These trees are a function of the thin soil, tight gray clay over glacial cobble, and the soil is a function of the bedrock, which is in turn a function of the earth's belly, the earth's anatomy—what she desires to belch up here in this spongy, lush river country.

At times it is more of a creek than a river, like a child's ride in a raft through an amusement park, with the theme of "jungle." You can reach out and touch either bank, in places. Deer rise from the tall grass to peer at you, only their heads visible over the banks: big-eyed does, wide-ribbed in pregnancy, and bucks in velvet nubs.

"Short casts," Tim tells the occasional wanderer who inquires about fishing the Yaak with him. "Short casts. Intimate. You can see everything. You can see the moss growing on the rocks. You can see the caddis nymphs, the stonefly nymphs, crawling under their rocks. You can see the fish. Intimate," he says.

Purple anvil-shaped thunderheads tower behind us, rising between the forested mountains all the way to the outer arc of the atmosphere, and perhaps beyond: we are so wet, so drenched, and it is still raining so steadily, that perhaps it is raining on the moon.

We pass beneath an old wooden covered bridge. Soon we will be out in the riffles where the rainbow trout leap. Black and silver, they look like anchovies.

We trade off riding in different boats and rafts, to chat; to get to know one another. It's not about fishing. It's about being in the Yaak. It's about feeling the magic of all the little feeder creeks, cedar streams, not so rich in nutrients, but rich in magic, emptying into the Yaak's little belly. Later in the summer there will be a drought, whose only saving grace will be that the temperatures never get too hot; though the river will drop drastically, lower than it's ever been mea- sured in white man's history; and in August, fires will move through on the south-facing slopes, cleaning out the underbrush, the dried-up buffalo berry that has grown up following old logging operations, and cleansing some of the lodgepole stands up high of pine beetles. And in September, on Labor Day, as on every Labor Day, the rains will return, extinguishing the fires, and beginning to give ease to the suffering creeks, and the fish will begin gathering at their mouths, readying to spawn in the fall rains, as they have almost every year through the millennia.

(Tim, a lover of waters, has moved up and down practically every creek in northwestern Montana, every backwater beaver-slough he can find, taking pictures of the occasional freak brook trout or the in- credibly rare wetslope cutthroat. Not surprisingly, those creeks that haven't been streamside- or headwaters-logged tolerate the droughts much better than the clearcut stretches.)

We pass beneath giant cedars. A few more fish. I hook a ten- inch rainbow, which will be the heavy of the day. Wild rainbows, and wild wetslope cutthroats, and the gorgeous little brook trout. It's not unusual, Tim says, to catch all three; while just below, in the Koote- nai, the bull trout breathing water breathed by sturgeon, and each year these creeks get filled in with more and more sediment, get lower and lower, and each year the bulls wait to make their heroic runs one more time.

We talk about books, we talk about politics, we talk about dogs and food and friends and assholes. We talk about the ocean and about Africa and about childhood. Charles is smoking a pipe now, and the smoke mixes with the fog. These damn little fish keep hooking them- selves on our casts. Some of us put our rods down and just ride. The water turns dark, deep. Like any small river, the Yaak can be over- fished by a single guy intent upon only meat, and in the past, it has been. The days of big fish in big holes are no longer with us, but be- cause the river's small, the little fish still hide behind almost every rock.

Later on, at supper, we'll hit the five gents up for letters to save this wild green place. We'll tell them how, in all the years, there's never been a single acre of wilderness protected; how the international timber companies have long had their way with this forgotten place. We'll tell them that it's time to hold the Montana delegation responsible. Tim will discuss the Kootenai, and the Libby Dam operations, at length. The sign-up sheet will be passed, and the new letter writers recruited before dessert is passed out—if they want any dessert. A trade; the army, the small battalion, growing by four.

All that will come later. Right now it's time only for river intimacy. Green drakes begin to rise from the water, and Tim is overjoyed: in seven years, he's never seen them on the Yaak. He wants to believe that the river is recovering. We're drifting through a meadow now, where every year before cattle had grazed, but this year the cattle are gone, and the willows have grown at least a foot, and the green drakes are swarming, landing on our arms as if trying to tell us things.

A purple thundercloud drifts up the river to meet us—lashes us with stinging rain. We laugh like school kids walking home in a storm. We come around one corner—aspens, white pine, alder, ash, all clinging to a rock outcrop—and turn into a cool dark tunnel of cedar and spruce. Another bend, and now an old spruce stretches across the little river, spiny limbs splayed everywhere, resting a few inches above the water and spanning it completely. The tree is so big that it must have been a giant before whites first moved into the valley in the early 1900s. It's probably fifty inches across; it's too low to go under, and too high for us to drag our boats up over it.

The current has quickened, here in this dark tunnel, and we back-paddle to avoid being drawn into the limbs and turned sideways. We're all aware of the furious, silent power of water, even relatively mild water—the strength of its mass—and the way things can turn bad quickly.

Carefully I climb up on top of the tree—thrashing through the maw of branches—and Tim anchors, and hands the saw up to me.

The saw's wet and won't start at first. We're a long way from anywhere. It's raining harder still. Finally the saw coughs, then ignites, with a belch of blue smoke and a roar, and I choke it back to a purr, then start blipping off branches to clear a working area. Sawdust showers all three boats, all five fishermen. The rain beating down quickly mixes with the sawdust to coat them all with a sodden paste.

A bit of bar oil drips into the river, sending heartbreaking iridescent rainbow downcurrent. So much for the pious talk of the afternoon.

I begin making my crosscuts in the huge tree. The roar is deafening. How will I be able to hear grouse flush this fall?

So much for intimate. The green wood sags. Our worst fear is of binding the saw, and I'm careful, but can't get beneath the log with the blade—not unless I put it underwater.

There's a creaking, and the log drops an inch, pinches the saw tight. Now we're screwed. We take turns clambering onto the log and pulling, wrenching and twisting—a fly-fisherman's version of *The Sword in the Stone*. A fly-fishing guide's nightmare. Surely he's wondering why he brought me.

The rain lashes at us. Finally Tim, in the strength of desperation, is able to free the saw. I start it back up. Nothing runs like a Stihl.

I'm standing in the bow of his new boat making a new cut, and making good progress, when a new sound begins to emanate from the saw, a splintery sound, accompanied by a certain bucking and vibration of the boat. *Ahh*, I think, *we're into the heartwood now.*

Out of the corner of my eye, I notice a new color of sawdust beginning to appear in the pile around our ankles: it's cream-colored, the same color as Tim's boat.

He's such a gentleman! "That's O.K.," he says, when I lift the saw and stare, aghast, at the cut in the gunwale: as if I aimed to sink us! "Just a ding," he says.

Tim doesn't belong up here, really. He's like those other four gents. He's too courteous, and too *professional*. I'm afraid of giving him my virus, the one that makes you fond of duct tape; afraid of infecting him somehow with a woods-piggishness, a kind of savagery that is not uncommon in Yaak. I want him to be immune from it: and so far, he is. His New England heritage, etc. I'd already torn up his truck; he'd parked it behind my old beater one day, and I backed into it. "Ah, that's O.K.," he'd said then, too. "Just a ding."

It's a different place, up here. There's a certain roughness of spirit; a wildness. You can see it in the old cars and trucks, in all the rotting things. A certain endurance, a willingness to go on, even when a bit crippled up by hard times, by deep snows, or whatever. But Tim's a pro, and such a nice guy: I feel guilty, as if my looseness, my Yaakness, might cramp his style. As if the valley might cramp his style.

He loves it, too. At least as much as I do. I guess if he were going to turn into a savage, it would have already happened.

I finish the cut, avoiding the boat this time. The log drops with a crash, swings free; the current surges. New structure—a new hole for the worm fishermen. We pull up anchor and release ourselves through the slot, like salmon through a gate. The rain finally lets up; sunlight pours down the mountains. We enter long, slow water—flat water, with much rowing to be done. We're cold, chilled to the deep bone. Fresh sawdust floats downriver with us, preceding us for a mile or so.

Shadows deepen. There's one touchy moment when we come to a spot in the river where a man has draped a 220-volt electrical line across the river at neck level, as if to electroshock us; but it turns out he's only doing some welding on the other side of the river. In the dimness, we might not have seen it. Tim knows the man, is friendly with him, as he is with everyone. He gives the magic password, and the man lifts his cable high enough for us to go by unelectrocuted.

We take out in deepening, buggy twilight, slapping mosquitoes, and go up to the tavern to watch one of the basketball playoffs. Later we feast on wild game accompanied by wine and cigars and stories.

Driving home that night, Tim will tell me, he saw a lynx with only three paws cross the road; the fourth paw was raw and stumpy, probably from a trap. But Tim said he could tell by the way the lynx crossed the road that it still wanted to go on. It would rest up, Tim thought, and recover.

FROM *Down an Unknown River*

Theodore Roosevelt

*T*he mightiest river in the world is the Amazon. It runs from west to east, from the sunset to the sunrise, from the Andes to the Atlantic. The main stream flows almost along the equator, while the basin which contains its affluents extends many degrees north and south of the equator. The gigantic equatorial river-basin is filled with an immense forest, the largest in the world, with which no other forest can be compared save those of western Africa and Malaysia. We were within the southern boundary of this great equatorial forest, on a river which was not merely unknown but unguessed at, no geographer having ever suspected its existence. This river flowed northward toward the equator, but whither it would go, whether it would turn one way or another, the length of its course, where it would come out, the character of the stream itself, and the character of the dwellers along its banks—all these things were yet to be discovered.

One morning while the canoes were being built Kermit and I walked a few kilometres down the river and surveyed the next rapids below. The vast still forest was almost empty of life. We found old Indian signs. There were very few birds and these in the tops of the tall trees. We saw a recent tapir track; and under a cajazeira-tree by the bank there were the tracks of capybaras which had been eating the fallen fruit. This fruit is delicious and would make a valuable addition to our orchards. The tree although tropical is hardy, thrives when domesticated, and propagates rapidly from shoots. The Department of Agriculture should try whether it would not grow in southern California and Florida. This was the tree from which the doctor's family name was taken. His parental grandfather, although of Portuguese blood, was an intensely patriotic Brazilian. He was a very young man when the independence of Brazil was declared, and did not wish to keep the Portuguese family name; so he changed it to that of the fine Brazilian tree in question. Such change of family names is common in Brazil. Doctor Vital Brazil, the student of poisonous serpents, was given his name by his father, whose own family name was entirely different; and his brother's name was again different.

There were tremendous downpours of rain, lasting for a couple of hours and accompanied by thunder and lightning. But on the whole it seemed as if the rains were less heavy and continuous than they had been. We all of us had to help in building the canoes now and then. Kermit, accompanied by Antonio the Parecís and João, crossed the river and walked back to the little river that had entered from the east, so as to bring back a report of it to Colonel Rondon. Lyra took observations, by the sun and by the stars. We were in about latitude eleven degrees twenty-one minutes south, and due north of where we had started. The river had wound so that we had gone two miles for every one we made northward. Our progress had been very slow; and until we got out of the region of incessant rapids, with their attendant labor and hazard, it was not likely that we should go much faster.

On the morning of March 22 we started in our six canoes. We made ten kilometres. Twenty minutes after starting we came to the first rapids. Here every one walked except the three best paddlers, who took the canoes down in succession—an hour's job. Soon after this we struck a bees' nest in the top of a tree overhanging the river; our steersman climbed out and robbed it, but, alas! lost the honey on the way back. We came to a small steep fall which we did not dare run in our overladen, clumsy, and cranky dugouts. Fortunately, we were able to follow a deep canal which led off for a kilometre, returning just below the falls, fifty yards from where it had started. Then, having been in the boats and in motion only one hour and a half, we came to a long stretch of rapids which it took us six hours to descend, and we camped at the foot. Everything was taken out of the canoes, and they were run down in succession. At one difficult and perilous place they were let down by ropes; and even thus we almost lost one.

We went down the right bank. On the opposite bank was an Indian village, evidently inhabited only during the dry season. The marks on the stumps of trees showed that these Indians had axes and knives; and there were old fields in which maize, beans, and cotton had been grown. The forest dripped and steamed. Rubber-trees were plentiful. At one point the tops of a group of tall trees were covered with yellow-white blossoms. Others bore red blossoms. Many of the big trees, of different kinds, were buttressed at the base with great thin walls of wood. Others, including both palms and ordinary trees, showed an even stranger peculiarity. The trunk, near the base, but sometimes six or eight feet from the ground, was split into a dozen or twenty branches or small trunks which sloped outward in tent-like shape, each becoming a root. The larger trees of this type looked as if their trunks were seated on the tops of the pole frames of Indian tepees. At one point in the stream, to our great surprise, we saw a flying-fish. It skimmed the water like a swallow for over twenty yards.

Although we made only ten kilometres we worked hard all day. The last canoes were brought down and moored to the bank at nightfall. Our tents were pitched in the darkness.

Next day we made thirteen kilometres. We ran, all told, a little over an hour and three quarters. Seven hours were spent in getting past a series of rapids at which the portage, over rocky and difficult ground, was a kilometre long. The canoes were run down empty—a hazardous run, in which one of them upset.

Yet while we were actually on the river, paddling and floating downstream along the reaches of swift, smooth water, it was very lovely. When we started in the morning the day was overcast and the air was heavy with vapor. Ahead of us the shrouded river stretched between dim walls of forest, half seen in the mist. Then the sun burned up the fog and loomed through it in a red splendor that changed first to gold and then to molten white. In the dazzling light, under the brilliant blue of the sky, every detail of the magnificent forest was vivid to the eye: the great trees, the network of bushropes, the caverns of greenery where thick-leaved vines covered all things else. Wherever there was a hidden boulder the surface of the current was broken by waves. In one place, in midstream, a pyramidal rock thrust itself six feet above the surface of the river. On the banks we found fresh Indian sign.

At home in Vermont, Cherrie is a farmer, with a farm of six hundred acres, most of it woodland. As we sat at the foot of the rapids, watching for the last dugouts with their naked paddlers to swing into sight round the bend through the white water, we talked of the northern spring that was just beginning. He sells cream, eggs, poultry, potatoes, honey, occasionally pork and veal; but at this season it was the time for the maple-sugar crop. He has a sugar-orchard, where he taps twelve hundred trees and hopes soon to tap as many more in addition. Said Cherrie: "It's a busy time now for Fred Rice"— Fred Rice is the hired man, and in sugar-time the Cherrie boys help him with enthusiasm, and, moreover, are paid with exact justice for the work they do. There is much wild life about the farm, although it is near Brattleboro. One night in early spring a bear left his tracks near the sugarhouse; and now and then in summer Cherrie has had to sleep in the garden to keep the deer away from the beans, cabbages, and beets.

There was not much bird life in the forest, but Cherrie kept getting species new to the collection. At this camp he shot an interesting little ant-thrush. It was the size of a warbler, jet-black, with white under-surfaces of the wings and tail, white on the tail-feathers, and a large spot of white on the back, normally almost concealed, the feathers on the back being long and fluffy. When he shot the bird, a male, it was showing off before a dull-colored little bird, doubtless the female; and the chief feature of the display was this white spot on the back. The white feathers were raised and displayed so that the spot flashed like the "chrysanthemum" on a prongbuck whose curiosity has been roused. In gloom of the forest the bird was hard to see, but the flashing of this patch of white feathers revealed it at once, attracting immediate attention. It was an excellent example of a coloration mark which served a purely advertising purpose; apparently it was part of a courtship display. The bird was about thirty feet up in the branches.

In the morning, just before leaving this camp, a tapir swam across stream a little way above us; but unfortunately we could not get a shot at it. An ample supply of tapir beef would have meant much to us. We had started with fifty days' rations; but this by no means meant full rations, in the sense of giving every man all he wanted to eat. We had two meals a day, and were on rather short commons—both our mess and the camaradas'—except when we got plenty of palm tops. For our mess we had the boxes chosen by Fiala, each containing a day's rations for six men, our number. But we made each box last a day and a half, or at times two days, and in addition we gave some of the food to the camaradas. It was only on the rare occasions when we had killed some monkeys or curassows, or caught some fish, that everybody had enough. We would have welcomed that tapir. So far the game, fish, and fruit had been too scarce to be an element of weight in our food-supply. In an exploring trip like ours, through a difficult and utterly unknown country, especially if densely forested, there is little time to halt, and game cannot be counted on. It is only in lands like our own West thirty years ago, like South Africa in the middle of the last century, like East Africa to-day that game can be made the chief food-supply. On this trip our only substantial food-supply from the country hitherto had been that furnished by the palm tops. Two men were detailed every day to cut down palms for food.

A kilometre and a half after leaving this camp we came on a stretch of big rapids. The river here twists in loops, and we had heard the roaring of these rapids the previous afternoon. Then we passed out of earshot of them; but Antonio Correa, our best waterman, insisted all along that the roaring meant rapids worse than any we had encountered for some days. "I was brought up in the water, and I know it like a fish, and all its sounds," said he. He was right. We had to carry the loads nearly a kilometre that afternoon, and the canoes were pulled out on the bank so that they might be in readiness to be dragged overland next day. Rondon, Lyra, Kermit, and Antonio Correa explored both sides of the river. On the opposite or left bank they found the mouth of a considerable river, bigger than the Rio Kermit, flowing in from the west and making its entrance in the middle of the rapids. This river we christened the Taunay, in honor of a distinguished Brazilian, an explorer, a soldier, a senator, who was also a writer of note. Kermit had with him two of his novels, and I had read one of his books dealing with a disastrous retreat during the Paraguayan war.

Next morning, the 25th, the canoes were brought down. A path was chopped for them and rollers laid: and half-way down the rapids Lyra and Kermit, who were overseeing the work as well as doing their share of the pushing and hauling, got them into a canal of smooth water, which saved much severe labor. As our food-supply lowered we were constantly more desirous of economizing the strength of the men. One day more would complete a month since we had embarked on the Dúvida—as we had started in February, the lunar and calendar months coincided. We had used up over half our provisions. We had come only a trifle over one hundred and sixty kilometres, thanks to the character and number of the rapids. We believed we had three or four times the distance yet to go before coming to a part of the river where we might hope to meet assistance, either from rubber-gatherers or from Pyrineus, if he were really coming up the river which we were going down. If the rapids continued to be as they had been it could not be much more than three weeks before we were in straits for food, aside from the ever-present danger of accident in the rapids; and if our progress were no faster than it had been—and we were straining to do our best—we would in such event still have several hundreds of kilometres of unknown river before us. We could not even hazard a guess at what was in front. The river was now a really big river, and it seemed impossible that it could flow either into the Gy-Paraná or the Tapajos. It was possible that it went into the Canumá, a big affluent of the Madeira low down and next to the Tapajos. It was more probable that it was the headwaters of the Aripuanan, a river which, as I have said, was not even named on the excellent English map of Brazil I carried. Nothing but the mouth had been known to any geographer; but the lower course had long been known to rubber-gatherers, and recently a commission from the government of Amazonas had part way ascended one branch of it—not as far as the rubber-gatherers had gone, and, as it turned out, not the branch we came down.

Two of our men were down with fever. Another man, Julio, a fellow of powerful frame, was utterly worthless, being an inborn, lazy shirk with the heart of a ferocious cur in the body of a bullock. The others were good men, some of them very good indeed. They were under the immediate supervision of Pedrinho Craveiro, who was first-class in every way.

This camp was very lovely. It was on the edge of a bay, into which the river broadened immediately below the rapids. There was a beach of white sand, where we bathed and washed our clothes. All around us, and across the bay, and on both sides of the long water-street made by the river, rose the splendid forest. There were flocks of parakeets colored green, blue, and red. Big toucans called overhead, lustrous green-black in color, with white throats, red gorgets, red-and-yellow tail-coverts, and huge black-and-yellow bills. Here the soil was fertile; it will be a fine site for a coffee-plantation when this region is open to settlement. Surely such a rich and fertile land cannot be permitted to remain idle, to lie as a tenantless wilderness, while there are such teeming swarms of human beings in the overcrowded, overpeopled countries of the Old World. The very rapids and waterfalls which now make the navigation of the river so difficult and dangerous would drive electric trolleys up and down its whole length and far out on either side, and run mills and factories, and lighten the labor on farms. With the incoming of settlement and with the steady growth of knowledge how to fight and control tropical diseases, fear of danger to health would vanish. A land like this is a hard land for the first explorers, and perhaps for their immediate followers, but not for the people who come after them.

In mid-afternoon we were once more in the canoes; but we had paddled with the current only a few minutes, we had gone only a kilometre, when the roar of rapids in front again forced us to haul up to the bank. As usual, Rondon, Lyra, and Kermit, with Antonio Correa, explored both sides while camp was being pitched. The rapids were longer and of steeper descent than the last, but on the opposite or western side there was a passage down which we thought we could get the empty dugouts at the cost of dragging them only a few yards at one spot. The loads were to be carried down the hither bank, for a kilometre, to the smooth water. The river foamed between great rounded masses of rock, and at one point there was a sheer fall of six or eight feet. We found and ate wild pineapples. Wild beans were in flower. At dinner we had a toucan and a couple of parrots, which were very good.

All next day was spent by Lyra in superintending our three best watermen as they took the canoes down the west side of the rapids, to the foot, at the spot to which the camp had meantime been shifted. In the forest some of the huge sipas, or rope vines, which were as big as cables, bore clusters of fragrant flowers. The men found several honey-trees, and fruits of various kinds, and small cocoanuts; they chopped down an ample number of palms, for the palm-cabbage; and, most important of all, they gathered a quantity of big Brazil-nuts, which when roasted tasted like the best of chestnuts and are nutritious; and they caught a number of big piranhas, which were good eating. So we all had a feast, and everybody had enough to eat and was happy.

By these rapids, at the fall, Cherrie found some strange carvings on a bare mass of rock. They were evidently made by men a long time ago. As far as is known, the Indians thereabouts make no such figures now. They were in two groups, one on the surface of the rock facing the land, the other on that facing the water. The latter were nearly obliterated. The former were in good preservation, the figures sharply cut into the rock. They consisted, upon the upper flat part of the rock, of four multiple circles with a dot in the middle very accurately made and about a foot and a half in diameter; and below them, on the side of the rock, four multiple m's or inverted w's. What these curious symbols represented or who made them, we could not, of course, form the slightest idea. It may be that in a very remote past some Indian tribes of comparatively advanced culture had penetrated to this lovely river, just as we had now come to it. Before white men came to South America there had already existed therein various semicivilizations, some rude, others fairly advanced, which rose, flourished, and persisted through immemorial ages, and then vanished. The vicissitudes in the history of humanity during its stay on this southern continent have been as strange, varied, and inexplicable as paleontology shows to have been the case, on the same continent, in the history of the higher forms of animal life during the age of mammals. Colonel Rondon stated that such figures as these are not found anywhere else in Matto Grosso where he has been, and therefore it was all the more strange to find them in this one place on the unknown river, never before visited by white men, which we were descending.

Next morning we went about three kilometres before coming to some steep hills, beautiful to look upon, clad as they were in dense, tall, tropical forest, but ominous of new rapids. Sure enough, at their foot we had to haul up and prepare for a long portage. The canoes we ran down empty. Even so, we were within an ace of losing two, the lashed couple in which I ordinarily journeyed. In a sharp bend of the rapids, between two big curls, they were swept among the boulders and under the matted branches which stretched out from the bank. They filled, and the racing current pinned them where they were, one partly on the other. All of us had to help get them clear. Their fastenings were chopped asunder with axes. Kermit and half a dozen of the men, stripped to the skin, made their way to a small rock island in the little falls just above the canoes, and let down a rope which we tied to the outermost canoe. The rest of us, up to our armpits and barely able to keep our footing as we slipped and stumbled among the boulders in the swift current, lifted and shoved while Kermit and his men pulled the rope and fastened the slack to a half-submerged tree. Each canoe in succession was hauled up the little rock island, baled, and then taken down in safety by two paddlers. It was nearly four o'clock before we were again ready to start, having been delayed by a rain-storm so heavy that we could not see across the river. Ten minutes' run took us to the head of another series of rapids; the exploring party returned with the news that we had an all-day's job ahead of us: and we made camp in the rain, which did not matter much, as we were already drenched through. It was impossible, with the wet wood, to make a fire sufficiently hot to dry all our soggy things, for the rain was still falling. A tapir was seen from our boat, but, as at the moment we were being whisked round in a complex circle by a whirlpool, I did not myself see it in time to shoot.

Next morning we went down a kilometre, and then landed on the other side of the river. The canoes were run down, and the loads carried to the other side of a little river coming in from the west, which Colonel Rondon christened Cherrie River. Across this we went on a bridge consisting of a huge tree felled by Macairo, one of our best men. Here we camped, while Rondon, Lyra, Kermit, and Antonio Correa explored what was ahead. They were absent until mid-afternoon. Then they returned with the news that we were among ranges of low mountains, utterly different in formation from the high plateau region to which the first rapids, those we had come to on the 2d of March, belonged. Through the first range of these mountains the river ran in a gorge, some three kilometres long, immediately ahead of us. The ground was so rough and steep that it would be impossible to drag the canoes over it and difficult enough to carry the loads; and the rapids were so bad, containing several falls, one of at least ten metres in height, that it was doubtful how many of the canoes we could not down them. Kermit, who was the only man with much experience of rope work, was the only man who believed we could get the canoes down at all; and it was, of course, possible that we should have to build new ones at the foot to supply the place of any that were lost or left behind. In view of the length and character of the portage and of all the unpleasant possibilities that were ahead and of the need of keeping every pound of food, it was necessary to reduce weight in every possible way and to throw away everything except the barest necessities.

We thought we had reduced our baggage before: but now we cut to the bones. We kept the fly for all six of us to sleep under. Kermit's shoes had gone, thanks to the amount of work in the water which he had been doing; and he took the pair I had been wearing, while I put on my spare pair. In addition to the clothes I wore, I kept one set of pajamas, a spare pair of drawers, a spare pair of socks, half a dozen handkerchiefs, my wash-kit, my pocket medicine case, and a little bag containing my spare spectacles, gun grease, some adhesive plaster, some needles and thread, the "fly dope," and my purse and letter of credit, to be used at Manaos. All of these went into the bag containing my cot, blanket, and mosquito-net. I also carried a cartridge bag containing my cartridges, head net, and gauntlets. Kermit cut down even closer; and the others about as close.

The last three days of March we spent in getting to the foot of the rapids in this gorge. Lyra and Kermit, with four of the best watermen, handled the empty canoes. The work was not only difficult and laborious in the extreme, but hazardous; for the walls of the gorge were so sheer that at the worst places they had to cling to narrow shelves on the face of the rock, while letting the canoes down with ropes. Meanwhile Rondon surveyed and cut a trail for the burden-bearers, and superintended the portage of the loads. The rocky sides of the gorge were too steep for laden men to attempt to traverse them. Accordingly the trail had to go over the top of the mountain, both the ascent and the descent of the rock-strewn, forest-clad slopes being very steep. It was hard work to carry loads over such a trail. From the top of the mountain, through an opening in the trees on the edge of a cliff, there was a beautiful view of the country ahead. All around and in front of us there were ranges of low mountains about the height of the lower ridges of the Alleghanies. Their sides were steep and they were covered with the matted growth of the tropical forest. Our next camping-place, at the foot of the gorge, was almost beneath us, and from thence the river ran in a straight line, flecked with white water, for about a kilometre. Then it disappeared behind and between mountain ridges, which we supposed meant further rapids. It was a view well worth seeing; but, beautiful although the country ahead of us was, its character was such as to promise further hardships, difficulty, and exhausting labor, and especially further delay; and delay was a serious matter to men whose food-supply was beginning to run short, whose equipment was reduced to the minimum, who for a month, with the utmost toil, had made very slow progress, and who had no idea of either the distance or the difficulties of the route in front of them.

There was not much life in the woods, big or little. Small birds were rare, although Cherrie's unwearied efforts were rewarded from time to time by a species new to the collection. There were tracks of tapir, deer, and agouti; and if we had taken two or three days to devote to nothing else than hunting them we might perchance have killed something; but the chance was much too uncertain, the work we were doing was too hard and wearing, and the need of pressing forward altogether too great to permit us to spend any time in such manner. The hunting had to come in incidentally. This type of well-nigh impenetrable forest is the one in which it is most difficult to get even what little game exists therein. A couple of curassows and a big monkey were killed by the colonel and Kermit. On the day the monkey was brought in Lyra, Kermit, and their four associates had spent from sunrise to sunset in severe and at moments dangerous toil among the rocks and in the swift water, and the fresh meat was appreciated. The head, feet, tail, skin, and entrails were boiled for the gaunt and ravenous dogs. The flesh gave each of us a few mouthfuls; and how good those mouthfuls tasted!

Cherrie, in addition to being out after birds in every spare moment, helped in all emergencies. He was a veteran in the work of the tropic wilderness. We talked together often, and of many things, for our views of life, and of a man's duty to his wife and children, to other men and to women, and to the State in peace and war, were in all essentials the same. His father had served all through the Civil War, entering an Iowa cavalry regiment as a private and coming out as a captain; his breast-bone was shattered by a blow from a musket butt, in hand-to-hand fighting at Shiloh.

During this portage the weather favored us. We were coming toward the close of the rainy season. On the last day of the month, when we moved camp to the foot of the gorge, there was a thunderstorm; but on the whole we were not bothered by rain until the last night, when it rained heavily, driving under the fly so as to wet my cot and bedding. However, I slept comfortably enough, rolled in the damp blanket. Without the blanket I should have been uncomfortable; a blanket is a necessity for health. On the third day Lyra and Kermit, with their daring and hard-working watermen, after wearing labor, succeeded in getting five canoes through the worst of the rapids to the chief fall. The sixth, which was frail and weak, had its bottom beaten out on the jagged rocks of the broken water. On this night, although I thought I had put my clothes out of reach, both the termites and the carregadores ants got at them, ate holes in one boot, ate one leg of my drawers, and riddled my handkerchief; and I now had nothing to replace anything that was destroyed.

Next day Lyra, Kermit, and their camaradas brought the five canoes that were left down to camp. They had in four days accomplished a work of incredible labor and of the utmost importance; for at the first glance it had seemed an absolute impossibility to avoid abandoning the canoes when we found that the river sank into a cataract-broken torrent at the bottom of a canyon-like gorge between steep mountains. On April 2 we once more started, wondering how soon we should strike other rapids in the mountains ahead, and whether in any reasonable time we should, as the aneroid indicated, be so low down that we should necessarily be in a plain where we could make a journey of at least a few days without rapids. We had been exactly a month going through an uninterrupted succession of rapids. During that month we had come only about one hundred and ten kilometres, and had descended nearly one hundred and fifty me-tres—the figures are approximate but fairly accurate.[1] We had lost four of the canoes with which we started, and one other, which we had built, and the life of one man; and the life of a dog which by its death had in all probability saved the life of Colonel Rondon. In a straight line northward toward our supposed destination, we had not made more than a mile and a quarter a day; at the cost of bitter toil for most of the party, of much risk for some of the party, and of some risk and some hardship for all the party. Most of the camaradas were downhearted, naturally enough, and occasionally asked one of us if we really believed that we should ever get out alive; and we had to cheer them up as best we could.

There was no change in our work for the time being. We made but three kilometres that day. Most of the party walked all the time; but the dugouts carried the luggage until we struck the head of the se-ries of rapids which were to take up the next two or three days. The river rushed through a wild gorge, a chasm or canyon, between two mountains. Its sides were very steep, mere rock walls, although in most places so covered with the luxuriant growth of the trees and bushes that clung in the crevices and with green moss that the naked rock was hardly seen. Rondon, Lyra, and Kermit, who were in front, found a small level spot with a beach of sand, and sent back word to camp there while they spent several hours in exploring the country ahead. The canoes were run down empty, and the loads carried

---

[1]The first four days, before we struck the upper rapids, and during which we made nearly seventy kilometres, are of course not included when I speak of our making our way down the rapids.

painfully along the face of the cliffs; so bad was the trail that I found it rather hard to follow, although carrying nothing but my rifle and cartridge bag. The explorers returned with the information that the mountains stretched ahead of us, and that there were rapids as far as they had gone. We could only hope that the aneroid was not hopelessly out of kilter, and that we should, therefore, fairly soon find ourselves in comparatively level country. The severe toil, on a rather limited food-supply, was telling on the strength as well as on the spirits of the men; Lyra and Kermit, in addition to their other work, performed as much actual physical labor as any of them.

Next day, the 3d of April, we began the descent of these sinister rapids of the chasm. Colonel Rondon had gone to the summit of the mountain in order to find a better trail for the burden-bearers, but it was hopeless, and they had to go along the face of the cliffs. Such an exploring expedition as that in which we were engaged of necessity involves hard and dangerous labor and perils of many kinds. To follow downstream an unknown river, broken by innumerable cataracts and rapids, rushing through mountains of which the existence has never even been guessed, bears no resemblance whatever to following even a fairly dangerous river which has been thoroughly explored and has become in some sort a highway, so that experienced pilots can be secured as guides, while the portages have been pioneered and trails chopped out, and every dangerous feature of the rapids is known beforehand. In this case no one could foretell that the river would cleave its way through steep mountain chains, cutting narrow clefts in which the cliff walls rose almost sheer on either hand. When a rushing river thus "canyons," as we used to say out West, and the mountains are very steep, it becomes almost impossible to bring the canoes down the river itself and utterly impossible to portage them along the cliff sides, while even to bring the loads over the mountain is a task of extraordinary labor and difficulty. Moreover, no one can tell how many times the task will have to be repeated or when it will end or whether the food will hold out; every hour of work in the rapids is fraught with the possibility of the gravest disaster, and yet it is imperatively necessary to attempt it; and all this is done in an uninhabited wilderness, or else a wilderness tenanted only by unfriendly savages, where failure to get through means death by disease and starvation. Wholesale disasters to South American exploring parties have been frequent. The first recent effort to descend one of the unknown rivers to the Amazon from the Brazilian highlands resulted in such a disaster. It was undertaken in 1889 by a party about as large as ours under a Brazilian engineer officer, Colonel Telles Peres. In descending some rapids they lost everything—canoes, food, medicine, implements—everything. Fever smote them and then starvation. All of them died except one officer and two men who were rescued months later. Recently, in Guiana, a wilderness veteran, André, lost two-thirds of his party by starvation. Genuine wilderness exploration is as dangerous as warfare. The conquest of wild nature demands the utmost vigor, hardihood, and daring, and takes from the conquerors a heavy toll of life and health.

Lyra, Kermit, and Cherrie, with four of the men, worked the canoes half-way down the canyon. Again and again it was touch and go whether they could get by a given point. At one spot the channel of the furious torrent was only fifteen yards across. One canoe was lost, so that of the seven with which we had started only two were left. Cherrie labored with the other men at times, and also stood as guard over them, for, while actually working, of course no one could carry a rifle. Kermit's experience in bridge-building was invaluable in enabling him to do the rope work by which alone it was possible to get the canoes down the canyon. He and Lyra had now been in the water for days. Their clothes were never dry. Their shoes were rotten. The bruises on their feet and legs had become sores. On their bodies some of the insect bites had become festering wounds, as indeed was the case with all of us. Poisonous ants, biting flies, ticks, wasps, bees were a perpetual torment. However, no one had yet been bitten by a venomous serpent, a scorpion, or a centipede, although we had killed all of the three within camp limits.

Under such conditions whatever is evil in men's natures comes to the front. On this day a strange and terrible tragedy occurred. One of the camaradas, a man of pure European blood, was the man named Julio, of whom I have already spoken. He was a very powerful fellow and had been importunately eager to come on the expedition; and he had the reputation of being a good worker. But, like so many men of higher standing, he had had no idea of what such an expedition really meant, and under the strain of toil, hardship, and danger his nature showed its true depths of selfishness, cowardice, and ferocity. He shirked all work. He shammed sickness. Nothing could make him do his share; and yet unlike his self-respecting fellows he was always shamelessly begging for favors. Kermit was the only one of our party who smoked; and he was continually giving a little tobacco to some of the camaradas, who worked especially well under him. The good men did not ask for it; but Julio, who shirked every labor, was always, and always in vain, demanding it. Colonel Rondon, Lyra, and Kermit each tried to get work out of him, and in order to do anything with him had to threaten to leave him in the wilderness. He threw all his tasks on his comrades, and, moreover, he stole their food as well as ours. On such an expedition the theft of food comes next to murder as a crime, and should by rights be punished as such. We could not trust him to cut down palms or gather nuts, because he would stay out and eat what ought to have gone into the common store. Finally, the men on several occasions themselves detected him stealing their food. Alone of the whole party, and thanks to the stolen food, he had kept in full flesh and bodily vigor.

One of our best men was a huge negro named Paixão—Paishon—a corporal and acting sergeant in the engineer corps. He had, by the way, literally torn his trousers to pieces, so that he wore only the tatters of a pair of old drawers until I gave him my spare trousers when we lightened loads. He was a stern disciplinarian. One evening he detected Julio stealing food and smashed him in the mouth. Julio came crying to us, his face working with fear and malignant hatred; but after investigation he was told that he had gotten off uncommonly lightly. The men had three or four carbines, which were sometimes carried by those who were not their owners.

On this morning, at the outset of the portage, Pedrinho discovered Julio stealing some of the men's dried meat. Shortly afterward Paishon rebuked him for, as usual, lagging behind. By this time we had reached the place where the canoes were tied to the bank and then taken down one at a time. We were sitting down, waiting for the last loads to be brought along the trail. Pedrinho was still in the camp we had left. Paishon had just brought in a load, left it on the ground with his carbine beside it, and returned on the trail for another load. Julio came in, put down his load, picked up the carbine, and walked back on the trail, muttering to himself but showing no excitement. We thought nothing of it, for he was always muttering; and occasionally one of the men saw a monkey or big bird and tried to shoot it, so it was never surprising to see a man with a carbine.

In a minute we heard a shot; and in a short time three or four of the men came up the trail to tell us that Paishon was dead, having been shot by Julio, who had fled into the woods. Colonel Rondon and Lyra were ahead; I sent a messenger for them, directed Cherrie and

Kermit to stay where they were and guard the canoes and provisions and started down the trail with the doctor—an absolutely cool and plucky man, with a revolver but no rifle—and a couple of the cama-radas. We soon passed the dead body of poor Paishon. He lay in a huddle, in a pool of his own blood, where he had fallen, shot through the heart. I feared that Julio had run amuck, and intended merely to take more lives before he died, and that he would begin with Pedrinho, who was alone and unarmed in the camp we had left. Accordingly I pushed on, followed by my companions, looking sharply right and left; but when we came to the camp the doctor quietly walked by me, remarking: "My eyes are better than yours, colonel: if he is in sight I'll point him out to you, as you have the rifle." However, he was not there, and the others soon joined us with the welcome news that they had found the carbine.

The murderer had stood to one side of the path and killed his victim, when a dozen paces off, with deliberate and malignant purpose. Then evidently his murderous hatred had at once given way to his innate cowardice, and, perhaps hearing some one coming along the path, he fled in panic terror into the wilderness. A tree had knocked the carbine from his hand. His footsteps showed that after going some rods he had started to return, doubtless for the carbine, but had fled again, probably because the body had then been discovered. It was questionable whether or not he would live to reach the Indian villages, which were probably his goal. He was not a man to feel remorse—never a common feeling; but surely that murderer was in a living hell, as, with fever and famine leering at him from the shadows, he made his way through the empty desolation of the wilderness. Franca, the cook, quoted out of the melancholy proverbial philosophy of the people the proverb, "No man knows the heart of any one"; and then expressed with deep conviction a weird ghostly belief I had never encountered before: "Paishon is following Julio now, and will follow him until he dies; Paishon fell forward on his hands and knees, and when a murdered man falls like that his ghost will follow the slayer as long as the slayer lives."

We did not attempt to pursue the murderer. We could not legally put him to death, although he was a soldier who in cold blood had just deliberately killed a fellow soldier. If we had been near civilization we would have done our best to bring him in and turn him over to justice. But we were in the wilderness, and how many weeks' journey was ahead of us we could not tell. Our food was running low, sickness was beginning to appear among the men, and both their courage and their strength were gradually ebbing. Our first duty was to save the lives and the health of the men of the expedition who had honestly been performing, and had still to perform, so much perilous labor. If we brought the murderer in he would have to be guarded night and day on an expedition where there were always loaded firearms about, and where there would continually be opportunity and temptation for him to make an effort to seize food and a weapon and escape, perhaps murdering some other good man. He could not be shackled while climbing along the cliff slopes; he could not be shackled in the canoes, where there was always chance of upset and drowning; and standing guard would be an additional and severe penalty on the weary, honest men already exhausted by overwork. The expedition was in peril, and it was wise to take every chance possible that would help secure success. Whether the murderer lived or died in the wilderness was of no moment compared with the duty of doing everything to secure the safety of the rest of the party. For the two days following we were always on the watch against his return, for he could have readily killed some one else by rolling rocks down on any of the men working on the cliff sides or in the bottom of the gorge. But we did not see him until the morning of the third day. We had passed the last of the rapids of the chasm, and the four boats were going downstream when he appeared behind some trees on the bank and called out that he wished to surrender and be taken aboard; for the murderer was an arrant craven at heart, a strange mixture of ferocity and cowardice. Colonel Rondon's boat was far in advance; he did not stop nor answer. I kept on in similar fashion with the rear boats, for I had no intention of taking the murderer aboard, to the jeopardy of the other members of the party, unless Colonel Rondon told me that it would have to be done in pursuance of his duty, as an officer of the army and a servant of the government of Brazil. At the first halt Colonel Rondon came up to me and told me that this was his view of his duty, but that he had not stopped because he wished first to consult me as the chief of the expedition. I answered that for the reasons enumerated above I did not believe that in justice to the good men of the expedition we should jeopardize their safety by taking the murderer along, and that if the responsibility were mine I should refuse to take him; but that he, Colonel Rondon, was the superior officer of both the murderer and of all the other enlisted men and army officers on the expedition, and in return was responsible for his actions to his own governmental superiors and to the laws of Brazil; and that in view of this responsibility he must act as his sense of duty bade him. Accordingly, at the next camp he sent back two men, expert woodsmen, to find the murderer and bring him in. They failed to find him.[2]

I have anticipated my narrative because I do not wish to recur to the horror more than is necessary. I now return to my story. After we found that Julio had fled, we returned to the scene of the tragedy. The murdered man lay with a handkerchief thrown over his face. We buried him beside the place where he fell. With axes and knives the camaradas dug a shallow grave while we stood by with bared heads. Then reverently and carefully we lifted the poor body which but half an hour before had been so full of vigorous life. Colonel Rondon and I bore the head and shoulders. We laid him in the grave, and heaped a mound over him, and put a rude cross at his head. We fired a volley for a brave and loyal soldier who had died doing his duty. Then we left him forever, under the great trees beside the lonely river.

That day we got only half-way down the rapids. There was no good place to camp. But at the foot of one steep cliff there was a narrow, boulder-covered slope where it was possible to sling hammocks and cook; and a slanting spot was found for my cot, which had sagged until by this time it looked like a broken-backed centiped. It rained a little during the night, but not enough to wet us much. Next day Lyra, Kermit, and Cherrie finished their job, and brought the four remaining canoes to camp, one leaking badly from the battering on the rocks. We then went downstream a few hundred yards, and camped on the opposite side; it was not a good camping-place, but it was better than the one we left.

The men were growing constantly weaker under the endless strain of exhausting labor. Kermit was having an attack of fever, and Lyra and Cherrie had touches of dysentery, but all three continued to work. While in the water trying to help with an upset canoe I had by my own clumsiness bruised my leg against a boulder; and the resulting inflammation was somewhat bothersome. I now had a sharp attack of fever, but thanks to the excellent care of the doctor, was over it in about forty-eight hours; but Kermit's fever grew worse and he too

---

[2]The above account of all the circumstances connected with the murder was read to and approved as correct by all six members of the expedition.

was unable to work for a day or two. We could walk over the portages, however. A good doctor is an absolute necessity on an exploring expedition in such a country as that we were in, under penalty of a frightful mortality among the members; and the necessary risks and hazards are so great, the chances of disaster so large, that there is no warrant for increasing them by the failure to take all feasible precautions.

The next day we made another long portage round some rapids, and camped at night still in the hot, wet, sunless atmosphere of the gorge. The following day, April 6, we portaged past another set of rapids, which proved to be the last of the rapids of the chasm. For some kilometres we kept passing hills, and feared lest at any moment we might again find ourselves fronting another mountain gorge; with, in such case, further days of grinding and perilous labor ahead of us, while our men were disheartened, weak, and sick. Most of them had already begun to have fever. Their condition was inevitable after over a month's uninterrupted work of the hardest kind in getting through the long series of rapids we had just passed; and a long further delay, accompanied by wearing labor, would have almost certainly meant that the weakest among our party would have begun to die. There were already two of the camaradas who were too weak to help the others, their condition being such as to cause us serious concern.

However, the hills gradually sank into a level plain, and the river carried us through it at a rate that enabled us during the remainder of the day to reel off thirty-six kilometres, a record that for the first time held out promise. Twice tapirs swam the river while we passed, but not near my canoe. However, the previous evening Cherrie had killed two monkeys and Kermit one, and we all had a few mouthfuls of fresh meat; we had already had a good soup made out of a turtle Kermit had caught. We had to portage by one short set of rapids, the unloaded canoes being brought down without difficulty. At last, at four in the afternoon, we came to the mouth of a big river running in from the right. We thought it was probably the Ananás, but, of course, could not be certain. It was less in volume than the one we had descended, but nearly as broad; its breadth at this point being ninety-five yards as against one hundred and twenty for the larger river. There were rapids ahead, immediately after the junction, which took place in latitude ten degrees fifty-eight minutes south. We had come two hundred and sixteen kilometres all told, and were nearly north of where we had started. We camped on the point of land between the two rivers. It was extraordinary to realize that here about the eleventh degree we were on such a big river, utterly unknown to the cartographers and not indicated by even a hint on any map. We named this big tributary Rio Cardozo, after a gallant officer of the commission who had died of beriberi just as our expedition began. We spent a day at this spot, determining our exact position by the sun, and afterward by the stars, and sending on two men to explore the rapids in advance. They returned with the news that there were big cataracts in them, and that they would form an obstacle to our progress. They had also caught a huge siluroid fish, which furnished an excellent meal for everybody in camp. This evening at sunset the view across the broad river, from our camp where the two rivers joined, was very lovely; and for the first time we had an open space in front of and above us, so that after nightfall the stars, and the great waxing moon, were glorious overhead, and against the rocks in mid-stream the broken water gleamed like tossing silver.

The huge catfish which the men had caught was over three feet and a half long, with the usual enormous head, out of all proportion to the body, and the enormous mouth, out of all proportion to the head. Such fish, although their teeth are small, swallow very large prey. This one contained the nearly digested remains of a monkey. Probably the monkey had been seized while drinking from the end of a branch; and once engulfed in that yawning cavern there was no escape. We Americans were astounded at the idea of a catfish making prey of a monkey; but our Brazilian friends told us that in the lower Madeira and the part of the Amazon near its mouth there is a still more gigantic catfish which in similar fashion occasionally makes prey of man. This is a grayish-white fish over nine feet long, with the usual disproportionately large head and gaping mouth, with a circle of small teeth; for the engulfing mouth itself is the danger, not the teeth. It is called the piraiba—pronounced in four syllables. While stationed at the small city of Itacoatiara, on the Amazon, at the mouth of the Madeira, the doctor had seen one of these monsters which had been killed by the two men it had attacked. They were fishing in a canoe when it rose from the bottom—for it is a ground fish—and raising itself half out of the water lunged over the edge of the canoe at them, with open mouth. They killed it with their *falcóns*, as machetes are called in Brazil. It was taken round the city in triumph in an ox-cart; the doctor saw it and said it was three metres long. He said that swimmers feared it even more than the big cayman, because they could see the latter, whereas the former lay hid at the bottom of the water. Colonel Rondon said that in many villages where he had been on the lower Madeira the people had built stockaded enclosures in the water in which they bathed, not venturing to swim in the open water for fear of the piraiba and the big cayman.

Next day, April 8, we made five kilometres only, as there was a succession of rapids. We had to carry the loads past two of them but ran the canoes without difficulty, for on the west side were long canals of swift water through the forest. The river had been higher but was still very high, and the current raced round the many islands that at this point divided the channel. At four we made camp at the head of another stretch of rapids, over which the Canadian canoes would have danced without shipping a teaspoonful of water, but which our dugouts could only run empty. Cherrie killed three monkeys and Lyra caught two big piranhas, so that we were again all of us well provided with dinner and breakfast. When a number of men, doing hard work, are most of the time on half-rations, they grow to take a lively interest in any reasonably full meal that does arrive.

On the 10th we repeated the proceedings: a short quick run; a few hundred metres' portage, occupying, however, at least a couple of hours; again a few minutes' run; again other rapids. We again made less than five kilometres; in the two days we had been descending nearly a metre for every kilometre we made in advance: and it hardly seemed as if this state of things could last, for the aneroid showed that we were getting very low down. How I longed for a big Maine birchbark, such as that in which I once went down the Mattawamkeag at high water! It would have slipped down these rapids as a girl trips through a country-dance. But our loaded dugouts would have shoved their noses under every curl. The country was lovely. The wide river, now in one channel, now in several channels, wound among hills; the shower-freshened forest glistened in the sunlight; the many kinds of beautiful palm fronds and the huge pacova-leaves stamped the peculiar look of the tropics on the whole landscape—it was like passing by water through a gigantic botanical garden. In the afternoon we got an elderly toucan, a piranha, and a reasonably edible side-necked river-turtle; so we had fresh meat again. We slept as usual in earshot of rapids. We had been out six weeks and almost all the time we had been engaged in wearily working our own way down and past rapid after rapid. Rapids are by far the most dangerous enemies of explorers and travelers who journey along these rivers.

Next day was a repetition of the same work. All the morning was spent in getting the loads to the foot of the rapids at the head of which we were encamped, down which the canoes were run empty. Then for thirty or forty minutes we ran down the swift, twisting river, the two lashed canoes almost coming to grief at one spot where a swirl of the current threw them against some trees on a small submerged island. Then we came to another set of rapids, carried the baggage down past them, and made camp long after dark in the rain—a good exercise in patience for those of us who were still suffering somewhat from fever. No one was in really buoyant health. For some weeks we had been sharing part of the contents of our boxes with the camaradas; but our food was not very satisfying to them. They needed quantity and the mainstay of each of their meals was a mass of palmitas; but on this day they had no time to cut down palms. We finally decided to run these rapids with the empty canoes, and they came down in safety. On such a trip it is highly undesirable to take any save necessary risks, for the consequences of disaster are too serious; and yet if no risks are taken the progress is so slow that disaster comes anyhow: and it is necessary perpetually to vary the term of the perpetual working compromise between rashness and overcaution. This night we had a very good fish to eat, a big silvery fellow called a pescada, of a kind we had not caught before.

One day Trigueiro failed to embark with the rest of us, and we had to camp where we were next day to find him. Easter Sunday we spent in the fashion with which we were altogether too familiar. We only ran in a clear course for ten minutes all told, and spent eight hours in portaging the loads past rapids down which the canoes were run; the balsa was almost swamped. This day we caught twenty-eight big fish, mostly piranhas, and everybody had all he could eat for dinner and for breakfast the following morning.

The forenoon of the following day was a repetition of this wearisome work; but late in the afternoon the river began to run in long and quiet reaches. We made fifteen kilometres, and for the first time in several weeks camped where we did not hear the rapids. The silence was soothing and restful. The following day, April 14, we made a good run of some thirty-two kilometres. We passed a little river which entered on our left. We ran two or three light rapids and portaged the loads by another. The river ran in long and usually tranquil stretches. In the morning when we started the view was lovely.

There was a mist, and for a couple of miles the great river, broad and quiet, ran between the high walls of tropical forest, the tops of the giant trees showing dim through the haze. Different members of the party caught many fish, and shot a monkey and a couple of jacu-tinga—birds kin to a turkey but the size of a fowl—so we again had a camp of plenty. The dry season was approaching, but there were still heavy, drenching rains. On this day the men found some new nuts of which they liked the taste: but the nuts proved unwholesome and half of the men were very sick and unable to work the following day. In the balsa only two were left fit to do anything, and Kermit plied a paddle all day long.

Accordingly, it was a rather sorry crew that embarked the fol-lowing morning, April 15. But it turned out a red-letter day. The day before, we had come across cuttings, a year old, which were probably but not certainly made by pioneer rubber men. But on this day—dur-ing which we made twenty-five kilometres—after running two hours and a half we found on the left bank a board on a post with the ini-tials J. A., to show the farthest-up point which a rubber man had reached and claimed as his own. An hour farther down we came on a newly built house in a little planted clearing; and we cheered heartily. No one was at home, but the house of palm thatch was clean and cool. A couple of dogs were on watch, and the belongings showed that a man, and a woman, and a child lived there and had only just left. Another hour brought us to a similar house where dwelt an old black man who showed the innate courtesy of the Brazilian peasant. We came on these rubber men and their houses in about latitude ten degrees twenty-four minutes.

In mid-afternoon we stopped at another clean, cool, pic-turesque house of palm thatch. The inhabitants all fled at our ap-proach, fearing an Indian raid; for they were absolutely unprepared to have any one come from the unknown regions upstream. They returned and were most hospitable and communicative; and we spent the night there. Said Antonio Correa to Kermit: "It seems like a dream to be in a house again and hear the voices of men and women, instead of being among those mountains and rapids." The river was known to them as the Castanho and was the main afflu-ent, or rather the left or western branch, of the Aripuanan; the Cas-tanho is a name used by the rubber-gatherers only; it is unknown to the geographers. We were, according to our informants, about fifteen days' journey from the confluence of the two rivers; but there were many rubber men along the banks, some of whom had become permanent settlers. We had come over three hundred kilometres in forty-eight days, over absolutely unknown ground; we had seen no human being, although we had twice heard Indians. Six weeks had been spent in steadily slogging our way down through the interminable series of rapids. It was astonishing before, when we were on a river of about the size of the upper Rhine or Elbe, to realize that no geographer had any idea of its existence. But, after all, no civilized man of any grade had ever been on it. Here, however, was a river with people dwelling along the banks, some of whom had lived in the neighborhood for eight or ten years; and yet on no standard map was there a hint of the river's existence. We were putting on the map a river, running through between five and six degrees of latitude—of between seven and eight if, as should properly be done, the lower Aripuanan is included as part of it—of which no geographer, in any map published in Europe or the United States or Brazil, had even admitted the possibility of the existence; for the place actually occupied by it was filled, on the maps, by other—imaginary—streams or by mountain ranges. Before we started, the Amazonas Boundary Commission had come up the lower Aripuanan and then the eastern branch, or upper Aripuanan, to eight degrees forty-eight minutes, following the course which for a couple of decades had been followed by the rubber men, but not going as high. An employee, either of this commission or of one of the big rubber men, had been up the Castanho, which is easy of ascent in its lower course, to about the same latitude, not going nearly as high as the rubber men had gone; this we found out while we ourselves were descending the lower Castanho. The lower main stream, and the lower portion of its main affluent, the Castanho, had been commercial highways for rubber men and settlers for nearly two decades, and, as we speedily found, were as easy to traverse as the upper stream, which we had just come down, was difficult to traverse; but the governmental and scientific authorities, native and foreign, remained in complete ignorance; and the rubber men themselves had not the slightest idea of the headwaters, which were in country never hitherto traversed by civilized man. Evidently the Castanho was, in length at least, substantially equal, and probably superior, to the upper Aripuanan; it now seemed even more likely that the Ananás was the headwaters of the main stream than of the Cardozo.[3] For the first time this great river, the greatest affluent of the Madeira, was to be put on the map; and the understanding of its real position and real relationship, and the clearing up of the complex problem of the sources of all these lower right-hand affluents of the Madeira, were rendered possible by the seven weeks of hard and dangerous labor we had spent in going down an absolutely unknown river, through an absolutely unknown wilderness. At this stage of the growth of world geography I esteemed it a great piece of good fortune to be able to take part in such a feat—a defeat which represented the capping of the pyramid which during the previous seven years had been built by the labor of the Brazilian Telegraphic Commission.

We had passed the period when there was a chance of peril, of disaster, to the whole expedition. There might be risk ahead to individuals, and some difficulties and annoyances for all of us; but there was no longer the least likelihood of any disaster to the expedition as a whole. We now no longer had to face continual anxiety, the need of constant economy with food, the duty of labor with no end in sight, and bitter uncertainty as to the future.

It was time to get out. The wearing work, under very unhealthy conditions, was beginning to tell on every one. Half of the camaradas had been down with fever and were much weakened; only a few of them retained their original physical and moral strength. Cherrie and Kermit had recovered; but both Kermit and Lyra still had bad sores on their legs from the bruises received in the water work. I was in worse shape. The after-effects of the fever still hung on; and the leg which had been hurt while working in the rapids with the sunken canoe had taken a turn for the bad and developed an abscess. The good doctor, to whose unwearied care and kindness I owe much, had cut it open and inserted a drainage-tube; an added charm being given the operation and the subsequent dressings by the enthusiasm with which the piums and boroshudas took part therein. I could hardly hobble and was pretty well laid up. But "there aren't no 'stop , conductor,' while a

---

[3]I hope that this year Ananás, or Pineapple, will also be put on the map. One of Colonel Rondon's subordinates is to attempt the descent of the river. We passed the headwaters of the Pineapple on the high plateau, very possibly we passed its mouth, although it is also possible that it empties into the Canumá or Tapajos. But it will not be "put on the map" until some one descends and finds out where, as a matter of fact, it really does go.

battery's changing ground." No man has any business to go on such a trip as ours unless he will refuse to jeopardize the welfare of his associates by any delay caused by a weakness or ailment of his. It is his duty to go forward, if necessary on all fours, until he drops. Fortunately, I was put to no such test. I remained in good shape until we had passed the last of the rapids of the chasms. When my serious trouble came we had only canoe-riding ahead of us. It is not ideal for a sick man to spend the hottest hours of the day stretched on the boxes in the bottom of a small open dugout, under the well-nigh intolerable heat of the torrid sun of the mid-tropics, varied by blinding, drenching downpours of rain; but I could not be sufficiently grateful for the chance. Kermit and Cherrie took care of me as if they had been trained nurses; and Colonel Rondon and Lyra were no less thoughtful.

The north was calling strongly to the three men of the north—Rocky Dell Farm to Cherrie, Sagamore Hill to me: and to Kermit the call was stronger still. After nightfall we could now see the Dipper well above the horizon—upside down, with the two pointers pointing to a north star below the world's rim; but the Dipper, with all its stars. In our home country spring had now come, the wonderful northern spring of long glorious days, of brooding twilights, of cool delightful nights. Robin and bluebird, meadow-lark and song-sparrow, were singing in the mornings at home; the maple buds were red: windflowers and bloodroot were blooming while the last patches of snow still lingered; the rapture of the hermit-thrush in Vermont, the serene golden melody of the wood-thrush on Long Island, would be heard before we were there to listen. Each man to his home, and to his true love! Each was longing for the homely things that were so dear to him, for the home people who were dearer still, and for the one who was dearest of all.

AND THE
SALMON SING

Louise Wagenknecht

My mother's mother grew up on the Mississippi River, where her father, a Danish immigrant, worked through the Iowa winters in his shirtsleeves, cutting great blocks of ice from the heart of the river. She died seventy-two years later in the Gold Rush country of California, below a wall of blue water held back by Oroville Dam. In between, she lived for thirty-four years in the valley of Cottonwood Creek, a tributary of the upper Klamath River, in the Klamath Mountains on the California-Oregon border.

I remember standing, in those days, beside the Klamath, watching Grandmother cast a dry fly over the water, and asking, "How wide is the Mississippi, Grandmother?" And she would answer, "At Clinton, about a mile across. Now be quiet, the fish can hear you."

I stared at the green water purling around her hip waders, across the fifty-yard width of the Klamath, and tried to picture a river—a *river!*—a mile wide. Impossible.

I saw the Mississippi when I was seven, a great sluggish mass of brown water with a line of round trees over on the Illinois shore. It doesn't even *move*, I thought, so how can it be a river? But Grandmother looked across it, her hand shading her light blue eyes, smiling as I had never seen her smile, as she told us about the catfish—as long as a man and able to swamp a rowboat—that the fishermen used to catch when she was a girl. Although she fished the Klamath, *her* river

81

was the Mississippi, and the things she loved about the Klamath were the things that reminded her—and how few they must have been—of that vast presence two thousand miles away.

I write looking out at a line of willows beside a little river in eastern Idaho, the Lemhi, one of the far headwaters of the strangled Columbia. It flows into the Salmon River, which flows into the Snake. The Columbia is one of only two rivers that rise east of the Cascade Range and empty into the Pacific Ocean. The other is the Klamath.

The Lemhi—fought over, channelized, dewatered by irrigation withdrawals, its salmon gone—tries to meander through a valley about forty-five miles long. Along its length, remnants of gallery cottonwood forests survive, thin ribbons of prehistory bordering beautiful, doomed meadows. From above, they glow like green jewels in this impoverished high desert of bentonite hills. I grieve for the Lemhi, but another river comes to me in dreams just when I think I have forgotten it; another name brings my head up across a crowded room like the voice of a lost lover; I hear other waters roaring in the night, across a thousand miles of mountains. Those things I begin to love about the Lemhi and its boisterous child the Salmon, are the things that remind me, however faintly, of my river, of the Klamath.

Rivers are more than hydrology; they have lives and souls and can be hurt. My life on the Klamath paralleled the river's flow, moving downstream as we both grew older. The river and I spent all our days in the midst of a play for which nobody ever gave us the script. The difference between us is that the Klamath channels its stubborn, violent energy into a patient synergism with the laws of physics, willing to wait a thousand years to cut away a point or straighten a bend. In the end, the waters prevail, though species die and little men believe they have won.

The Klamath begins with the Williamson and Sprague Rivers, rising in southeastern Oregon, in the volcanic country behind the Cascades. They empty into Upper Klamath Lake in the cold, dry Klamath basin. At the lake's southern outlet, the waters suddenly fall eighty-seven feet in less than two miles, constituting the whole length of the Link River, a stream entirely within the city limits of Klamath Falls, Oregon.

Below the city, the Link River widens into Lake Ewauna, and leaving it, is born as the Klamath proper, turns southwest, and heads at last for California. After a journey of almost three hundred miles, it enters the Pacific Ocean near a tired little town called Requa. On its way, it cuts through the Klamath Mountains, a jumbled collage of geologic formations, folded and lifted and peneplained into a huge dissected plateau through which flow parts of the Klamath and Sacramento Rivers, as well as parts of Oregon's Rogue River.

Carving its way through the old, old mountains, bearing steadily southwest, it suddenly, on meeting the Trinity, its largest tributary, swings sharply north, pouring into a dark canyon only twenty miles from the coast, but so formidable that when Jedediah Smith reached the confluence on May 19, 1828, it took him until June 3 to reach the ocean by land.

The Klamath's first white explorers frequently got lost. Although the region around Upper Klamath Lake was known to the Hudson's Bay Company as "the Klamath Country" for years before Peter Skene Ogden actually explored it in 1826–27, what he called the "Clammitte" River was actually the Williamson. Subject to the creative spelling of the early nineteenth century, the name was written as Tlamet, Tlameth, Clamet, Clammitte, or Klamath, its actual meaning lost in the variations. The people known to whites as the Klamaths called themselves Maklaks, meaning "the people."

"My provisions are fast decreasing. The hunters are discouraged," Ogden confided morosely to his journal in November, just before some thirty Maklaks visited his camp. They told him that the river which emptied into the ocean was "yet far distant." By January the price of dogs for victuals had skyrocketed and Ogden was frankly depressed. His party worked their way downstream, trapping but taking few beaver until February, when a huge white mountain rose above the southern horizon as they reached the main Klamath River.

"I have named this river Sastise River," Ogden wrote, feeling better now that there were forty beaver pelts in camp. "There is a mountain equal in height to Mount Hood or Vancouver, I have named Mount Sastise. I have given these names from the tribes of Indians."

Ogden sent advance parties farther down the Klamath; they returned with hundreds of beaver and tales of large villages of plank houses with friendly inhabitants who owned large canoes of redwood.

His name for the river stuck for at least another decade, evolving into "Chasta" or "Shasta." The river now known as the Shasta rises near the great mountain and joins the Klamath a few miles downstream from the ford where Ogden's scouting parties crossed the river on their way back to Upper Klamath Lake. You can see it even now, across from Interstate 5, where the freeway leaves the river a few miles north of Yreka, California, and heads straight for Oregon.

Our fishing grounds stretched from the old ford upstream to just below Copco Lake, where the river, barely three miles south of the state line, slackens and widens behind Copco No. 1 Dam. Those sixteen or seventeen miles were all I knew of the Klamath before 1957. We lived ten miles north of the river, in a little company-owned lumber town called Hilt, just barely in California.

All week Grandfather worked in the lumber mill, my mother worked in the company office, and my Grandmother kept house and looked after my younger sister and me. But on Saturdays, from spring until the onset of winter, Grandmother and Grandfather got up early to pack a lunch, load the fishing gear into the Oldsmobile, and head south to the river. Here the Klamath runs through a gentle country, with alfalfa fields and pastures near the river bottoms, and steep grassy hills dotted with oak and juniper beyond. On the highest ridges and peaks, the remains of a pine forest that in the late nineteenth century supported a town beside the river called Klamathon, peeked from fields of brush. The town site was only another pasture on an old river bar, in a land of barbed wire and cows.

Just west of Hilt the rainfall increased, and the dark forests of pine and fir began again. Some were privately owned: by Fruit Growers Supply Company, which owned Hilt; by the Southern Pacific Railroad, which had been awarded alternate sections of land back in the 1880s, when the railroad between Sacramento and Portland was built; and by small ranches and mines that cut what timber they needed. But most was National Forest land, managed by the Klamath National Forest ever since the National Forests were organized in 1905.

Back in 1914, the Forest managers, overwhelmed by just how much timber they had, tried to sell more than two billion board feet growing north of the Klamath River, from the mouth of the Shasta River to the mouth of Indian Creek, sixty-four miles west at the town of Happy Camp. By building a railroad downriver from the main Southern Pacific line, they thought, the timber could be sold in three units, with mills spaced out along its length. No bids were ever received. "Too rugged, too much low quality timber," scoffed the lumbermen, still busily chewing their way through the vast groves of privately owned spruce and redwood and Douglas fir near the coast.

Abashed, the Forest Service realized that it could sell no great amounts of its timber reserves until a Forest road system existed. To this end they bent their efforts. Beginning in 1919, they pulled every string, used every law, and greased every wheel to have the federal and state governments build a road system that would make the un-counted millions of board feet of old growth conifers available to the saw. As my grandmother cast her fly into the water in the 1950s, the basic infrastructure was in place: the state highway that paralleled the Klamath River down to its confluence with the Trinity River and there linked with another highway that led to the coast, and a dozen other roads built with federal dollars up the main tributaries of the Klamath. Aggressive politicking by several Klamath National Forest Supervisors paid off; the post-war rises in lumber prices had already begun. The Forest needed only the right catalyst to spark a feeding frenzy, and we were about to watch it happen from our front yards.

On Labor Day weekend in 1955, we went fishing as usual. Grandfather, a sweat-stained fedora on his bald head, quickly disap-peared upstream. Grandmother fished closer to the car, a six-year-old and a four-year-old following her along the bank. My sister and I in-evitably jammed the tip of any fishing rod given to us into the rocks, or ensnarled the line into huge balls which Aunt Jo, taking a break from painting her nails and listening to the car radio, patiently un-wound, exclaiming, "How the *hell* did you do that?" while we giggled because nobody except Grandfather was supposed to say "hell."

Our river outings followed a pattern. Elizabeth and I followed Grandmother along the river, searching for agates or the opalescent shells of freshwater mussels and trying to catch the trout fry trapped in drying shoreline pools with doomed tadpoles. We poked at decay-ing fish carcasses, captured the mud-colored, yellow-legged frogs, and returned at last to the car with sticky hair and sneakers full of sand, which we dumped on the carpet.

Grandmother was a fine fly tyer and a skillful fisherwoman, bringing in trout after trout, which wiggled frantically as she gently removed the barbed hook and measured the fish against the flattened palm of her hand, which was the exact legal size, six inches. She in-spected their flanks for the ugly round wounds left on so many fish by the sharp mouths of lampreys. She slid the keepers into her wicker creel, seized her walking stick and waded further into the river, cast-ing, the line snaking out into the riffles, flinging shards of sparkling water into the sun.

Between May and October the limit was ten fish per day, almost all of them steelhead smolts. Unlike the young of the chinook and silver salmon, which fled straight to the ocean in early spring, the steelhead children started for salt water in June and moved slowly, growing fat along the way on the orange salmon flies of early summer. In drought years, they might not go to the ocean at all but take refuge in the cool waters off the mouths of the Klamath's main tributaries, waiting for the autumn rains.

Sometimes Grandmother put her fly rod aside and brought out her newfangled spinning outfit, with its clacking reel and monofilament line, which Grandfather initially despised and mocked until she began to catch more fish than he did. Then he got one of his own. In winter, Grandmother's big wet flies, wrapped with orange thread and trailing a hackle of polar-bear hair, were deadly when attached to a flashing silver spoon. In summer, to her disgust, the spinning outfit's lures sometimes attracted suckers, which she tossed back, disappointed, for they often weighed several pounds. We watched them drift downstream, their strange downcast mouths working, their beady, worried eyes staring back at us as they sank slowly away.

The river was life, and the river was death. Quail called softly, skittering in the dry leaves under the poison-oak thickets, while the red-tailed hawks wheeled overhead and the rattlesnakes waited for the coolness of evening to glide down to the river. Blacktail deer came to drink just at dark, and as we drove home at dusk, jackrabbits the size of fawns crossed the road ahead of us, their eyes insane. The great blue herons rose, croaking, at our approach, flying with their necks bent back along their shoulders. Killdeer cried and ran ahead, the mud flies scattering as they dragged one wing to lure us from their eggs.

Grandmother gutted her catch on the shore, while I watched and knew the finality of killing. The summer I was seven, I found a pocket knife in the road, which Grandfather sharpened for me. After that I squatted with Grandmother and cleaned fish, scraping against the grain of the scales until the speckled skin lay smooth beneath my fingers, then slicing upward from the vent to the gills. Cutting through the cartilage under the lower jaw, I hooked a finger in the gap and pulled, tearing loose the pectoral fins and the innards. I ran my thumbnail up the inside of the backbone, scraping away the kidneys and blood, and finally rinsed the carcass in the river before stripping away the last little piece of intestine from the vent. Lastly, I checked a stomach or two to see what the fish were eating that day and hurled the waste into the current.

Our mother, who preferred sketching to fishing, sat on fallen cottonwood logs, filling page after page with pencil drawings and watercolors, enjoying the freedom of slacks and sneakers after girdles and high heels all week, and keeping a wary eye on the river. For the first and great commandment of the Klamath was that it could not be trusted. Below Copco Lake, the river was subject to sudden rises of as much as four or five feet. When demand for electricity rose, huge amounts of water surged through the dam turbines. Fly fishermen were sometimes drowned in midstream in their waders. So we never trusted the dark pools and whirling eddies of the Klamath.

We never swam in it, either, but this had less to do with Copco than with the character of the water. Born in a land of erodible volcanic soils, passed through a lake laden with waterfowl—to which the silt and runoff from croplands and cattle pastures is added, and the whole broth stirred to froth by dam turbines—the Klamath is never too clean. The native tribes of the middle and lower Klamath, the Karuks and Yuroks, never drank from it even before the white men came. Watch the emerald waters of the sparkling Salmon River mingling with the dark waters of the Klamath in July, when the verges of the larger stream are laden with the fuzzy white corpses of spawned-out lampreys, and you'd never drink from it, either.

The summer Klamath was a dark translucent green, the rocks slippery with algae, its quiet stretches sharp with the smell of fermenting water plants. Cattle stood up to their bellies in the water, inhaling green slime. Trout from the Klamath had a slightly muddy taste that you didn't really notice until you ate fish from another river or tasted a steelhead fresh from the ocean. And in truth our summer fishing trips were just recreation. *Real* fishing began with the October rains, when the steelhead came home.

"I have seen salmon so thick . . . that fishermen would bait their hooks for steelhead that followed the salmon and . . . the bait would ride on the salmon backs for some time before it could get into deeper water," said an old-timer from Klamathon of the fishing in the early 1900s before the California-Oregon Power Company tamed the upper river.

Those magnificent runs of salmon and steelhead were gone before my time, after decades of decline, punctuated by occasional good years when it seemed as though the worst was over. In 1932, commercial salmon fishermen took thirty thousand pounds of salmon off the mouth of the Klamath. The 1920s and 1930s brought a spate of state laws to ban salmon spearing, regulate the timing of hydraulic gold mining, and forbid the construction of any dams on the Klamath River below the mouth of the Shasta River: but still the salmon runs fell.

The steelhead, hardier and more adaptable, seemed resilient and were still numerous. I saw a few salmon rolling like saturated logs, but because they stopped feeding after entering the river, they were seldom caught except by snagging. Steelhead were the preferred quarry; silver torpedoes leaping and twisting above the current, their reentry splashes like gunshots across the water.

Labor Day of 1955 was hot and dry and too windy. Stiff breezes ruffled the river pools, blowing the fishing line back so that Grandmother could scarcely cast. She gave up at about three o'clock and sat with us under the cottonwoods on the beach, pulling off her waders and sitting barefooted on the edge of the open trunk, sipping a can of beer. We watched the thunderheads building up over to the north and east. The air was cracklingly dry, the clouds an unhealthy purple beneath, and a taut, expectant feeling hung over the grove. Grandmother began sucking her gold bridgework, always a sign of nervousness, and Grandfather came walking briskly back down the bar as the wind thrashed the trees and the first rumbles of thunder rolled down the hills.

We drove back to Hilt and unloaded the car while Grandmother made ham sandwiches, which by some sort of mutual consent were consumed on the front porch, facing southwest toward Cottonwood Peak and Sterling Mountain. Behind them was the vast Beaver Creek drainage. We watched the dry lightning popping on the ridges, not a drop of rain falling. A few miles away, Clara Williams, the Forest Service fireguard on Hungry Creek Lookout, had just reported a smoke over the radio when the Fruit Growers Supply Company fuel dump on Mount Sterling was struck by lightning. "A big ball of fire came up from there," she remembered. "I got some action right away on that Cow Creek fire but when the men got up there . . . they couldn't do a thing because all their gas tanks on their equipment had exploded. . . . everything was so dry and the wind was so strong, they couldn't hold it, and it burned toward Dry Lake. Then it reversed itself and came back down the mountain and across Beaver Creek and up over Buckhorn Mountain. . . . We were all sent down from the lookouts the next day because the Dutch Creek fire was coming right toward us about three miles away. . . ."

The next day, virtually all the company's young men were out on the firelines. Building a fire of any kind was forbidden in Hilt, with every pumper truck in town gone. Grandfather had to sneak cigarettes in the bathroom like a guilty eighth grader. For several days, we watched the Beaver Creek drainage burn, glowing red in the night behind the ridgeline, the smoke reducing visibility to fifty yards by day. The fires jumped the Klamath and burned within two miles of Yreka, the county seat. On one memorable day, the Haystack Burn, as it came to be known, consumed twenty thousand acres of timber between three o'clock in the afternoon and ten o'clock at night.

The fires had scarcely cooled under the rains of October when the Forest Service auctioned the first batch of fire-damaged timber. The following spring, Fruit Growers hired more foresters to survey the roads and mark the skid trails for the logging to come. The millions of board feet of timber inventory that were supposed to last Fruit Growers for fifty years now had to be cut within two, or be lost to bugs and rot. One of the new foresters would marry my mother in 1957 and change our lives forever.

Below the mouth of the Shasta River, the Klamath growls and rushes, a wild child forced into a narrow channel by encroaching rock walls, dropping fast in elevation. As it falls, the canyon grows deeper, and the junipers and oaks and sagebrush grow fewer and fewer until finally they cease. In their place grow ponderosa pine and Douglas fir. As the river meets the pathway of the Pacific storms, rainfall rises steadily, reaching sixty inches at Happy Camp and eighty inches at the mouth of the Trinity.

Too steep to farm except on isolated river terraces, much of the land away from the river had never passed into private hands, and was almost entirely National Forest. The gold-bearing Klamath was everywhere marked by piles of dredger tailings, ponds, and the naked walls of old hydraulic mines.

When John Brannon married our mother, the world of the middle Klamath opened up to us. One of his favorite places to take his new family was Humbug Point, about six miles downriver from the mouth of the Shasta, where a narrow, steep little dirt road bailed off the edge of the Klamath River Highway, which here ran far above the river and crept downhill to an old homestead, where a ruined barn still stood and a rancher fed his cattle on the river bar in the winter.

We seldom saw other fishermen here except at the height of the steelhead run. An old dredger pond full of bullfrogs and perch afforded amusement when the river trout weren't biting. The river, deep in its canyon, was suddenly louder, wider, and entirely indifferent to us. On the south side of the river, a great arrowhead of Douglas firs pointed at the river, foreshadowing the heavier forests downstream. In the homesteader's fields, wet weather brought flakes of obsidian to the surface of the silty soil. An old ranch gelding dozed away his final summers under the witchy apple trees and lipped the fruit cores from our hands.

Dad bought me my first real fishing outfit, a rod and a good spinning reel, when I turned eight years old. I caught my first steelhead with it at Humbug Point three years later, on the first weekend in May. She was a spring-run fish, and I landed her on an eight-pound test line after an epic battle that brought the whole family down to watch. Dad coached me, urging me to keep the pole up, to try not to horse her in, until finally, worn out, I beached her, backing up on the sandpit, while Dad slipped a finger through her gills and tossed her up on the beach.

Mom ran to get the camera, and there I stood, a chubby eleven-year-old in dirty glasses, hair wild and coat askew, holding up a three-and-a-half-pound fish in triumph.

I never did learn to cast a dry fly. When I was in high school and Grandmother knew she was dying but hadn't told anyone yet, she gave me her old fly-fishing tackle but never taught me to cast. I succeeded only in snapping the barbs off a dozen precious flies. Embarrassed, I said nothing and went back to the spinning outfit for river fishing, using the fly rod only in mountain creeks where I could pull the line out by hand and let it drift toward the tiny pools overhung with willows.

Twenty-two miles downriver from Humbug Point, the forest closes in around the Klamath entirely. The river turns introspective and fierce, and even larger, as the Scott River pours in from the south. Above the mouth of the Scott, the implacable snows of the Scott Bar Mountains loom, resisting summer. The Scott River, always muddy after a storm, muddied the Klamath, too, and I wondered why, briefly, as we drove past it for the first time in 1962. I was thirteen, and Dad had just joined the Forest Service and had been assigned to the District office in Happy Camp.

In the 1850s, gangs of white miners turned the entire Scott River out of its bed with a series of wing dams for three miles upstream from its mouth. Some of the largest nuggets ever found in California, it was said, came from the Scott. Granville Stuart, who died a cattle king in Montana, passed through Scott Valley, twenty-three miles south of the river's junction with the Klamath, in the autumn of 1854. He wrote in his journal:

"Camped in Scott's valley which is perfectly beautiful, with a clear stream flowing through. The valley is different from most we have seen . . . all the valley proper is covered with yellow bunch grass, knee high, and waving in the wind like fields of grain . . . in the night we were awakened by our mules snorting and trying to break loose from the picket line . . . we saw a grizzly bear shambling off and disappearing in the brush along the stream. . . . During the night we heard continual splashing in the water near where we were sleeping, and couldn't imagine what kind of animal was in the stream all night, as we had seen no sign of beavers in California . . . In the morning we . . . found that all that splashing in the river was caused by salmon fish, from three to four feet long, flopping and jumping in, forcing their way up the stream over the riffles where the water was not deep enough for them to swim . . . we were told that every fall these large fish came up from the Pacific Ocean to the upper branches of all the streams as far as they can possibly go and there lay their eggs, then start back to the ocean, but most of them are so bruised and exhausted that they die on the way."

Of all the Klamath's tributaries, the Scott has perhaps suffered the most. Even the lovely valley of waving yellow grass was the result of an earlier intrusion by beaver hunters like Stephen Meek, who accompanied a Hudson's Bay Company party to the valley in 1836.

"The richest place for beaver I ever saw," Meek said, describing the valley as "all one swamp" and "full of huts" (beaver lodges). They took eighteen hundred beaver in one month from Scott Valley, and moved on. Other trappers came, and when Stuart saw the valley, all the beavers were dead, their dams washed out, and the wetlands they had maintained for ten thousand years were drying and turning to meadows.

Thirty years after Stuart saw it, Scott Valley produced so much wheat and barley that its towns boasted breweries and flour mills. The river was diverted into irrigation ditches that stranded both adult salmon and ocean-bound smolts. Siltation of spawning beds, logging of the headwaters streams, and high water temperatures doomed still more fish. And every year of the new century, there were more and more roads.

The little summer trout, the gravel beds where they hatched, the riffles where they fed, the places where I first knew the Klamath, were drowned by a filling reservoir in 1961 when Iron Gate Dam blocked the river just above Bogus Creek. Built to regulate the river flow and eliminate the dangerous water-level rises below Copco, it completed the destruction of the upriver spawning and rearing habitat for salmon and steelhead. Returning fish were taken out just below Iron Gate, milked of their eggs and sperm, their offspring raised artificially. Last year, 13,622 chinook salmon and 3,546 coho salmon returned to Iron Gate, but only 165 steelhead.

In the year that Iron Gate set its teeth against the river, Grandfather retired and took Grandmother two hundred miles south to Oroville. In the ten years of life left to her, she struggled to convert a quarter acre of red hardpan around her new suburban house to lawn and flowers, and never fished again except on brief visits to the Klamath. She and Grandfather took many trips up the Feather River Canyon to visit the quiet places deep in the digger pines, soon to be lost forever behind the great dam, capstone of California's water dreams.

In Happy Camp we lived for the first time in country that the Karuks knew as the middle of the world. Their ancient territory extended from Seiad Valley, twenty miles upriver from Happy Camp and downriver almost to the mouth of the Trinity. Beyond that was Yurok land; the Hupa lived on the Trinity River.

About thirty miles downriver from Happy Camp, near the mouth of the Salmon River, was the site of the sacred village of Katimin. Between Katimin and the Salmon stands a conical peak known as Sugarloaf to the whites and as Auich to the Karuk.

On top of Auich lived Aikren, "he who dwells above," the immortal peregrine falcon who every year flew away with his hatchlings, following the ridge up which go the souls of the Karuk dead before returning in the spring. The Yurok also reverenced the bird, which they called Kerernit, and his two wives, black bear and grizzly bear.

At Katimin, the great dances and ceremonies that stabilized the physical world and prevented pestilence and famine were no longer held. Even the great summer new year ceremony at the time of the salmon runs, *isivsanen pikiavish*, "earth making," had been stilled. And one year, even Aikren failed to return from the land of the dead. But the Karuks still dipnetted salmon at Ishi Pishi Falls below Katimin; and we drove down to watch one day, standing deafened by the falls, astounded at seeing our Happy Camp neighbors balancing unafraid on the rocks, wet with mist, scooping up thrashing salmon in their nets and tossing them onto the rocks only to be heaved aloft by our grinning schoolmates, belonging utterly to an ancient world that we could never enter.

For Karuk and Yurok alike agreed that salmon were first made at a small village just downstream from Ishi Pishi Falls, and there were old people yet alive who would point out the very place where it happened.

All the salmon in the world, and the Klamath River itself, were once kept in a box by two old women. When they wanted salmon to eat, they took one out and cooked it. Widower-across-the-ocean saw them one day. He waited until they left their house, then found the box inside and tipped it over. Water and salmon ran out, rushing downhill. The two angry women pursued Widower, and he called on two tanoak trees to help him. They grew around him, joining, to hide him. He called out, "Let the river run downstream!" and blew downhill. And the Klamath flowed, where before there was no river, and the salmon with it, to the sea.

That the Forest Service might have had a great deal to do with the construction of the Klamath River Highway and the county roads stemming from it never occurred to me in those days, however often we drove their interminable, twisting lengths. But in fact the Forest Service had everything to do with them. The men who managed the Klamath National Forest, from the very beginning, thought about timber and how to extract it when the timber famine should come at last. The famine never came, but the roads did, for the Forest Service brought them.

Foresters tend to regard old growth forests not as assets but as liabilities, not as ecosystems but as sinks of diminishing returns. Any tree not putting on volume is wasting space, wasting time, and should be replaced as soon as possible. But in the first decades of the Klamath National Forest, the problem was how to make cutting its timber worthwhile for lumbermen. From the day in 1919 when Supervisor Huestis persuaded coastal Humboldt County to lobby the state for a highway connecting the Klamath River with the coast, to the day in 1947 that Supervisor James pushed through a plan to reroute part of the Klamath River Highway on the north side of the river in order to access the untouched National Forest timber in Beaver Creek, the goal of replacing all the old growth in the Forest never changed.

Russ Bower, a retired Forest Supervisor who I knew as a gentle white-haired old man much honored at Forest Service social functions, reminisced about the process many years later.

"The reason the Klamath National Forest was able to get such a large portion of Federal highway funds was interesting," Russ mused. "The allocation of such funds within the state of California was guided by a three-way agreement of the Forest Service . . . the State Division of Highways and the U.S. Bureau of Public Roads. The State Highway engineers' guidelines for funding was based on traffic counts exclusively. The Klamath River Highway was near the bottom of their list . . . and was also far down on (the Bureau of Public Roads) list. The Forest Service had it as their top priority due to the selling job done by former Klamath Supervisor George James who was now on the Regional Forester's staff. We needed one more vote to get the funds directed to the Klamath Highway. In the winter of 1950-51, I sat down to review the program with State Senator Randolph Collier of Yreka who represented Siskiyou County in the Senate and was also Chairman of the Joint Legislative Committee on Transportation. He agreed that the project would be of great economic benefit to Siskiyou County but he would need some leverage to get it through the Highway Commission over the objection of the engineers . . . I was chairman of the local Chamber of Commerce Transportation Committee. I prepared an economic analysis of the probable benefits to the economy of Siskiyou County from increased logging, lumber and mineral development, with a plea to the Highway Commission to vary their normal basis for priority of allocation of funds . . . When [the request] came up for consideration by the State Highway Commission, Senator Collier was able to persuade them to accept the proposal . . . Senator Collier and I informally and verbally agreed that if I would continue to push for Federal Funds for the portion of the Highway from Pacific Highway 99 to Happy Camp, he would try to get a State Inmate road camp assigned to the portion of the highway from Happy Camp to Orleans . . ."

The Forest Service got its highway and the convict labor to maintain it, and the timber fell. By the 1970s, when the spawning beds in many of the Klamath's tributaries had been fatally damaged, the Forest Service blamed the county road department and the California Department of Transportation, which over the years had indeed shoved many a load of dirt into the stream during maintenance and construction. But the private deals of thirty years before were conveniently forgotten.

The logging roads that fed into the county roads and the state highways ran red and brown in the winter rains. Culverts washed out, slides tore out whole drainages, clear-cuts stripped bare the little creeks. But the logs came out of the woods, hundreds of thousands of board feet a day, fifty-five million board feet a year from the Happy Camp district alone. The Forest Service hired more foresters and more engineers to build wider logging roads. Dad, who as a gyppo logger in Oregon had learned that wider roads were expensive to build and maintain, complained about engineers who never saw a bigger road they didn't like.

But the big timber sales attracted bigger companies, which built bigger mills, and even before we moved to Happy Camp all but one of the family-owned mills on the river were gone, replaced by Josephine Plywood and Siskiyou Mills and Carolina Pacific, and still later by Stone Industries. In 1953 the Forest Service, looking ahead, built the largest two-lane bridge in the Forest over the Klamath River at Happy Camp. Two billion board feet of timber lay on the other side, sealing the fate of Elk Creek. Hundreds of miles of road later, Happy Camp's municipal waterworks frequently shut down after a storm to avoid sucking mud into the system.

When Dad was transferred upriver to the Seiad Ranger District in 1966, he and Mother bought a house near the mouth of Walker Creek, a mile east of Seiad Valley. For the first time, we lived within sight and sound of the river, all the time. In the summer, a pair of ospreys, recolonizing the river after the ravages of DDT, fished below the house, their young screaming over the noise of the water.

In winter, I fished a deep quiet stretch, the color of kelp, using some of Grandmother's last steelhead flies. Beaver swam silently past me as I stood between the willows, then slapped their tails on the water in panic and dove for their burrows in the riverbank. Tundra swans flew overhead, and sometimes an otter or muskrat slid by my line as it cut through the water. I caught a four- or five-pound steelhead about every other day, sometimes with a half pounder thrown in. I brought them home and baked them in the oven with lemon and dried parsley, or froze them in milk cartons filled with water, but I didn't really care if I caught anything or not. I fished for five or six hours every weekend and every day of the Christmas vacation deeply in love with this creature, the river, and knowing, with the finality of any opinion we hold at the age of seventeen, that I would never want anything more than this, ever.

The 1964 flood changed the face of the river and its tributaries. Creeks too cold to swim in before the flood grew warmer when the floodwaters ripped out overhanging trees and filled deep holes with sand. We knew that our swimming holes were warmer, but not that it meant the death of entire populations of young salmon and steelhead, which could not hatch out in fine sand or survive in the warmed water.

The flood took out the entire log deck of Sharp's Mill on Indian Creek, north of Happy Camp. Six million board feet swept to the ocean, slamming into bridges, hammering down anything in the way. Near the town of Klamath, which was simply erased, the big north-south highway bridge was torn in half, the water swirling past the gilded statues of California grizzlies on either end.

Large segments of the river road, sliced away like cake, fell into the floodwaters. The river ran the color of latte for months. Two years later, as my sister and I rode the school bus every day from Walker Creek to Happy Camp, we ran a gauntlet of muddy, unstable construction areas, where rocks the size of Volkswagens tumbled down the cuts, sometimes bouncing in front of the fragile yellow bus before splashing into the river.

The epic battle over the fate of the last roadless watersheds in the Klamath River country lay in the future, but late in the summer of 1943, a small group of Klamath National Forest managers climbed into two redwood canoes, handled by Yurok guides, and took a strange trip down the lower Klamath River. The Klamath canyon

below the confluence with the Trinity River was then entirely un-
roaded, and while the Klamath National Forest had lands within the
river canyon, it had no actual river frontage.

The men had met to decide what to do about a proposal by the
state to extend the Klamath River Highway all the way down the
river canyon to the mouth. Astonishingly enough, the Forest Service
now wanted the lower Klamath River canyon left alone. But the Klamath National Forest had trained the Highway Department too well,
so if they couldn't block construction entirely, they decided, they
would at least try to have it located high enough on the ridges to preserve the natural beauty of the canyon. Perhaps, they agreed, they
could acquire strategically located parcels of land on the lower river
and enter into negotiations with the state. Later, they did scrape together funds to buy three parcels, and the state took the hint, eventually dropping the project from the planned road system, thanks to
seven men in a couple of boats. But I wonder what the Yurok boatmen thought, or if anyone even asked them?

That representatives of the Forest Service did this is astonishing
in itself; but to delve into their reasons is to suspect a chilling reality:
that they wished to protect the last canyon because they had no intention of protecting any of the others. At one time, Dad told me, the
Forest planned a logging road every thousand feet wherever timber
grew. Had they known that they would someday be deprived of that
goal, they might not have tried to save the lower canyon at all. In the
beginning they didn't know how much timber they had; in the end,
they didn't know how little they had left, or how many other things
had already been lost.

So the Klamath flows ungated to the sea, through that one last
stretch between the mountains, and roars at last under the four
golden bears staring sightlessly where Aikren's wives once fished.

I was born into the generation for whom the roads were built,
the rivers dammed, the old growth cut, entire races of salmon destroyed, and ten thousand years of wealth consumed in a moment of
time. Yet, in a handful of years, we will be gone, too. A few hundred
more, and Iron Gate and Copco will fill with silt; and the Klamath
will find its own way around or over or under, and flow on, untrou-
bled. In a million years, when our very species is dust, it will still meet
the ocean, somewhere off what was once the coast of California.

The bones of my grandmother lie beneath a lawn on an ancient terrace left by the Feather River, which was not her river, and on which she never cast a fly. Above her grave rises the massive bulk of Oroville Dam, built of the dredger tailings left by an earlier destruction. Over millions of years, water crushed and smoothed the very rocks that built the dam, tumbling the bones of forgotten mountains.

Some say the Feather was killed so that the Klamath might live, but it only waits, like the Klamath, for us all to go away. Yet to see it so drained and constrained, to see a whole river sent hundreds of miles to the south to be pumped over the Tehachapi Mountains, to see it falling at last into a thirsty land that will never know a salmon, is to stand stupefied before our parents, and to wonder if even a river might want only to go home.

> I'll love you, dear, I'll love you
> Till China and Africa meet,
> And the river jumps over the mountain
> And the salmon sing in the street.
> —W. H. Auden

The Allegash and East Branch

Henry David Thoreau

An Indian at Oldtown had told us that we should be obliged to carry ten miles between Telos Lake on the St. John and Second Lake on the East Branch of the Penobscot; but the lumberers whom we met assured us that there would not be more than a mile of carry. It turned out that the Indian, who had lately been over this route, was nearest right, as far as we were concerned. However, if one of us could have assisted the Indian in managing the canoe in the rapids, we might have run the greater part of the way; but as he was alone in the management of the canoe in such places, we were obliged to walk the greater part. I did not feel quite ready to try such an experiment on Webster Stream, which has so bad a reputation. According to my observation, a batteau, properly manned, shoots rapids as a matter of course, which a single Indian with a canoe carries round.

My companion and I carried a good part of the baggage on our shoulders, while the Indian took that which would be least injured by wet in the canoe. We did not know when we should see him again, for he had not been this way since the canal was cut, nor for more than thirty years. He agreed to stop when he got to smooth water, come up and find our path if he could, and halloo for us, and after waiting a reasonable time go on and try again,—and we were to look out in like manner for him.

He commenced by running through the sluiceway and over the dam, as usual, standing up in his tossing canoe, and was soon out of sight behind a point in a wild gorge. This Webster Stream is well known to lumbermen as a difficult one. It is exceedingly rapid and rocky, and also shallow, and can hardly be considered navigable, unless that may mean that what is launched in it is sure to be carried swiftly down it, though it may be dashed to pieces by the way. It is somewhat like navigating a thunderspout. With commonly an irresistible force urging you on, you have got to choose your own course each moment, between the rocks and shallows, and to get into it, moving forward always with the utmost possible moderation, and often holding on, if you can, that you may inspect the rapids before you.

By the Indian's direction we took an old path on the south side, which appeared to keep down the stream, though at a considerable distance from it, cutting off bends, perhaps to Second Lake, having first taken the course from the map with a compass, which was north-easterly, for safety. It was a wild wood-path, with a few tracks of oxen which had been driven over it, probably to some old camp clearing, for pasturage, mingled with the tracks of moose which had lately used it. We kept on steadily for about an hour without putting down our packs, occasionally winding around or climbing over a fallen tree, for the most part far out of sight and hearing of the river; till, after walking about three miles, we were glad to find that the path came to the river again at an old camp ground, where there was a small opening in the forest, at which we paused. Swiftly as the shallow and rocky river ran here, a continuous rapid with dancing waves, I saw, as I sat on the shore, a long string of sheldrakes, which something scared, run up the opposite side of the stream by me, with the same ease that they commonly did down it, just touching the surface of the waves, and getting an impulse from them as they flowed from under them; but they soon came back, driven by the Indian, who had fallen a little behind us on account of the windings. He shot round a point just above, and came to land by us with considerable water in his canoe. He had found it, as he said, "very strong water," and had been obliged to land once before to empty out what he had taken in. He complained that it strained him to paddle so hard in order to keep his canoe straight in its course, having no one in the bows to aid him, and, shallow as it was, said that it would be no joke to upset there, for the force of the water was such that he had as lief I would strike him over the head with a paddle as have that water strike him. Seeing him come out of that gap was as if you should pour water down an inclined and zigzag trough, then drop a nutshell into it, and, taking a short cut to the bottom, get there in time to see it come out, notwithstanding the rush and tumult, right side up, and only partly full of water.

After a moment's breathing-space, while I held his canoe, he was soon out of sight again around another bend, and we, shouldering our packs, resumed our course.

We did not at once fall into our path again, but made our way with difficulty along the edge of the river, till at length, striking inland through the forest, we recovered it. Before going a mile we heard the Indian calling to us. He had come up through the woods and along the path to find us, having reached sufficiently smooth water to warrant his taking us in. The shore was about one fourth of a mile distant, through a dense, dark forest, and as he led us back to it, winding rapidly about to the right and left, I had the curiosity to look down carefully, and found that he was following his steps backward. I could only occasionally perceive his trail in the moss, and yet he did not appear to look down nor hesitate an instant, but led us out exactly to his canoe. This surprised me, for without a compass, or the sight or noise of the river to guide us, we could not have kept our course many minutes, and could have retraced our steps but a short distance, with a great deal of pains and very slowly, using a laborious circumspection. But it was evident that he could go back through the forest wherever he had been during the day.

After this rough walking in the dark woods it was an agreeable change to glide down the rapid river in the canoe once more. This river, which was about the size of our Assabet (in Concord), though still very swift, was almost perfectly smooth here, and showed a very visible declivity, a regularly inclined plane, for several miles, like a mirror set a little aslant, on which we coasted down. This very obvious regular descent, particularly plain when I regarded the water-line against the shores, made a singular impression on me, which the swiftness of our motion probably enhanced, so that we seemed to be gliding down a much steeper declivity than we were, and that we could not save ourselves from rapids and falls if we should suddenly come to them. My companion did not perceive this slope, but I have a surveyor's eyes, and I satisfied myself that it was no ocular illusion. You could tell at a glance on approaching such a river, which way the water flowed, though you might perceive no motion. I observed the angle at which a level line would strike the surface, and calculated the amount of fall in a rod, which did not need to be remarkably great to produce this effect.

It was very exhilarating, and the perfection of traveling, quite unlike floating on our dead Concord River, the coasting down this inclined mirror, which was now and then gently winding, down a mountain, indeed, between two evergreen forests, edged with lofty dead white-pines, sometimes slanted halfway over the stream, and destined soon to bridge it. I saw some monsters there, nearly destitute of branches, and scarcely diminishing in diameter for eighty or ninety feet.

As we thus swept along, our Indian repeated in a deliberate and drawling tone the words "Daniel Webster, great lawyer," apparently reminded of him by the name of the stream, and he described his calling on him once in Boston, at what he supposed was his boarding-house. He had no business with him, but merely went to pay his respects, as we should say. In answer to our questions, he described his person well enough. It was on the day after Webster delivered his Bunker Hill oration, which I believe Polis heard. The first time he called he waited till he was tired without seeing him, and then went away. The next time, he saw him go by the door of the room in which he was waiting several times, in his shirt-sleeves, without noticing him. He thought that if he had come to see Indians, they would not have treated him so. At length, after very long delay, he came in, walked toward him, and asked in a loud voice, gruffly, "What do you want?" and he, thinking at first, by the motion of his hand, that he was going to strike him, said to himself, "You'd better take care, if you try that I shall know what to do." He did not like him, and declared that all he said "was not worth talk about a musquash." We suggested that probably Mr. Webster was very busy, and had a great many visitors just then.

Coming to falls and rapids, our easy progress was suddenly terminated. The Indian went along shore to inspect the water, while we climbed over the rocks, picking berries. The peculiar growth of blueberries on the tops of large rocks here made the impression of high land, and indeed this was the Height-of-land Stream. When the Indian came back, he remarked, "You got to walk; very strong water." So, taking out his canoe, he launched it again below the falls, and was soon out of sight. At such times, he would step into the canoe, take up his paddle, and, with an air of mystery, start off, looking far down stream, and keeping his own counsel, as if absorbing all the intelligence of forest and stream into himself; but I sometimes detected a little fun in his face, which could yield to my sympathetic smile, for he was thoroughly good-humored. We meanwhile scrambled along the shore with our packs, without any path. This was the last of *our* boating for the day.

The prevailing rock here was a kind of slate, standing on its edges, and my companion, who was recently from California, thought it exactly like that in which the gold is found, and said that if he had had a pan he would have liked to wash a little of the sand here.

The Indian now got along much faster than we, and waited for us from time to time. I found here the only cool spring that I drank at anywhere on this excursion, a little water filling a hollow in the sandy bank. It was a quite memorable event, and due to the elevation of the country, for wherever else we had been the water in the rivers and the streams emptying in was dead and warm, compared with that of a mountainous region. It was very bad walking along the shore over fallen and drifted trees and bushes, and rocks, from time to time swinging ourselves round over the water, or else taking to a gravel bar or going inland. At one place, the Indian being ahead, I was obliged to take off all my clothes in order to ford a small but deep stream emptying in, while my companion, who was inland, found a rude bridge, high up in the woods, and I saw no more of him for some time. I saw there very fresh moose tracks, found a new goldenrod to me (perhaps *Solidago thyrsoidea*), and I passed one white-pine log, which had lodged, in the forest near the edge of the stream, which was quite five feet in diameter at the butt. Probably its size detained it.

Shortly after this I overtook the Indian at the edge of some burnt land, which extended three or four miles at least, beginning about three miles above Second Lake, which we were expecting to reach that night, and which is about ten miles from Telos Lake. This burnt region was still more rocky than before, but, though comparatively open, we could not yet see the lake. Not having seen my companion for some time, I climbed, with the Indian, a singular high rock on the edge of the river, forming a narrow ridge only a foot or two wide at top, in order to look for him; and, after calling many times, I at length heard him answer from a considerable distance inland, he having taken a trail which led off from the river, perhaps directly to the lake, and being now in search of the river again. Seeing a much higher rock, of the same character, about one third of a mile farther east, or down stream, I proceeded toward it, through the burnt land, in order to look for the lake from its summit, supposing that the Indian would keep down the stream in his canoe, and hallooing all the while that my companion might join me on the way. Before we came together I noticed where a moose, which possibly I had scared by my shouting, had apparently just run along a large rotten trunk of a pine, which made a bridge, thirty or forty feet long, over a hollow, as convenient for him as for me. The tracks were as large as those of an ox, but an ox could not have crossed there. This burnt land was an exceedingly wild and desolate region. Judging by the weeds and sprouts, it appeared to have been burnt about two years before. It was covered with charred trunks, either prostrate or standing, which crocked our clothes and hands, and we could not easily have distinguished a bear there by his color. Great shells of trees, sometimes unburnt without, or burnt on one side only, but black within, stood twenty or forty feet high. The fire had run up inside, as in a chimney, leaving the sapwood. Sometimes we crossed a rocky ravine fifty feet wide, on a fallen trunk; and there were great fields of fire-weed (*Epilobium angustifolium*) on all sides, the most extensive that I ever saw, which presented great masses of pink. Intermixed with these were blueberry and raspberry bushes.

Having crossed a second rocky ridge like the first, when I was beginning to ascend the third, the Indian, whom I had left on the shore some fifty rods behind, beckoned to me to come to him, but I made sign that I would first ascend the highest rock before me, whence I expected to see the lake. My companion accompanied me to the top. This was formed just like the others. Being struck with the perfect parallelism of these singular rock hills, however much one might be in advance of another, I took out my compass and found that they lay northwest and southeast, the rock being on its edge, and sharp edges they were. This one, to speak from memory, was perhaps a third of a mile in length, but quite narrow, rising gradually from the northwest to the height of about eighty feet, but steep on the southeast end. The southwest side was as steep as an ordinary roof, or as we could safely climb, the northeast was an abrupt precipice from which you could jump clean to the bottom, near which the river flowed; while the level top of the ridge, on which you walked along, was only from one to three or four feet in width. For a rude illustration, take the half of a pear cut in two lengthwise, lay it on its flat side, the stem to the northwest, and then halve it vertically in the direction of its length, keeping the southwest half. Such was the general form.

There was a remarkable series of these great rock-waves revealed by the burning; breakers, as it were. No wonder that the river that found its way through them was rapid and obstructed by falls. No doubt the absence of soil on these rocks, or its dryness where there was any, caused this to be a very thorough burning. We could see the lake over the woods, two or three miles ahead, and that the river made an abrupt turn southward around the northwest end of the cliff on which we stood, or a little above us, so that we had cut off a bend, and that there was an important fall in it a short distance below us. I could see the canoe a hundred rods behind, but now on the opposite shore, and supposed that the Indian had concluded to take out and carry round some bad rapids on that side, and that that might be what he had beckoned to me for; but after waiting a while I could still see nothing of him, and I observed to my companion that I wondered where he was, though I began to suspect that he had gone inland to look for the lake from some hill-top on that side, as we had done. This proved to be the case; for after I had started to return to the canoe, I heard a faint halloo, and descried him on the top of a distant rocky hill on that side. But as, after a long time had elapsed, I still saw his canoe in the same place, and he had not returned to it, and appeared in no hurry to do so, and, moreover, as I remembered that he had previously beckoned to me, I thought that there might be something more to delay him than I knew, and began to return northwest, along the ridge, toward the angle in the river. My companion, who had just been separated from us, and had even contemplated the necessity of camping alone, wishing to husband his steps, and yet to keep with us, inquired where I was going; to which I answered that I was going far enough back to communicate with the Indian, and that then I thought we had better go along the shore together, and keep him in sight.

When we reached the shore, the Indian appeared from out the woods on the opposite side, but on account of the roar of the water it was difficult to communicate with him. He kept along the shore westward to his canoe, while we stopped at the angle where the stream turned southward around the precipice. I again said to my companion, that we would keep along the shore and keep the Indian in sight. We started to do so, being close together, the Indian behind us having launched his canoe again, but just then I saw the latter, who had crossed to our side, forty or fifty rods behind, beckoning to me, and I called to my companion, who had just disappeared behind large rocks at the point of the precipice, three or four rods before me, on his way down the stream, that I was going to help the Indian a moment. I did so,—helped get the canoe over a fall, lying with my breast over a rock, and holding one end while he received it below,—and within ten or fifteen minutes at most I was back again at the point where the river turned southward, in order to catch up with my companion, while Polis glided down the river alone, parallel with me. But to my surprise, when I rounded the precipice, though the shore was bare of trees, without rocks, for a quarter of a mile at least, my companion was not to be seen. It was as if he had sunk into the earth. This was the more unaccountable to me, because I knew that his feet were, since our swamp walk, very sore, and that he wished to keep with the party; and besides this was very bad walking, climbing over or about the rocks. I hastened along, hallooing and searching for him, thinking he might be concealed behind a rock, yet doubting if he had not taken the other side of the precipice, but the Indian had got along still faster in his canoe, till he was arrested by the falls, about a quarter of a mile below. He then landed, and said that we could go no farther that night. The sun was setting, and on account of falls and rapids we should be obliged to leave this river and carry a good way into another farther east. The first thing then was to find my companion, for I was now very much alarmed about him, and I sent the Indian along the shore down stream, which began to be covered with unburnt wood again just below the falls, while I searched backward about the precipice which we had passed. The Indian showed some unwillingness to exert himself, complaining that he was very tired, in consequence of his day's work, that it had strained him very much getting down so many rapids alone; but he went off calling somewhat like an owl. I remembered that my companion was near-sighted, and I feared that he had either fallen from the precipice, or fainted and sunk down amid the rocks beneath it. I shouted and searched above and below this precipice in the twilight till I could not see, expecting nothing less than to find his body beneath it. For half an hour I anticipated and believed only the worst. I thought what I should do the next day, if I did not find him, what I *could* do in such a wilderness, and how his relatives would feel, if I should return without him. I felt that if he were really lost away from the river there, it would be a desperate undertaking to find him; and where were they who could help you? What would it be to raise the country, where there were only two or three camps, twenty or thirty miles apart, and no road, and perhaps nobody at home? Yet we must try the harder, the less the prospect of success.

I rushed down from this precipice to the canoe in order to fire the Indian's gun, but found that my companion had the caps. I was still thinking of getting it off when the Indian returned. He had not found him, but said that he had seen his tracks once or twice along the shore. This encouraged me very much. He objected to firing the gun, saying that if my companion heard it, which was not likely, on account of the roar of the stream, it would tempt him to come toward us, and he might break his neck in the dark. For the same reason we refrained from lighting a fire on the highest rock. I proposed that we should both keep down the stream to the lake, or that I should go at any rate, but the Indian said, "No use, can't do anything in the dark; come morning, then we find 'em. No harm,—he make 'em camp. No bad animals here, no gristly bears, such as in California, where he's been,—warm night,—he well off as you and I." I considered that if he was well he could do without us. He had just lived eight years in California, and had plenty of experience with wild beasts and wilder men, was peculiarly accustomed to make journeys of great length, but if he were sick or dead, he was near where we were. The darkness in the woods was by this so thick that it alone decided the question. We must camp where we were. I knew that he had his knapsack, with blankets and matches, and, if well, would fare no worse than we, except that he would have no supper nor society.

This side of the river being so encumbered with rocks, we crossed to the eastern or smoother shore, and proceeded to camp there, within two or three rods of the falls. We pitched no tent, but lay on the sand, putting a few handfuls of grass and twigs under us, there being no evergreen at hand. For fuel we had some of the charred stumps. Our various bags of provisions had got quite wet in the rapids, and I arranged them about the fire to dry. The fall close by was the principal one on this stream, and it shook the earth under us. It was a cool, because dewy, night; the more so, probably, owing to the nearness of the falls. The Indian complained a good deal, and thought afterward that he got a cold there which occasioned a more serious illness. We were not much troubled by mosquitoes at any rate. I lay awake a good deal from anxiety, but, unaccountably to myself, was at length comparatively at ease respecting him. At first I had apprehended the worst, but now I had little doubt but that I should find him in the morning. From time to time I fancied that I heard his voice calling through the roar of the falls from the opposite side of the river; but it is doubtful if we could have heard him across the stream there. Sometimes I doubted whether the Indian had really seen his tracks, since he manifested an unwillingness to make much of a search, and then my anxiety returned.

It was the most wild and desolate region we had camped in, where, if anywhere, one might expect to meet with befitting inhabitants, but I heard only the squeak of a nighthawk flitting over. The moon in her first quarter, in the fore part of the night, setting over the bare rocky hills garnished with tall, charred, and hollow stumps or shells of trees, served to reveal the desolation.

LOOD

Annie Dillard

It's summer. We had some deep spring sunshine about a month ago, in a drought; the nights were cold. It's been gray sporadically, but not oppressively, and rainy for a week, and I would think: When is the real hot stuff coming, the mind-melting weeding weather? It was rainy again this morning, the same spring rain, and then this afternoon a different rain came: a pounding, three-minute shower. And when it was over, the cloud dissolved to haze. I can't see Tinker Mountain. It's summer now: the heat is on. It's summer now all summer long.

The season changed two hours ago. Will my life change as well? This is a time for resolutions, *revolutions*. The animals are going wild. I must have seen ten rabbits in as many minutes. Baltimore orioles are here; brown thrashers seem to be nesting down by Tinker Creek across the road. The coot is still around, big as a Thanksgiving turkey, and as careless; it doesn't even glance at a barking dog.

The creek's up. When the rain stopped today I walked across the road to the downed log by the steer crossing. The steers were across the creek, a black clot on a distant hill. High water had touched my log, the log I sit on, and dumped a smooth slope of muck in its lee. The water itself was an opaque pale green, like pulverized jade, still high and very fast, lightless, like no earthly water. A dog I've never seen before, thin as death, was flushing rabbits.

A knot of yellow, fleshy somethings had grown up by the log. They didn't seem to have either proper stems or proper flowers, but instead only blind, featureless growth, like etiolated potato sprouts in a root cellar. I tried to dig one up from the crumbly soil, but they all apparently grew from a single, well-rooted corn, so I let them go.

Still, the day had an air of menace. A broken whiskey bottle by the log, the brown tip of a snake's tail disappearing between two rocks on the hill at my back, the rabbit the dog nearly caught, the rabies I knew was in the county, the bees who kept unaccountably fumbling at my forehead with their furred feet . . .

I headed over to the new woods by the creek, the motorbike woods. They were strangely empty. The air was so steamy I could barely see. The ravine separating the woods from the field had filled during high water, and a dead tan mud clogged it now. The horny orange roots of one tree on the ravine's jagged bank had been stripped of soil; now the roots hung, an empty net in the air, clutching an incongruous light bulb stranded by receding waters. For the entire time that I walked in the woods, four jays flew around me very slowly, acting generally odd, and screaming on two held notes. There wasn't a breath of wind.

Coming out of the woods, I heard loud shots; they reverberated ominously in the damp air. But when I walked up the road, I saw what it was, and the dread quality of the whole afternoon vanished at once. It was a couple of garbage trucks, huge trash compacters humped like armadillos, and they were making their engines backfire to impress my neighbors' pretty daughters, high school girls who had just been let off the school bus. The long-haired girls strayed into giggling clumps at the corner of the road; the garbage trucks sped away gloriously, as if they had been the Tarleton twins on thoroughbreds cantering away from the gates of Tara. In the distance a white vapor was rising from the waters of Carvin's Cove and catching in trailing tufts in the mountains' sides. I stood on my own porch, exhilarated, unwilling to go indoors.

It was just this time last year that we had the flood. It was Hurricane Agnes, really, but by the time it got here, the weather bureau had demoted it to a tropical storm. I see by a clipping I saved that the date was June twenty-first, the solstice, midsummer's night, the longest daylight of the year; but I didn't notice it at the time. Everything was so exciting, and so very dark.

All it did was rain. It rained, and the creek started to rise. The creek, naturally, rises every time it rains; this didn't seem any different. But it kept raining, and, that morning of the twenty-first, the creek kept rising.

That morning I'm standing at my kitchen window. Tinker Creek is out of its four-foot banks, way out, and it's still coming. The high creek doesn't look like our creek. Our creek splashes transparently over a jumble of rocks; the high creek obliterates everything in flat opacity. It looks like somebody else's creek that has usurped or eaten our creek and is roving frantically to escape, big and ugly, like a black-snake caught in a kitchen drawer. The color is foul, a rusty cream. Water that has picked up clay soils looks worse than other muddy waters, because the particles of clay are so fine; they spread out and cloud the water so that you can't see light through even an inch of it in a drinking glass.

Everything looks different. Where my eye is used to depth, I see the flat water, near, too near. I see trees I never noticed before, the black verticals of their rain-soaked trunks standing out of the pale water like pilings for a rotted dock. The stillness of grassy banks and stony ledges is gone; I see rushing, a wild sweep and hurry in one direction, as swift and compelling as a waterfall. The Atkins kids are out in their tiny rain gear, staring at the monster creek. It's risen up to their gates; the neighbors are gathering; I go out.

I hear a roar, a high windy sound more like air than like water, like the run-together whaps of a helicopter's propeller after the engine is off, a high million rushings. The air smells damp and acrid, like fuel oil, or insecticide. It's raining.

I'm in no danger; my house is high. I hurry down the road to the bridge. Neighbors who have barely seen each other all winter are there, shaking their heads. Few have ever seen it before: the water is *over* the bridge. Even when I see the bridge now, which I do every day, I still can't believe it: the water was *over* the bridge, a foot or two over the bridge, which at normal times is eleven feet above the surface of the creek.

Now the water is receding slightly; someone has produced empty metal drums, which we roll to the bridge and set up in a square to keep cars from trying to cross. It takes a bit of nerve even to stand on the bridge; the flood has ripped away a wedge of concrete that buttressed the bridge on the bank. Now one corner of the bridge hangs apparently unsupported while water hurls in an arch just inches below.

It's hard to take it all in, it's all so new. I look at the creek at my feet. It smashes under the bridge like a fist, but there is no end to its force; it hurtles down as far as I can see till it lurches round the bend, filling the valley, flattening, mashing, pushed, wider and faster, till it fills my brain.

It's like a dragon. Maybe it's because the bridge we are on is chancy, but I notice that no one can help imagining himself washed overboard, and gauging his chances for survival. You couldn't live. Mark Spitz couldn't live. The water arches where the bridge's supports at the banks prevent its enormous volume from going wide, forcing it to go high; that arch drives down like a diving whale, and would butt you on the bottom. "You'd never know what hit you," one of the men says. But if you survived that part and managed to surface . . .? How fast can you live? You'd need a windshield. You couldn't keep your head up; the water under the surface is fastest. You'd spin around like a sock in a clothes dryer. You couldn't grab onto a tree trunk without leaving that arm behind. No, you couldn't live. And if they ever found you, your gut would be solid red clay.

It's all I can do to stand. I feel dizzy, drawn, mauled. Below me the floodwater roils to a violent froth that looks like dirty lace, a lace that continuously explodes before my eyes. If I look away, the earth moves backwards, rises and swells, from the fixing of my eyes at one spot against the motion of the flood. All the familiar land looks as though it were not solid and real at all, but painted on a scroll like a backdrop, and that unrolled scroll has been shaken, so the earth sways and the air roars.

Everything imaginable is zipping by, almost too fast to see. If I stand on the bridge and look downstream, I get dizzy; but if I look upstream, I feel as though I am looking up the business end of an avalanche. There are dolls, split wood and kindling, dead fledgling songbirds, bottles, whole bushes and trees, rakes and garden gloves. Wooden, rough-hewn railroad ties charge by faster than any express. Lattice fencing bobs along, and a wooden picket gate. There are so many white plastic gallon milk jugs that when the flood ultimately recedes, they are left on the grassy banks looking from a distance like a flock of white geese.

I expect to see anything at all. In this one way, the creek is more like itself when it floods than at any other time: mediating, bringing things down. I wouldn't be at all surprised to see John Paul Jones coming round the bend, standing on the deck of the *Bon Homme Richard*, or Amelia Earhart waving gaily from the cockpit of her floating Lockheed. Why not a cello, a basket of breadfruit, a casket of antique coins? Here comes the Franklin expedition on snowshoes, and the three magi, plus camels, afloat on a canopied barge!

The whole world is in flood, the land as well as the water. Water streams down the trunks of trees, drips from hat-brims, courses across roads. The whole earth seems to slide like sand down a chute; water pouring over the least slope leaves the grass flattened, silver side up, pointing downstream. Everywhere windfall and flotsam twigs and leafy boughs, wood from woodpiles, bottles, and saturated straw spatter the ground or streak it in curving windrows. Tomatoes in flat gardens are literally floating in mud; they look as though they have been dropped whole into a boiling, brown-gravy stew. The level of the water table is at the top of the toe of my shoes. Pale muddy water lies on the flat so that it all but drowns the grass; it looks like a hideous parody of a light snow on the field, with only the dark tips of the grass blades visible.

When I look across the street, I can't believe my eyes. Right behind the road's shoulder are waves, waves whipped in rhythmically peaking scallops, racing downstream. The hill where I watched the praying mantis lay her eggs is a waterfall that splashes into a brown ocean. I can't even remember where the creek usually runs—it is everywhere now. My log is gone for sure, I think—but in fact, I discover later, it holds, rammed between growing trees. Only the cable suspending the steers' fence is visible, and not the fence itself; the steers' pasture is entirely in flood, a brown river. The river leaps its banks and smashes into the woods where the motorbikes go, devastating all but the sturdiest trees. The water is so deep and wide it seems as though you could navigate the *Queen Mary* in it, clear to Tinker Mountain.

What do animals do in these floods? I see a drowned muskrat go by like he's flying, but they all couldn't die; the water rises after every hard rain, and the creek is still full of muskrats. This flood is higher than their raised sleeping platforms in the banks; they must just race for high ground and hold on. Where do the fish go, and what do they do? Presumably their gills can filter oxygen out of this muck, but I don't know how. They must hide from the current behind any barriers they can find, and fast for a few days. They must: otherwise we'd have no fish; they'd all be in the Atlantic Ocean. What about herons and kingfishers, say? They can't see to eat. It usually seems to me that when I see any animal, its business is urgent enough that it couldn't easily be suspended for forty-eight hours. Crayfish, frogs, snails, rotifers? Most things must simply die. They couldn't live. Then I suppose that when the water goes down and clears, the survivors have a field day with no competition. But you'd think the bottom would be knocked out of the food chain—the whole pyramid would have no base plankton, and it would crumble, or crash with a thud. Maybe enough spores and larvae and eggs are constantly being borne down from slower upstream waters to repopulate . . . I don't know.

Some little children have discovered a snapping turtle as big as a tray. It's hard to believe that this creek could support a predator that size: its shell is a foot and a half across, and its head extends a good seven inches beyond the shell. When the children—in the company of a shrunken terrier—approach it on the bank, the snapper rears up on its thick front legs and hisses very impressively. I had read earlier that since turtles' shells are rigid, they don't have bellows lungs; they have to gulp for air. And, also since their shells are rigid, there's only room for so much inside, so when they are frightened and planning a retreat, they have to expel air from their lungs to make room for head and feet—hence the malevolent hiss.

The next time I look, I see that the children have somehow maneuvered the snapper into a washtub. They're waving a broom handle at it in hopes that it will snap the wood like a matchstick, but the creature will not deign to oblige. The kids are crushed; all their lives they've heard that this is the one thing you do with a snapping turtle—you shove a broom handle near it, and it "snaps it like a matchstick." It's nature's way; it's sure-fire. But the turtle is having none of it. It avoids the broom handle with an air of patiently repressed rage. They let it go, and it beelines down the bank, dives unhesitatingly into the swirling floodwater, and that's the last we see of it.

A cheer comes up from the crowd on the bridge. The truck is here with a pump for the Bowerys' basement, hooray! We roll away the metal drums, the truck makes it over the bridge, to my amazement—the crowd cheers again. State police cruise by; everything's fine here; downstream people are in trouble. The bridge over by the Bings' on Tinker Creek looks like it's about to go. There's a tree trunk wedged against its railing, and a section of concrete is out. The Bings are away, and a young couple is living there, "taking care of the house." What can they do? The husband drove to work that morning as usual; a few hours later, his wife was evacuated from the front door in a *motorboat*.

I walk to the Bings'. Most of the people who•are on our bridge eventually end up over there; it's just down the road. We straggle along in the rain, gathering a crowd. The men who work away from home are here, too; their wives have telephoned them at work this morning to say that the creek is rising fast, and they'd better get home while the getting's good.

There's a big crowd already there; everybody knows that the Bings' is low. The creek is coming in the recreation-room windows; it's halfway up the garage door. Later that day people will haul out everything salvageable and try to dry it: books, rugs, furniture—the lower level was filled from floor to ceiling. Now on this bridge a road crew is trying to chop away the wedged tree trunk with a long-handled ax. The handle isn't so long that they don't have to stand on the bridge, in Tinker Creek. I walk along a low brick wall that was built to retain the creek away from the house at high water. The wall holds just fine, but now that the creek's receding, it's retaining water around the house. On the wall I can walk right out into the flood and stand in the middle of it. Now on the return trip I meet a young man who's going in the opposite direction. The wall is one brick wide; we can't pass. So we clasp hands and lean out backwards over the turbulent water; our feet interlace like teeth on a zipper, we pull together, stand, and continue on our ways. The kids have spotted a rattlesnake draping itself out of harm's way in a bush; now they all want to walk over the brick wall to the bush, to get bitten by the snake.

The little Atkins kids are here, and they are hopping up and down. I wonder if I hopped up and down, would the bridge go? I could stand at the railing as at the railing of a steamboat, shouting deliriously, "Mark three! Quarter-less-three! Half twain! Quarter twain! . . ." as the current bore the broken bridge out of sight around the bend before she sank.

Everyone else is standing around. Some of the women are carrying curious plastic umbrellas that look like diving bells—umbrellas they don't put up, but on; they don't get under, but in. They can see out dimly, like goldfish in bowls. Their voices from within sound distant, but with an underlying cheerfulness that plainly acknowledges, "Isn't this ridiculous?" Some of the men are wearing their fishing hats. Others duck their heads under folded newspapers held not very high in an effort to compromise between keeping their heads dry and letting rain run up their sleeves. Following some form of courtesy, I guess, they lower these newspapers when they speak with you, and squint politely into the rain.

Women are bringing coffee in mugs to the road crew. They've barely made a dent in the tree trunk, and they're giving up. It's a job for power tools; the water's going down anyway, and the danger is past. Some kid starts doing tricks on a skateboard; I head home.

On the same day that I was standing on bridges here over Tinker Creek, a friend, Lee Zacharias, was standing on a bridge in Richmond over the James River. It was a calm day there, with not a cloud in the skies. The James River was up a mere nine feet, which didn't look too unusual. But floating in the river was everything under the bright sun. As Lee watched, chicken coops raced by, chunks of houses, porches, stairs, whole uprooted trees—and finally a bloated dead horse. Lee knew, all of Richmond knew; it was coming.

There the James ultimately rose thirty-two feet. The whole town was under water, and all the electrical power was out. When Governor Holton signed the emergency relief bill—which listed our county among the federal disaster areas—he had to do it by candlelight.

That night a curious thing happened in the blacked-out Governor's mansion. Governor Holton walked down an upstairs hall and saw, to his disbelief, a lightbulb glowing in a ceiling fixture. It was one of three bulbs, all dead—the whole city was dead—but that one bulb was giving off a faint electrical light. He stared at the thing, scratched his head, and summoned an electrician. The electrician stared at the thing, scratched his head, and announced, "Impossible." The governor went back to bed, and the electrician went home. No explanation has ever been found.

Later Agnes would move on up into Maryland, Pennsylvania, and New York, killing people and doing hundreds of millions of dollars worth of damage. Here in Virginia alone it killed twelve people and ruined 166 million dollars' worth of property. But it hit Pennsylvania twice, coming and going. I talked to one of the helicopter pilots who had helped airlift ancient corpses from a flooded cemetery in Wilkes-Barre, Pennsylvania. The flood left the bodies stranded on housetops, in trees; the pilots, sickened, had to be relieved every few hours. The one I talked to, in a little sandwich shop at the Peaks of Otter on the Blue Ridge Parkway, preferred Vietnam. We were lucky here.

Flood

∞

This winter I heard a final flood story, about an extra dividend that the flood left the Bings, a surprise as unexpected as a baby in a basket on a stoop.

The Bings came home and their house was ruined, but somehow they managed to salvage almost everything, and live as before. One afternoon in the fall a friend went to visit them; as he was coming in, he met a man coming out, a professor with a large volume under his arm. The Bings led my friend inside and into the kitchen, where they proudly opened the oven door and showed him a giant mushroom—which they were baking to serve to guests the following day. The professor with the book had just been verifying its edibility. I imagined the mushroom, wrinkled, black, and big as a dinner plate, erupting overnight mysteriously in the Bings' living room—from the back of an upholstered couch, say, or from a still-damp rug under an armchair.

Alas, the story as I had fixed it in my mind proved to be only partly true. The Bings often cook wild mushrooms, and they know what they're doing. This particular mushroom had grown outside, under a sycamore, on high ground that the flood hadn't touched. So the flood had nothing to do with it. But it's still a good story, and I like to think that the flood left them a gift, a consolation prize, so that for years to come they will be finding edible mushrooms here and there about the house, dinner on the bookshelf, hors d'oeuvres in the piano. It would have been nice.

FROM *EXPLORATION OF THE COLORADO RIVER AND ITS CANYONS*

John Wesley Powell

FROM THE LITTLE COLORADO TO THE FOOT OF THE GRAND CANYON

August 13.—We are now ready to start on our way down the Great Unknown. Our boats, tied to a common stake, chafe each other as they are tossed by the fretful river. They ride high and buoyant, for their loads are lighter than we could desire. We have but a month's rations remaining. The flour has been resifted through the mosquito-net sieve; the spoiled bacon has been dried and the worst of it boiled; the few pounds of dried apples have been spread in the sun and reshrunken to their normal bulk. The sugar has all melted and gone on its way down the river. But we have a large sack of coffee. The lightening of the boats has this advantage: they will ride the waves better and we shall have but little to carry when we make a portage.

We are three quarters of a mile in the depths of the earth, and the great river shrinks into insignificance as it dashes its angry waves against the walls and cliffs that rise to the world above; the waves are but puny ripples, and we but pigmies, running up and down the sands or lost among the boulders.

We have an unknown distance yet to run, an unknown river to explore. What falls there are, we know not; what rocks beset the channel, we know not; what walls rise over the river, we know not. Ah, well! we may conjecture many things. The men talk as cheerfully as ever; jests are bandied about freely this morning; but to me the cheer is somber and the jests are ghastly.

With some eagerness and some anxiety and some misgiving we enter the canyon below and are carried along by the swift water through walls which rise from its very edge. They have the same structure that we noticed yesterday—tiers of irregular shelves below, and, above these, steep slopes to the foot of marble cliffs. We run six miles in a little more than half an hour and emerge into a more open portion of the canyon, where high hills and ledges of rock intervene between the river and the distant walls. Just at the head of this open place the river runs across a dike; that is, a fissure in the rocks, open to depths below, was filled with eruptive matter, and this on cooling was harder than the rocks through which the crevice was made, and when these were washed away the harder volcanic matter remained as a wall, and the river has cut a gateway through it several hundred feet high and as many wide. As it crosses the wall, there is a fall below and a bad rapid, filled with boulders of trap; so we stop to make a portage. Then on we go, gliding by hills and ledges, with distant walls in view; sweeping past sharp angles of rock; stopping at a few points to examine rapids, which we find can be run, until we have made another five miles, when we land for dinner.

Then we let down with lines over a long rapid and start again. Once more the walls close in, and we find ourselves in a narrow gorge, the water again filling the channel and being very swift. With great care and constant watchfulness we proceed, making about four miles this afternoon, and camp in a cave.

August 14.—At daybreak we walk down the bank of the river, on a little sandy beach, to take a view of a new feature in the canyon. Heretofore hard rocks have given us bad river; soft rocks, smooth water; and a series of rocks harder than any we have experienced sets in. The river enters the gneiss! We can see but a little way into the granite gorge, but it looks threatening.

After breakfast we enter on the waves. At the very introduction it inspires awe. The canyon is narrower than we have ever before seen it: the water is swifter; there are but few broken rocks in the channel; but the walls are set, on either side, with pinnacles and crags; and sharp, angular buttresses, bristling with wind- and wave-polished spires, extend far out into the river.

Ledges of rock jut into the stream, their tops sometimes just below the surface, sometimes rising a few or many feet above; and island ledges and island pinnacles and island towers break the swift course of the stream into chutes and eddies and whirlpools. We soon reach a place where a creek comes in from the left, and, just below, the channel is choked with boulders, which have washed down this lateral canyon and formed a dam, over which there is a fall of 30 or 40 feet; but on the boulders foothold can be had, and we make a portage. Three more such dams are found. Over one we make a portage; at the other two are chutes through which we can run.

As we proceed the granite rises higher, until nearly a thousand feet of the lower part of the walls are composed of this rock.

About eleven o'clock we hear a great roar ahead, and approach it very cautiously. The sound grows louder and louder as we run, and at last we find ourselves above a long, broken fall, with ledges and pinnacles of rock obstructing the river. There is a descent of perhaps 75 or 80 feet in a third of a mile, and the rushing waters break into great waves on the rocks, and lash themselves into a mad, white foam. We can land just above, but there is no foothold on either side by which we can make a portage. It is nearly a thousand feet to the top of the granite; so it will be impossible to carry our boats around, though we can climb to the summit up a side gulch and, passing along a mile or two, descend to the river. This we find on examination; but such a portage would be impracticable for us, and we must run the rapid or abandon the river. There is no hesitation. We step into our boats, push off, and away we go, first on smooth but swift water, then we strike a glassy wave and ride to its top, down again into the trough, up again on a higher wave, and down and up on waves higher and still higher until we strike one just as it curls back, and a breaker rolls over our little boat. Still on we speed, shooting past projecting rocks, till the little boat is caught in a whirlpool and spun round several times. At last we pull out again into the stream. And now the other boats have passed us. The open compartment of the *Emma Dean* is filled with water and every breaker rolls over us. Hurled back from a rock, now on this side, now on that, we are carried into an eddy, in which we struggle for a few minutes, and are then out again, the breakers still rolling over us. Our boat is unmanageable, but she cannot sink, and we drift down another hundred yards through breakers—how, we scarcely know. We find the other boats have turned into an eddy at the foot of the fall and are waiting to catch us as we come, for the men have seen that our boat is swamped. They push out as we come near and pull us in against the wall. Our boat bailed, on we go again.

The walls now are more than a mile in height—a vertical distance difficult to appreciate. Stand on the south steps of the Treasury building in Washington and look down Pennsylvania Avenue to the Capitol; measure this distance overhead, and imagine cliffs to extend to that altitude, and you will understand what is meant; or stand at Canal Street in New York and look up Broadway to Grace Church, and you have about the distance; or stand at Lake Street bridge in Chicago and look down to the Central Depot, and you have it again.

A thousand feet of this is up through granite crags; then steep slopes and perpendicular cliffs rise one above another to the summit. The gorge is black and narrow below, red and gray and flaring above, with crags and angular projections on the walls, which, cut in many places by side canyons, seem to be a vast wilderness of rocks. Down in these grand, gloomy depths we glide, ever listening, for the mad waters keep up their roar; ever watching, ever peering ahead, for the narrow canyon is winding and the river is closed in so that we can see but a few hundred yards, and what there may be below we know not; so we listen for falls and watch for rocks, stopping now and then in the bay of a recess to admire the gigantic scenery; and ever as we go there is some new pinnacle or tower, some crag or peak, some distant view of the upper plateau, some strangely shaped rock, or some deep, narrow side canyon.

Then we come to another broken fall, which appears more difficult than the one we ran this morning. A small creek comes in on the right, and the first fall of the water is over boulders, which have been carried down by this lateral stream. We land at its mouth and stop for an hour or two to examine the fall. It seems possible to let down with lines, at least a part of the way, from point to point, along the right-hand wall. So we make a portage over the first rocks and find footing on some boulders below. Then we let down one of the boats to the end of her line, when she reaches a corner of the projecting rock, to which one of the men clings and steadies her while I examine an eddy below. I think we can pass the other boats down by us and catch them in the eddy. This is soon done, and the men in the boats in the eddy pull us to their side. On the shore of this little eddy there is about two feet of gravel beach above the water. Standing on this beach, some of the men take the line of the little boat and let it drift down against another projecting angle. Here is a little shelf, on which a man from my boat climbs, and a shorter line is passed to him, and he fastens the boat to the side of the cliff; then the second one is let down, bringing the line of the third. When the second boat is tied up, the two men standing on the beach above spring into the last boat, which is pulled up alongside of ours; then we let down the boats for 25 or 30 yards by walking along the shelf, landing them again in the mouth of a side canyon. Just below this there is another pile of boulders, over which we make another portage. From the foot of these rocks we can climb to another shelf, 40 or 50 feet above the water.

On this bench we camp for the night. It is raining hard, and we have no shelter, but find a few sticks which have lodged in the rocks, and kindle a fire and have supper. We sit on the rocks all night, wrapped in our *ponchos*, getting what sleep we can.

August 15.—This morning we find we can let down for 300 or 400 yards, and it is managed in this way: we pass along the wall by climbing from projecting point to point, sometimes near the water's edge, at other places 50 or 60 feet above, and hold the boat with a line while two men remain aboard and prevent her from being dashed against the rocks and keep the line from getting caught on the wall. In two hours we have brought them all down, as far as it is possible, in this way. A few yards below, the river strikes with great violence against a projecting rock and our boats are pulled up in a little bay above. The little boat is held by the bow obliquely up the stream. We jump in and pull out only a few strokes, and sweep clear of the dangerous rock. The other boats follow in the same manner and the rapid is passed.

It is not easy to describe the labor of such navigation. We must prevent the waves from dashing the boats against the cliffs. Sometimes, where the river is swift, we must put a bight of rope about a rock, to prevent the boat from being snatched from us by a wave; but where the plunge is too great or the chute too swift, we must let her leap and catch her below or the undertow will drag her under the falling water and sink her. Where we wish to run her out a little way from shore through a channel between rocks, we first throw in little sticks of driftwood and watch their course, to see where we must steer so that she will pass the channel in safety. And so we hold, and let go, and pull, and lift, and ward—among rocks, around rocks, and over rocks.

And now we go on through this solemn, mysterious way. The river is very deep, the canyon very narrow, and still obstructed, so that there is no steady flow of the stream; but the waters reel and roll and boil, and we are scarcely able to determine where we can go. Now the boat is carried to the right, perhaps close to the wall; again, she is shot into the stream, and perhaps is dragged over to the other side, where, caught in a whirlpool, she spins about. We can neither land nor run as we please. The boats are entirely unmanageable; no order in their running can be preserved; now one, now another, is ahead, each crew laboring for its own preservation. In such a place we come to another rapid. Two of the boats run it perforce. One succeeds in landing, but there is no foothold by which to make a portage and she is pushed out again into the stream. The next minute a great reflex wave fills the open compartment; she is water-logged, and drifts unmanageable. Breaker after breaker rolls over her and one capsizes her. The men are thrown out; but they cling to the boat, and she drifts down some distance alongside of us and we are able to catch her. She is soon bailed out and the men are aboard once more; but the oars are lost, and so a pair from the *Emma Dean* is spared. Then for two miles we find smooth water.

Clouds are playing in the canyon to-day. Sometimes they roll down in great masses, filling the gorge with gloom; sometimes they hang aloft from wall to wall and cover the canyon with a roof of impending storm, and we can peer long distances up and down this canyon corridor, with its cloud-roof overhead, its walls of black granite, and its river bright with the sheen of broken waters. Then a gust of wind sweeps down a side gulch and, making a rift in the clouds, reveals the blue heavens, and a stream of sunlight pours in. Then the clouds drift away into the distance, and hang around crags and peaks and pinnacles and towers and walls, and cover them with a mantle that lifts from time to time and sets them all in sharp relief. Then baby clouds creep out of side canyons, glide around points, and creep back again into more distant gorges. Then clouds arrange in strata across the canyon, with intervening vista views to cliffs and rocks beyond. The clouds are children of the heavens, and when they play among the rocks they lift them to the region above.

It rains! Rapidly little rills are formed above, and these soon grow into brooks, and the brooks grow into creeks and tumble over the walls in innumerable cascades, adding their wild music to the roar of the river. When the rain ceases the rills, brooks, and creeks run dry.

The waters that fall during a rain on these steep rocks are gathered at once into the river; they could scarcely be poured in more suddenly if some vast spout ran from the clouds to the stream itself. When a storm bursts over the canyon a side gulch is dangerous, for a sudden flood may come, and the inpouring waters will raise the river so as to hide the rocks.

Early in the afternoon we discover a stream entering from the north—a clear, beautiful creek, coming down through a gorgeous red canyon. We land and camp on a sand beach above its mouth, under a great, overspreading tree with willow-shaped leaves.

August 16.—We must dry our rations again to-day and make oars.

The Colorado is never a clear stream, but for the past three or four days it has been raining much of the time, and the floods poured over the walls have brought down great quantities of mud, making it exceedingly turbid now. The little affluent which we have discovered here is a clear, beautiful creek, or river, as it would be termed in this western country, where streams are not abundant. We have named one stream, away above, in honor of the great chief of the "Bad Angels," and as this is in beautiful contrast to that, we conclude to name it "Bright Angel."

Early in the morning the whole party starts up to explore the Bright Angel River, with the special purpose of seeking timber from which to make oars. A couple of miles above we find a large pine log, which has been floated down from the plateau, probably from an altitude of more than 6,000 feet, but not many miles back. On its way it must have passed over many cataracts and falls, for it bears scars in evidence of the rough usage which it has received. The men roll it on skids, and the work of sawing oars is commenced.

This stream heads away back under a line of abrupt cliffs that terminates the plateau, and tumbles down more than 4,000 feet in the first mile or two of its course; then runs through a deep, narrow canyon until it reaches the river.

Late in the afternoon I return and go up a little gulch just above this creek, about 200 yards from camp, and discover the ruins of two or three old houses, which were originally of stone laid in mortar. Only the foundations are left, but irregular blocks, of which the houses were constructed, lie scattered about. In one room I find an old mealing-stone, deeply worn, as if it had been much used. A great deal of pottery is strewn around, and old trails, which in some places are deeply worn into the rocks, are seen.

It is ever a source of wonder to us why these ancient people sought such inaccessible places for their homes. They were, doubtless, an agricultural race, but there are no lands here of any considerable extent that they could have cultivated. To the west of Oraibi, one of the towns in the Province of Tusayan, in northern Arizona, the inhabitants have actually built little terraces along the face of the cliff where a spring gushes out, and thus made their sites for gardens. It is possible that the ancient inhabitants of this place made their agricultural lands in the same way. But why should they seek such spots? Surely the country was not so crowded with peoples to demand the utilization of so barren a region. The only solution suggested of the problem is this: We know that for a century or two after the settlement of Mexico many expeditions were sent into the country now comprising Arizona and New Mexico, for the purpose of bringing the town-building people under the dominion of the Spanish government. Many of their villages were destroyed, and the inhabitants fled to regions at that time unknown; and there are traditions among the people who inhabit the pueblos that still remain that the canyons were these unknown lands. It may be these buildings were erected at that time; sure it is that they have a much more modern appearance than the ruins scattered over Nevada, Utah, Colorado, Arizona, and New Mexico. Those old Spanish conquerors had a monstrous greed for gold and a wonderful lust for saving souls. Treasures they must have, if not on earth, why, then, in heaven; and when they failed to find heathen temples bedecked with silver, they propitiated Heaven by seizing the heathen themselves. There is yet extant a copy of a record made by a heathen artist to express his conception of the demands of the conquerors. In one part of the picture we have a lake, and near by stands a priest pouring water on the head of a native. On the other side, a poor Indian has a cord about his throat. Lines run from these two groups to a central figure, a man with beard and full Spanish panoply. The interpretation of the picture-writing is this: "Be baptized as this saved heathen, or be hanged as that damned heathen." Doubtless, some of these people preferred another alternative, and rather than be baptized or hanged they chose to imprison themselves within these canyon walls.

August 17.—Our rations are still spoiling; the bacon is so badly injured that we are compelled to throw it away. By an accident, this morning, the saleratus was lost overboard. We have now only musty flour sufficient for ten days and a few dried apples, but plenty of coffee. We must make all haste possible. If we meet with difficulties such as we have encountered in the canyon above, we may be compelled to give up the expedition and try to reach the Mormon settlements to the north. Our hopes are that the worst places are passed, but our barometers are all so much injured as to be useless, and so we have lost our reckoning in altitude, and know not how much descent the river has yet to make.

The stream is still wild and rapid and rolls through a narrow channel. We make but slow progress, often landing against a wall and climbing around some point to see the river below. Although very anxious to advance, we are determined to run with great caution, lest by another accident we lose our remaining supplies. How precious that little flour has become! We divide it among the boats and carefully store it away, so that it can be lost only by the loss of the boat itself.

We make ten miles and a half, and camp among the rocks on the right. We have had rain from time to time all day, and have been thoroughly drenched and chilled; but between showers the sun shines with great power and the mercury in our thermometers stands at 115°, so that we have rapid changes from great extremes, which are very disagreeable. It is especially cold in the rain to-night. The little canvas we have is rotten and useless; the rubber *ponchos* with which we started from Green River City have all been lost; more than half the party are without hats, not one of us has an entire suit of clothes, and we have not a blanket apiece. So we gather driftwood and build a fire; but after supper the rain, coming down in torrents, extinguished it, and we sit up all night on the rocks, shivering, and are more exhausted by the night's discomfort than by the day's toil.

August 18.—The day is employed in making portages and we advance but two miles on our journey. Still it rains.

While the men are at work making portages I climb up the granite to its summit and go away back over the rust-colored sandstones and greenish-yellow shales to the foot of the marble wall. I climb so high that the men and boats are lost in the black depths below and the dashing river is a rippling brook, and still there is more canyon above than below. All about me are interesting geologic records. The book is open and I can read as I run. All about me are grand views, too, for the clouds are playing again in the gorges. But somehow I think of the nine days' rations and the bad river, and the lesson of the rocks and the glory of the scene are but half conceived.

I push on to an angle, where I hope to get a view of the country beyond, to see if possible what the prospect may be of our soon running through this plateau, or at least of meeting with some geologic change that will let us out of the granite; but, arriving at the point, I can see below only a labyrinth of black gorges.

August 19.—Rain again this morning. We are in our granite prison still, and the time until noon is occupied in making a long, bad portage.

After dinner, in running a rapid the pioneer boat is upset by a wave. We are some distance in advance of the larger boats. The river is rough and swift and we are unable to land, but cling to the boat and are carried down stream over another rapid. The men in the boats above see our trouble, but they are caught in whirlpools and are spinning about in eddies, and it seems a long time before they come to our relief. At last they do come; our boat is turned right side up and bailed out; the oars, which fortunately have floated along in company with us, are gathered up, and on we go, without even landing. The clouds break away and we have sunshine again.

Soon we find a little beach with just room enough to land. Here we camp, but there is no wood. Across the river and a little way above, we see some driftwood lodged in the rocks. So we bring two boat loads over, build a huge fire, and spread everything to dry. It is the first cheerful night we have had for a week—a warm, drying fire in the midst of the camp, and a few bright stars in our patch of heavens overhead.

August 20.—The characteristics of the canyon change this morning. The river is broader, the walls more sloping, and composed of black slates that stand on edge. These nearly vertical slates are washed out in places—that is, the softer beds are washed out between the harder, which are left standing. In this way curious little alcoves are formed, in which are quiet bays of water, but on a much smaller scale than the great bays and buttresses of Marble Canyon.

The river is still rapid and we stop to let down with lines several times, but make greater progress, as we run ten miles. We camp on the right bank. Here, on a terrace of trap, we discover another group of ruins. There was evidently quite a village on this rock. Again we find mealing-stones and much broken pottery, and up on a little natural shelf in the rock back of the ruins we find a globular basket that would hold perhaps a third of a bushel. It is badly broken, and as I attempt to take it up it falls to pieces. There are many beautiful flint chips, also, as if this had been the home of an old arrow-maker.

August 21.—We start early this morning, cheered by the prospect of a fine day and encouraged also by the good run made yesterday. A quarter of a mile below camp the river turns abruptly to the left, and between camp and that point is very swift, running down in a long, broken chute and piling up against the foot of the cliff, where it turns to the left. We try to pull across, so as to go down on the other side, but the waters are swift and it seems impossible for us to escape the rock below; but, in pulling across, the bow of the boat is turned to the farther shore, so that we are swept broadside down and are prevented by the rebounding waters from striking against the wall. We toss about for a few seconds in these billows and are then carried past the danger. Below, the river turns again to the right, the canyon is very narrow, and we see in advance but a short distance. The water, too, is very swift, and there is no landing-place. From around this curve there comes a mad roar, and down we are carried with a dizzying velocity to the head of another rapid. On either side high over our heads there are overhanging granite walls, and the sharp bends cut off our view, so that a few minutes will carry us into unknown waters. Away we go on one long, winding chute. I stand on deck, supporting myself with a strap fastened on either side of the gunwale. The boat glides rapidly where the water is smooth, then, striking a wave, she leaps and bounds like a thing of life, and we have a wild, exhilarating ride of ten miles, which we make in less than an hour. The excitement is so great that we forget the danger until we hear the roar of a great fall below; then we back on our oars and are carried slowly toward its head and succeed in landing just above and find that we have to make another portage. At this we are engaged until some time after dinner.

Just here we run out of the granite. Ten miles in less than half a day, and limestone walls below. Good cheer returns; we forget the storms and the gloom and the cloud-covered canyons and the black granite and the raging river, and push our boats from shore in great glee.

Though we are out of the granite, the river is still swift, and we wheel about a point again to the right, and turn, so as to head back in the direction from which we came; this brings the granite in sight again, with its narrow gorge and black crags; but we meet with no more great falls or rapids. Still, we run cautiously and stop from time to time to examine some places which look bad. Yet we make ten miles this afternoon; twenty miles in all to-day.

August 22.—We come to rapids again this morning and are occupied several hours in passing them, letting the boats down from rock to rock with lines for nearly half a mile, and then have to make a long portage. While the men are engaged in this I climb the wall on the northeast to a height of about 2,500 feet, where I can obtain a good view of a long stretch of canyon below. Its course is to the southwest. The walls seem to rise very abruptly for 2,500 or 3,000 feet, and then there is a gently sloping terrace on each side for two or three miles, when we again find cliffs, 1,500 or 2,000 feet high. From the brink of these the plateau stretches back to the north and south for a long distance. Away down the canyon on the right wall I can see a group of mountains, some of which appear to stand on the brink of the canyon. The effect of the terrace is to give the appearance of a narrow winding valley with high walls on either side and a deep, dark, meandering gorge down its middle. It is impossible from this point of view to determine whether or not we have granite at the bottom; but from geologic considerations, I conclude that we shall have marble walls below.

After my return to the boats we run another mile and camp for the night. We have made but little over seven miles to-day, and a part of our flour has been soaked in the river again.

August 23.—Our way to-day is again through marble walls. Now and then we pass for a short distance through patches of granite, like hills thrust up into the limestone. At one of these places we have to make another portage, and, taking advantage of the delay, I go up a little stream to the north, wading it all the way, sometimes having to plunge in to my neck, in other places being compelled to swim across little basins that have been excavated at the foot of the falls. Along its course are many cascades and springs, gushing out from the rocks on either side. Sometimes a cottonwood tree grows over the water. I come to one beautiful fall, of more than 150 feet, and climb around it to the right on the broken rocks. Still going up, the canyon is found to narrow very much, being but 15 or 20 feet wide; yet the walls rise on either side many hundreds of feet, perhaps thousands; I can hardly tell.

In some places the stream has not excavated its channel down vertically through the rocks, but has cut obliquely, so that one wall overhangs the other. In other places it is cut vertically above and obliquely below, or obliquely above and vertically below, so that it is impossible to see out overhead. But I can go no farther; the time which I estimated it would take to make the portage has almost expired, and I start back on a round trot, wading in the creek where I must and plunging through basins. The men are waiting for me, and away we go on the river.

Just after dinner we pass a stream on the right, which leaps into the Colorado by a direct fall of more than 100 feet, forming a beautiful cascade. There is a bed of very hard rock above, 30 or 40 feet in thickness, and there are much softer beds below. The hard beds above project many yards beyond the softer, which are washed out, forming a deep cave behind the fall, and the stream pours through a narrow crevice above into a deep pool below. Around on the rocks in the cavelike chamber are set beautiful ferns, with delicate fronds and enameled stalks. The frondlets have their points turned down to form spore cases. It has very much the appearance of the maidenhair fern, but is much larger. This delicate foliage covers the rocks all about the fountain, and gives the chamber great beauty. But we have little time to spend in admiration; so on we go.

We make fine progress this afternoon, carried along by a swift river, shooting over the rapids and finding no serious obstructions. The canyon walls for 2,500 or 3,000 feet are very regular, rising almost perpendicularly, but here and there set with narrow steps, and occasionally we can see away above the broad terrace to distant cliffs.

We camp to-night in a marble cave, and find on looking at our reckoning that we have run 22 miles.

August 24.—The canyon is wider to-day. The walls rise to a vertical height of nearly 3,000 feet. In many places the river runs under a cliff in great curves, forming amphitheaters half-dome shaped.

Though the river is rapid, we meet with no serious obstructions and run 20 miles. How anxious we are to make up our reckoning every time we stop, now that our diet is confined to plenty of coffee, a very little spoiled flour, and very few dried apples! It has come to be a race for a dinner. Still, we make such fine progress that all hands are in good cheer, but not a moment of daylight is lost.

August 25.—We make 12 miles this morning, when we come to monuments of lava standing in the river,—low rocks mostly, but some of them shafts more than a hundred feet high. Going on down three or four miles, we find them increasing in number. Great quantities of cooled lava and many cinder cones are seen on either side; and then we come to an abrupt cataract. Just over the fall on the right wall a cinder cone, or extinct volcano, with a well-defined crater, stands on the very brink of the canyon. This, doubtless, is the one we saw two or three days ago, From this volcano vast floods of lava have been poured down into the river, and a stream of molten rock has run up the canyon three or four miles and down we know not how far. Just where it poured over the canyon wall is the fall. The whole north side as far as we can see is lined with the black basalt, and high up on the opposite wall are patches of the same material, resting on the benches and filling old alcoves and caves, giving the wall a spotted appearance.

The rocks are broken in two along a line which here crosses the river, and the beds we have seen while coming down the canyon for the last 30 miles have dropped 800 feet on the lower side of the line, forming what geologists call a "fault." The volcanic cone stands directly over the fissure thus formed. On the left side of the river, opposite, mammoth springs burst out of this crevice, 100 or 200 feet above the river, pouring in a stream quite equal in volume to the Colorado Chiquito.

This stream seems to be loaded with carbonate of lime, and the water, evaporating, leaves an incrustation on the rocks; and this process has been continued for a long time, for extensive deposits are noticed in which are basins with bubbling springs. The water is salty.

We have to make a portage here, which is completed in about three hours; then on we go.

We have no difficulty as we float along, and I am able to observe the wonderful phenomena connected with this flood of lava. The canyon was doubtless filled to a height of 1,200 or 1,500 feet, perhaps by more than one flood. This would dam the water back; and in cutting through this great lava bed, a new channel has been formed, sometimes on one side, sometimes on the other. The cooled lava, being of firmer texture than the rocks of which the walls are composed, remains in some places; in others a narrow channel has been cut, leaving a line of basalt on either side. It is possible that the lava cooled faster on the sides against the walls and that the center ran out; but of this we can only conjecture. There are other places where almost the whole of the lava is gone, only patches of it being seen where it has caught on the walls. As we float down we can see that it ran out into side canyons. In some places this basalt has a fine, columnar structure, often in concentric prisms, and masses of these concentric columns have coalesced. In some places, when the flow occurred the canyon was probably about the same depth that it is now, for we can see where the basalt has rolled out on the sands, and—what seems curious to me—the sands are not melted or metamorphosed to any appreciable extent. In places the bed of the river is of sandstone or limestone, in other places of lava, showing that it has all been cut out again where the sandstones and limestones appear; but there is a little yet left where the bed is of lava.

What a conflict of water and fire there must have been here! Just imagine a river of molten rock running down into a river of melted snow. What a seething and boiling of the waters; what clouds of steam rolled into the heavens!

Thirty-five miles to-day. Hurrah!

August 26.—The canyon walls are steadily becoming higher as we advance. They are still bold and nearly vertical up to the terrace. We still see evidence of the eruption discovered yesterday, but the thickness of the basalt is decreasing as we go down stream; yet it has been reinforced at points by streams that have come down from volcanoes standing on the terrace above, but which we cannot see from the river below.

Since we left the Colorado Chiquito we have seen no evidences that the tribe of Indians inhabiting the plateaus on either side ever come down to the river; but about eleven o'clock to-day we discover an Indian garden at the foot of the wall on the right, just where a little stream with a narrow flood plain comes down through a side canyon. Along the valley the Indians have planted corn, using for irrigation the water which bursts out in springs at the foot of the cliff. The corn is looking quite well, but it is not sufficiently advanced to give us roasting ears; but there are some nice green squashes. We carry ten or a dozen of these on board our boats and hurriedly leave, not willing to be caught in the robbery, yet excusing ourselves by pleading our great want. We run down a short distance to where we feel certain no Indian can follow, and what a kettle of squash sauce we make! True, we have no salt with which to season it, but it makes a fine addition to our unleavened bread and coffee. Never was fruit so sweet as these stolen squashes.

After dinner we push on again and make fine time, finding many rapids, but none so bad that we cannot run them with safety; and when we stop, just at dusk, and foot up our reckoning, we find we have run 35 miles again. A few days like this, and we are out of prison.

We have a royal supper—unleavened bread, green squash sauce, and strong coffee. We have been for a few days on half rations, but now have no stint of roast squash.

August 27.—This morning the river takes a more southerly direction. The dip of the rocks is to the north and we are running rapidly into lower formations. Unless our course changes we shall very soon run again into the granite. This gives some anxiety. Now and then the river turns to the west and excites hopes that are soon destroyed by another turn to the south. About nine o'clock we come to the dreaded rock. It is with no little misgiving that we see the river enter these black, hard walls. At its very entrance we have to make a portage; then let down with lines past some ugly rocks. We run a mile or two farther, and then the rapids below can be seen.

About eleven o'clock we come to a place in the river which seems much worse than any we have yet met in all its course. A little creek comes down from the left. We land first on the right and clamber up over the granite pinnacles for a mile or two, but can see no way by which to let down, and to run it would be sure destruction. After dinner we cross to examine on the left. High above the river we can walk along on the top of the granite, which is broken off at the edge and set with crags and pinnacles, so that it is very difficult to get a view of the river at all. In my eagerness to reach a point where I can see the roaring fall below, I go too far on the wall, and can neither advance nor retreat. I stand with one foot on a little projecting rock and cling with my hand fixed in a little crevice. Finding I am caught here, suspended 400 feet above the river, into which I must fall if my footing fails, I call for help. The men come and pass me a line, but I cannot let go of the rock long enough to take hold of it. Then they bring two or three of the largest oars. All this takes time which seems very precious to me; but at last they arrive. The blade of one of the oars is pushed into a little crevice in the rock beyond me in such a manner that they can hold me pressed against the wall. Then another is fixed in such a way that I can step on it; and thus I am extricated.

Still another hour is spent in examining the river from this side, but no good view of it is obtained; so now we return to the side that was first examined, and the afternoon is spent in clambering among the crags and pinnacles and carefully scanning the river again. We find that the lateral streams have washed boulders into the river, so as to form a dam, over which the water makes a broken fall of 18 or 20 feet; then there is a rapid, beset with rocks, for 200 or 300 yards, while on the other side, points of the wall project into the river. Below, there is a second fall; how great, we cannot tell. Then there is a rapid, filled with huge rocks, for 100 or 200 yards. At the bottom of it, from the right wall, a great rock projects quite halfway across the river. It has a sloping surface extending up stream, and the water, coming down with all the momentum gained in the falls and rapids above, rolls up this inclined plane many feet, and tumbles over to the left. I decide that it is possible to let down over the first fall, then run near the right cliff to a point just above the second, where we can pull out into a little chute, and, having run over that in safety, if we pull with all our power across the stream, we may avoid the great rock below. On my return to the boat I announce to the men that we are to run it in the morning. Then we cross the river and go into camp for the night on some rocks in the mouth of the little side canyon.

After supper Captain Howland asks to have a talk with me. We walk up the little creek a short distance, and I soon find that his object is to remonstrate against my determination to proceed. He thinks that we had better abandon the river here. Talking with him, I learn that he, his brother, and William Dunn have determined to go no farther in the boats. So we return to camp. Nothing is said to the other men.

For the last two days our course has not been plotted. I sit down and do this now, for the purpose of finding where we are by dead reckoning. It is a clear night, and I take out the sextant to make observation for latitude, and I find that the astronomic determination agrees very nearly with that of the plot—quite as closely as might be expected from a meridian observation on a planet. In a direct line, we must be about 45 miles from the mouth of the Rio Virgen. If we can reach that point, we know that there are settlements up that river about 20 miles. This 45 miles in a direct line will probably be 80 or 90 by the meandering line of the river. But then we know that there is comparatively open country for many miles above the mouth of the Virgen, which is our point of destination.

As soon as I determine all this, I spread my plot on the sand and wake Howland, who is sleeping down by the river, and show him where I suppose we are, and where several Mormon settlements are situated.

We have another short talk about the morrow, and he lies down again; but for me there is no sleep. All night long I pace up and down a little path, on a few yards of sand beach, along by the river. Is it wise to go on? I go to the boats again to look at our rations. I feel satisfied that we can get over the danger immediately before us; what there may be below I know not. From our outlook yesterday on the cliffs, the canyon seemed to make another great bend to the south, and this, from our experience heretofore, means more and higher granite walls. I am not sure that we can climb out of the canyon here, and, if at the top of the wall, I know enough of the country to be certain that it is a desert of rock and sand between this and the nearest Mormon town, which, on the most direct line, must be 75 miles away. True, the late rains have been favorable to us, should we go out, for the probabilities are that we shall find water still standing in holes; and at one time I almost conclude to leave the river. But for years I have been contemplating this trip. To leave the exploration unfinished, to say that there is a part of the canyon which I cannot explore, having already nearly accomplished it, is more than I am willing to acknowledge, and I determine to go on.

I wake my brother and tell him of Howland's determination, and he promises to stay with me; then I call up Hawkins, the cook, and he makes a like promise; then Sumner and Bradley and Hall, and they all agree to go on.

August 28.—At last daylight comes and we have breakfast without a word being said about the future. The meal is as solemn as a funeral. After breakfast I ask the three men if they still think it best to leave us. The elder Howland thinks it is, and Dunn agrees with him. The younger Howland tries to persuade them to go on with the party; failing in which, he decides to go with his brother.

Then we cross the river. The small boat is very much disabled and unseaworthy. With the loss of hands, consequent on the departure of the three men, we shall not be able to run all of the boats; so I decide to leave my *Emma Dean*.

Two rifles and a shotgun are given to the men who are going out. I ask them to help themselves to the rations and take what they think to be a fair share. This they refuse to do, saying they have no fear but that they can get something to eat; but Billy, the cook, has a pan of biscuits prepared for dinner, and these he leaves on a rock.

Before starting, we take from the boat our barometers, fossils, the minerals, and some ammunition and leave them on the rocks. We are going over this place as light as possible. The three men help us lift our boats over a rock 25 or 30 feet high and let them down again over the first fall, and now we are all ready to start. The last thing before leaving, I write a letter to my wife and I give it to Howland. Sumner gives him his watch, directing that it be sent to his sister should he not be heard from again. The records of the expedition have been kept in duplicate. One set of these is given to Howland; and now we are ready. For the last time they entreat us not to go on, and tell us that it is madness to set out in this place; that we can never get safely through it; and, further, that the river turns again to the south into the granite, and a few miles of such rapids and falls will exhaust our entire stock of rations, and then it will be too late to climb out. Some tears are shed; it is rather a solemn parting; each party thinks the other is taking the dangerous course.

My old boat left, I go on board of the *Maid of the Canyon.* The three men climb a crag that overhangs the river to watch us off. The *Maid of the Canyon* pushes out. We glide rapidly along the foot of the wall, just grazing one great rock, then pull out a little into the chute of the second fall and plunge over it. The open compartment is filled when we strike the first wave below, but we cut through it, and then the men pull with all their power toward the left wall and swing clear of the dangerous rock below all right. We are scarcely a minute in running it, and find that, although it looked bad from above, we have passed many places that were worse.

The other boat follows without more difficulty. We land at the first practicable point below, and fire our guns, as a signal to the men above that we have come over in safety. Here we remain a couple of hours, hoping that they will take the smaller boat and follow us. We are behind a curve in the canyon and cannot see up to where we left them, and so we wait until their coming seems hopeless, and then push on.

And now we have a succession of rapids and falls until noon, all of which we run in safety. Just after dinner we come to another bad place. A little stream comes in from the left, and below there is a fall, and still below another fall. Above, the river tumbles down, over and among the rocks, in whirlpools and great waves, and the waters are lashed into mad, white foam. We run along the left, above this, and soon see that we cannot get down on this side, but it seems possible to let down on the other. We pull up stream again for 200 or 300 yards and cross. Now there is a bed of basalt on this northern side of the canyon, with a bold escarpment that seems to be a hundred feet high. We can climb it and walk along its summit to a point where we are just at the head of the fall. Here the basalt is broken down again, so it seems to us, and I direct the men to take a line to the top of the cliff and let the boats down along the wall. One man remains in the boat to keep her clear of the rocks and prevent her line from being caught on the projecting angles. I climb the cliff and pass along to a point just over the fall and descend by broken rocks, and find that the break of the fall is above the break of the wall, so that we cannot land, and that still below the river is very bad, and that there is no possibility of a portage. Without waiting further to examine and determine what shall be done, I hasten back to the top of the cliff to stop the boats from coming down. When I arrive I find the men have let one of them down to the head of the fall. She is in swift water and they are not able to pull her back; nor are they able to go on with the line, as it is not long enough to reach the higher part of the cliff which is just before them; so they take a bight around a crag. I send two men back for the other line The boat is in very swift water, and Bradley is stand-ing in the open compartment, holding out his oar to prevent her from striking against the foot of the cliff. Now she shoots out into the stream and up as far as the line will permit, and then, wheeling, drives headlong against the rock, and then out and back again, now strain-ing on the line, now striking against the rock. As soon as the second line is brought, we pass it down to him; but his attention is all taken up with his own situation, and he does not see that we are passing him the line. I stand on a projecting rock, waving my hat to gain his attention, for my voice is drowned by the roaring of the falls. Just at this moment I see him take his knife from its sheath and step forward to cut the line. He has evidently decided that it is better to go over with the boat as it is than to wait for her to be broken to pieces. As he leans over, the boat sheers again into the stream, the stem-post breaks away and she is loose. With perfect composure Bradley seizes the great scull oar, places it in the stern rowlock, and pulls with all his power (and he is an athlete) to turn the bow of the boat down stream, for he wishes to go bow down, rather than to drift broadside on. One, two strokes he makes, and a third just as she goes over, and the boat is fairly turned, and she goes down almost beyond our sight, though we are more than a hundred feet above the river. Then she comes up again on a great wave, and down and up, then around behind some great rocks, and is lost in the mad, white foam below. We stand frozen with fear, for we see no boat. Bradley is gone! so it seems. But now, away below, we see something coming out of the waves. It is evidently a boat. A moment more, and we see Bradley standing on deck, swing-ing his hat to show that he is all right. But he is in a whirlpool. We have the stem-post of his boat attached to the line. How badly she may be disabled we know not. I direct Sumner and Powell to pass along the cliff and see if they can reach him from below. Hawkins, Hall, and myself run to the other boat, jump aboard, push out, and away we go over the falls. A wave rolls over us and our boat is un-manageable. Another great wave strikes us, and the boat rolls over, and tumbles and tosses, I know not how. All I know is that Bradley is picking us up. We soon have all right again, and row to the cliff and wait until Sumner and Powell can come. After a difficult climb they reach us. We run two or three miles farther and turn again to the northwest, continuing until night, when we have run out of the gran-ite once more.

August 29.—We start very early this morning. The river still continues swift, but we have no serious difficulty, and at twelve o'-clock emerge from the Grand Canyon of the Colorado. We are in a valley now, and low mountains are seen in the distance, coming to the river below. We recognize this as the Grand Wash.

A few years ago a party of Mormons set out from St. George, Utah, taking with them a boat, and came down to the Grand Wash, where they divided, a portion of the party crossing the river to ex-plore the San Francisco Mountains. Three men—Hamblin, Miller, and Crosby—taking the boat, went on down the river to Callville, landing a few miles below the mouth of the Rio Virgen. We have their manuscript journal with us, and so the stream is comparatively well known.

To-night we camp on the left bank, in a mesquite thicket.

The relief from danger and the joy of success are great. When he who has been chained by wounds to a hospital cot until his canvas tent seems like a dungeon cell, until the groans of those who lie about tortured with probe and knife are piled up, a weight of horror on his ears that he cannot throw off, cannot forget, and until the stench of festering wounds and anaesthetic drugs has filled the air with its loathsome burthen,—when he at last goes out into the open field, what a world he sees! How beautiful the sky, how bright the sunshine, what "floods of delirious music" pour from the throats of birds, how sweet the fragrance of earth and tree and blossom! The first hour of convalescent freedom seems rich recompense for all pain and gloom and terror.

Something like these are the feelings we experience to-night. Ever before us has been an unknown danger, heavier than immediate peril. Every waking hour passed in the Grand Canyon has been one of toil. We have watched with deep solicitude the steady disappearance of our scant supply of rations, and from time to time have seen the river snatch a portion of the little left, while we were a-hungered. And danger and toil were endured in those gloomy depths, where oft-times clouds hid the sky by day and but a narrow zone of stars could be seen at night. Only during the few hours of deep sleep, consequent on hard labor, has the roar of the waters been hushed. Now the danger is over, now the toil has ceased, now the gloom has disappeared, now the firmament is bounded only by the horizon, and what a vast expanse of constellations can be seen!

The river rolls by us in silent majesty; the quiet of the camp is sweet; our joy is almost ecstasy. We sit till long after midnight talking of the Grand Canyon, talking of home, but talking chiefly of the three men who left us. Are they wandering in those depths, unable to find a way out? Are they searching over the desert lands above for water? Or are they nearing the settlements?

ℛEVERSING THE 𝒯IDES

Lisa Couturier

There was a child went forth every day,
And the first object he looked upon and received with wonder or
    pity or love or dread, that object he became, . . .
The horizon's edge, the flying seacrow, the fragrance of saltmarsh
    and shoremud . . .

                                   —Walt Whitman, "Leaves of Grass"

𝒯he story is told in my family that when I was a year old my parents took me to the beach at Sandy Hook, New Jersey, which from the shoreline has a view of Manhattan. They took me out to the edge, where the sand meets the rocks, marking the intersection of Sandy Hook Bay, Lower New York Bay, and the Atlantic Ocean. My father lifted me up on his shoulders and my parents pointed to New York City. They say I looked. They say I saw the city then, on a clear day.

I now live in Manhattan and every day I walk to the East River—which, although big and wide as most people might imagine a river to be, is technically a tidal strait and part of the larger Hudson estuary ecosystem that surrounds Manhattan.

On my walks to the river, the wind, carrying the water's salt scent, surrounds me; and I am pulled toward its estuarine currents. To get near the river's side I must walk along a tar path that begins at the end of my street and winds through a manicured park, around the mayor's mansion, and over a small grassy hill. Coming to the top of the hill, I anticipate what the water will be like at my favorite spot on the river—Hell's Gate, named so for the tangling of tides that mix

141

here: the Atlantic tide travels up the Manhattan arm of the East River to collide with the tide of the Long Island Sound and the current of the Harlem River. Some days the tides look as though they're fighting. Dark olive-green waters hit and chop at each other and swirl and spiral all at once. Other times nothing, every drop of water seems to be just strolling along, friendly—as if water could sigh. I clear the hill, walk under an American basswood tree growing in a triangle of grass, and stop to let the wind blow over me. I take the air into my body, consciously swallow it, give my lungs—my entire being—a fix of the river's essence.

The smell of the water is as close as I will get to the river itself. There is no access, no great green shoreline. Looking at the river is more like looking at a mangy pound dog when you really want to see a shiny-furred, well-muscled purebred, its tail wagging. This body of water, like most of the waters around New York City, is for the most part surrounded by the dirty environment of the human world—fuel tanks, abandoned buildings, highways, skyscrapers and such. But recently nature's presence has returned to the river: butterflies, seaweed swaying over rocks, seagulls laughing, Canada geese flying in their autumn V, striped bass passing through from the Long Island Sound to the Hudson River, snapping turtles who've survived the last four centuries in New York waters, American eels who swim to the Sargasso Sea to lay their eggs and whose young make the one-thousand-mile return trip to the city, peregrine falcons who nest twenty blocks down river but hunt and fly up my way, cormorants, herons, and egrets.

When I'm by the river, which itself has been so stripped—of its wetlands, of its shoreline, of its purity through pollution and abuse—I shed my own urban skin, a general impatience with things slow moving, to listen to the movement of the river and to its waves against the rocks. The rippling of the water soothes me, as though its sound fuses with my blood to calm me. Often, when the sun reflects pink and orange on the river in early evening, flocks of starlings or sparrows explode from the park's trees and circle out over the water as though they are riding an airborne roller coaster. They fly back over me, their wings beating against their bodies, and return to the park. As the sky darkens, the birds settle in for the night and I begin my walk home, envious that the birds, unlike me, are safe in the park at night by the river. If it is a summer evening, I leave the river's side during a concert of cricket song with a light show of fireflies—a performance worthy of Madison Square Garden.

It's been a while since I stopped being surprised by nature in New York City, which is, after all, simply a name we've given this landscape—a label meaningless to the birds, the turtles, the river. Besides, said James Hillman, the Jungian psychologist, the "Greek word for city, *polis*, . . . draws from a pool of meanings related to water . . . *polis* locates city in the wet regions of the soul . . . We need but remember that the city, the *metro-polis* means at root a streaming, flowing, thronging Mother. We are her children, and she can nourish our imaginations if we nourish hers."

Walking the river's promenade and looking across at Roosevelt Island, I think of a local legend, Thomas Maxey. He knew something about the wet regions of his soul, from whence his feelings and dreams informed his life and helped him nourish the riverscape. It is said he was a bit of a madman who was quite fond of birds. Shortly after the Civil War, Maxey built a fort at the tip of Roosevelt Island, just below Hell's Gate; and in front of the fort, he erected a gate that was somehow designed to be used as a nesting site for wild geese. On the gate he wrote this message: I INVITE THE FOWLS AND THE BIRDS OF THE AIR TO ENTER.

Could it be that Maxey wasn't mad, but just in love with birds and the river? Perhaps he simply sensed then what writer Thomas Moore says now: "Maybe one function of love is to cure us of an anemic imagination, a life emptied of romantic attachment and abandoned to reason."

Of course there must be biological reasons the animals have returned to the East River—a body of water that, according to some accounts, was so toxic it would burn a ship's hull clean by docking it here for a few days. Even as recently as the 1950s, sewage and pollutants from manufacturing plants were poured into the river. And it wasn't until the Clean Water Act of 1972 that New York finally stopped thinking of the river as its toilet. Until then we were dumping raw sewage into it daily. (Even now, when it rains more than an inch and a half, sewage treatment plants along the river overflow into it.) And today, although there are still PCBs and other toxins remaining in the river's sediments, the East River is staging a comeback, which, according to local news reports, has environmental officials somewhat mystified. Nevertheless, oxygen levels are up; coliform bacteria (indicating the level of sewage) is down; amphipods—food for fish—are back, as are the crabs and minnows herons feed on; apparently, biodiversity is on the rise.

The river is making enormous changes, as is the city. The New York City Department of Environmental Protection will soon invest over a billion dollars to research the contamination of the East River and other parts of the estuary.

Environmental science: What is it but a way to rationalize our longings for interdependence and interrelationship?

Environmental legislation: What is it if not a desire for deep change, a kind of compassion for the earth?

For years I thought of the East River as nothing more than a polluted, liquefied roadway on which rode huge foreign tankers, garbage barges, speedboats, the yachts of the rich, and a few sailboats. Now I stand alongside Hell's Gate, breathing the river into me, gazing at it, waiting for its turtles, geese, herons—the innocents we more often associate with Heaven's Gate. Thomas Berry the eco-theologian, says that by pursuing what we love—our allurements—we help bind the universe together. Am I a madwoman now to think, like Maxey, that my allurement for the river might help her call in her creatures?

As a tugboat chugs down the river, I see a cormorant sitting on a dilapidated pier. It's not far from where I recently saw a snapping turtle swimming close to the surface of the water and almost mistook it for a deflated, discarded soccer ball. The cormorant extends his black wings to dry in the sunlight, and from the back looks much like the silhouette of Dracula. I watch him and remember the time I spent three years ago traveling through the underworld of the East River's sister waterway: the Arthur Kill. It is the place from whence the cormorant had flown, a place that most would agree is more deserving of the name Hell's Gate, and a place where all my ideas of nature as resplendent were abducted from me.

It is the faintest of sounds—a tiny tic, tic, tic—I hear as I hold to my ear an egg from which a seagull chick is pipping.

I am on the pebbly, scrubby, sandy shoreline of an island in the Arthur Kill—another large tidal strait in the Hudson estuary that runs through a polluted wetland along the western side of New York City's Staten Island, separating it from New Jersey. It is the end of my second summer as a volunteer assistant to two biologists for the Harbor Herons Project, and today we are searching for Canada goose nests. The search is a break in our usual routine of studying the more glamorous and elusive long-legged wading birds who, since the mid-

'70s, have made a miraculous comeback in the wooded interiors of isolated islands in the East River and the Arthur Kill.

As I place the seagull chick back into its nest on the shore, I silently laugh at myself for missing the messy research we do in the heronry. Going into the birds' seasonal nesting area as quickly and quietly as possible, we gently lift the baby birds from their nests in gray birches and quaking aspens to weigh and measure them. We handle just a small sampling of the nestlings of the four thousand great egrets, snowy egrets, cattle egrets, little blue herons, black-crowned night herons, green-backed herons, yellow-crowned night herons, and glossy ibises who are living and raising their young quite invisibly within the boundaries of New York City. We count how many young are born and how many fledge. The birds are an indicator species—as they are at the top of the food chain in their environment, their health indicates the health of the estuary.

Across from the heronry and the seagull nest, on the New Jersey side of the Kill, the giants of the oil and chemical companies—Du Pont, Citgo, Cyanamid, Exxon, and others—make house. Their huge white storage tanks stand silent in the tall, lime-green salt-marsh grasses, while their smokestacks spew out EPA-approved amounts of waste into the air over the marsh.

The history of the Arthur Kill, like that of the East River, should render it essentially lifeless from centuries of oil spills, raw sewage, and chemical dumping. The soft turf of the salt marsh has absorbed (and will probably continue to absorb) so many oil spills—such as the several in 1990 that totaled 794,500 gallons (one hundred thousand gallons is considered a major spill) and caused the collapse of the fragile and already badly bruised ecosystem. Only recently has the Kill begun to bounce back. Still, when I glance down at my footprints in the sand I see oil that will persist for decades. It is buried but not benign.

I picture the mother herons fishing in the shallow depths of the Kill, their long bills poised to skewer fish, crab, shrimp: invertebrates who themselves have ingested the toxic and carcinogenic oils. The poison will be passed, and in part explains why many of our nestlings fail to survive.

Scattered along the shore and hidden in the marsh grasses is a veritable Walmart of used plastic products: empty plastic containers of dishwashing detergent, shampoo, yogurt, toilet-bowl cleaner, and Chinese takeout, as well as balls, toys, kitchen sinks, anything and everything I could ever imagine having in my apartment. The trash has slipped off garbage barges that every day carry thirteen thousand tons of New York City's trash through the New York Harbor and down the Arthur Kill to be dumped in the world's largest landfill that, as it happens, sits next to the heronry.

Not far from the hatching seagull are children's baby dolls. They dot the shoreline. One is stranded in the stark sunlight, half-buried in the sand with a hand in the air. Another is missing its eyes and a leg. A third is just a head. We are several women on this island investigating the birth of birds, and we are of course acquainted with dolls, symbolic plastic bundles of the life within us—our own children, healthy, happy, living in a world abundant. But there is something sinister about the dolls' presence here, as though they are lost little ambassadors from the human world, living not in a foreign country but in humanity's damaged future.

When our work is finished, we emerge from the heronry carrying an assortment of dog ticks on our bodies and splattered with what we call "splooj" (our word for the large and liquid bowel movements of baby birds), bird pee, and regurgitant (which is often a concoction of undigested invertebrates or, if it's that of a cattle egret or black-crowned night heron, maybe a few pieces of Kentucky Fried Chicken or a small mouse or two that the mother bird picked from the landfill).

But I also carry a gift: an intimacy with the spirits, sounds, and touches of birds. The snowy egret nestlings, so fearful even as I try to calm them, wrap their long reptilian-skinned toes around my fingers in an effort, I guess, to feel safe. The excruciatingly shy glossy ibises lay limp in my lap while I stroke their dark brown feathers. And although the black-crowned night herons assertively nip at me, I admire their aggressiveness; it helps them survive. The colors, habits, feathers, pecks, personalities, smells, movements, eyes, and cries of these birds are inside of me. I, quite simply, love them.

"Tic, tic, tic." The seagull chick works tirelessly in the late morning sun to release itself. Using the powerful hatching muscles that run along the back of its neck and head, it is able to force a special egg tooth (a sort of temporary hatchet that has grown on the chick's upper mandible) against its beige and brown speckled shell to break it open—bit by bit by bit.

It is time to search for goose nests. As I gather up my binoculars and notebooks, I realize that after traveling through the Arthur Kill for two summers, I have given up trying to hate it. It both stuns and offends me. I cannot describe the chick's place of birth as ugly or beautiful: such labels seem too simple. I walk away from the chick knowing only that I feel deeply for this wasteland, where through the birth of birds I've witnessed a kind of magic.

The tugboat on the East River sounds a loud honk to a passing oil freighter and the cormorant flies off to animate the sky. Another day and still no snapping turtle. Tomorrow I will wait again.

My attachment to the East River has nothing to do with dipping my toes into it, with skipping stones over it, with riding it on an inner tube, with swimming in it, with cooling my face with a splash of it, with walking along its shores, with even sitting close to it the way I imagine rural folk might do on lazy summer afternoons.

I feel sympathy for the East River, for everything it has lost, but I love it for the same reason I love the Arthur Kill: for its magic. In all their woundedness, these resilient waterways are managing to give life. I can't accept the injuries New Yorkers have caused this estuary, but I feel there's a need to cherish what is left.

Who knows, maybe when my father lifted me up on his shoulders all those years ago, my eyes focused not on the city, but on its surrounding dark and damaged olive-green waters.

FROM TRAVELS OF WILLIAM BARTRAM

William Bartram

The Indian not returning this morning, I set sail alone. The coasts on each side had much the same appearance as already described. The Palm trees here seem to be of a different species from the Cabbage tree; their strait trunks are sixty, eighty or ninety feet high, with a beautiful taper of a bright ash colour, until within six or seven feet of the top, where it is a fine green colour, crowned with an orb of rich green plumed leaves: I have measured the stem of these plumes fifteen feet in length, besides the plume, which is nearly of the same length.

The little lake, which is an expansion of the river, now appeared in view; on the East side are extensive marshes, and on the other high forests and Orange groves, and then a bay, lined with vast Cypress swamps, both coasts gradually approaching each other, to the opening of the river again, which is in this place about three hundred yards wide; evening now drawing on, I was anxious to reach some high bank of the river, where I intended to lodge, and agreeably to my wishes, I soon after discovered on the West shore, a little promontory, at the turning of the river, contracting it here to about one hundred and fifty yards in width. This promontory is a peninsula, containing about three acres of high ground, and is one entire Orange grove, with a few Live Oaks, Magnolias and Palms. Upon doubling the point, I arrived at the landing, which is a circular harbour, at the foot of the bluff, the top of which is about twelve feet high; and back of it is a large Cypress swamp, that spreads each way, the right wing forming the West coast of the little lake, and the left stretching up the river many miles, and encompassing a vast space of low grassy marshes. From this promontory, looking Eastward across the river, we behold a landscape of low country, unparalleled as I think; on the left is the East coast of the little lake, which I had just passed, and from the Orange bluff at the lower end, the high forests begin, and increase in breadth from the shore of the lake, making a circular sweep to the right, and contain many hundred thousand acres of meadow, and this grand sweep of high forests encircles, as I apprehend, at least twenty miles of these green fields, interspersed with hommocks or islets of evergreen trees, where the sovereign Magnolia and lordly Palm stand conspicuous. The islets are high shelly knolls, on the sides of creeks or branches of the river, which wind about and drain off the superabundant waters that cover these meadows, during the winter season.

The evening was temperately cool and calm. The crocodiles began to roar and appear in uncommon numbers along the shores and in the river. I fixed my camp in an open plain, near the utmost projection of the promontory, under the shelter of a large Live Oak, which stood on the highest part of the ground and but a few yards from my boat. From this open, high situation, I had a free prospect of the river, which was a matter of no trivial consideration to me, having good reason to dread the subtle attacks of the alligators, who were crowding about my harbour. Having collected a good quantity of wood for the purpose of keeping up a light and smoke during the night, I began to think of preparing my supper, when, upon examining my stores, I found but a scanty provision, I thereupon determined, as the most expeditious way of supplying my necessities, to take my bob and try for some trout. About one hundred yards above my harbour, began a cove or bay of the river, out of which opened a large lagoon. The mouth or entrance from the river to it was narrow, but the waters soon after spread and formed a little lake, extending into the marshes, its entrance and shores within I observed to be verged with floating lawns of the Pistia and Nymphea and other aquatic plants; these I knew were excellent haunts for trout.

The verges and islets of the lagoon were elegantly embellished with flowering plants and shrubs; the laughing coots with wings half spread were tripping over the little coves and hiding themselves in the tufts of grass; young broods of the painted summer teal, skimming the still surface of the waters, and following the watchful parent unconscious of danger, were frequently surprised by the voracious trout, and he in turn, as often by the subtle, greedy alligator. Behold him rushing forth from the flags and reeds. His enormous body swells. His plaited tail brandished high, floats upon the lake. The waters like a cataract descend from his opening jaws. Clouds of smoke issue from his dilated nostrils. The earth trembles with his thunder. When immediately from the opposite coast of the lagoon, emerges from the deep his rival champion. They suddenly dart upon each other. The boiling surface of the lake marks their rapid course, and a terrific conflict commences. They now sink to the bottom folded together in horrid wreaths. The water becomes thick and discoloured. Again they rise, their jaws clap together, re-echoing through the deep surrounding forests. Again they sink, when the contest ends at the muddy bottom of the lake, and the vanquished makes a hazardous escape, hiding himself in the muddy turbulent waters and sedge on a distant shore. The proud victor exulting returns to the place of action. The shores and forests resound his dreadful roar, together with the triumphing shouts of the plaited tribes around, witnesses of the horrid combat.

My apprehensions were highly alarmed after being a spectator of so dreadful a battle; it was obvious that every delay would but tend to encrease my dangers and difficulties, as the sun was near setting, and the alligators gathered around my harbour from all quarters; from these considerations I concluded to be expeditious in my trip to the lagoon, in order to take some fish. Not thinking it prudent to take my fusee with me, lest I might lose it overboard in case of a battle, which I had every reason to dread before my return, I therefore furnished myself with a club for my defence, went on board, and penetrating the first line of those which surrounded my harbour, they gave way; but being pursued by several very large ones, I kept strictly on the watch, and paddled with all my might towards the entrance of the lagoon, hoping to be sheltered there from the multitude of my assailants; but ere I had half-way reached the place, I was attacked on all sides, several endeavouring to overset the canoe. My situation now became precarious to the last degree: two very large ones attacked me closely, at the same instant, rushing up with their heads and part of their bodies above the water, roaring terribly and belching floods of water over me. They struck their jaws together so close to my ears, as almost to stun me, and I expected every moment to be dragged out of the boat and instantly devoured, but I applied my weapons so effectually about me, though at random, that I was so successful as to beat them off a little; when, finding that they designed to renew the battle, I made for the shore, as the only means left me for my preservation, for, by keeping close to it, I should have my enemies on one side of me only, whereas I was before surrounded by them, and there was a probability, if pushed to the last extremity, of saving myself, by jumping out of the canoe on shore, as it is easy to outwalk them on land, although comparatively as swift as lightning in the water. I found this last expedient alone could fully answer my expectations, for as soon as I gained the shore they drew off and kept aloof. This was a happy relief, as my confidence was, in some degree recovered by it. On recollecting myself, I discovered that I had almost reached the entrance of the lagoon, and determined to venture in, if possible to take a few fish and then return to my harbour, while day-light continued; for I could now, with caution and resolution, make my way with safety along shore, and indeed there was no other way to regain my camp, without leaving my boat and making my retreat through the marshes and reeds, which, if I could even effect, would have been in a manner throwing myself away, for then there would have been no hopes of ever recovering my bark, and returning in safety to any settlements of men. I accordingly proceeded and made good my entrance into the lagoon, though not without opposition from the alligators, who formed a line across the entrance, but did not pursue me into it, nor was I molested by any there, though there were some very large ones in a cove at the upper end. I soon caught more trout than I had present occasion for, and the air was too hot and sultry to admit of their being kept for many hours, even though salted or barbecued. I now prepared for my return to camp, which I succeeded in with but little trouble, by keeping close to the shore, yet I was opposed upon re-entering the river out of the lagoon, and pursued near to my landing (though not closely attacked) particularly by an old daring one, about twelve feet in length, who kept close after me, and when I stepped on shore and turned about, in order to draw up my canoe, he rushed up near my feet and lay there for some time, looking me in the face, his head and shoulders out of water; I resolved he should pay for his temerity, and having a heavy load in my fusee, I ran to my camp, and returning with my piece, found him with his foot on the gunwale of the boat, in search of fish, on my coming up he withdrew sullenly and slowly into the water, but soon returned and placed himself in his former position, looking at me and seeming neither fearful or any way disturbed. I soon dispatched him by lodging the contents of my gun in his head, and then proceeded to cleanse and prepare my fish for supper, and accordingly took them out of the boat, laid them down on the sand close to the water, and began to scale them, when, raising my head, I saw before me, through the clear water, the head and shoulders of a very large alligator, moving slowly towards me; I instantly stepped back, when, with a sweep of his tail, he brushed off several of my fish. It was certainly most providential that I looked up at that instant, as the monster would probably, in less than a minute, have seized and dragged me into the river. This incredible boldness of the animal disturbed me greatly, supposing there could now be no reasonable safety for me during the night, but by keeping continually on the watch; I therefore, as soon as I had prepared the fish, proceeded to secure myself and effects in the best manner I could: in the first place, I hauled my bark upon the shore, almost clear out of the water, to prevent their oversetting or sinking her, after this every moveable was taken out and carried to my camp, which was but a few yards off; then ranging some dry wood in such order as was the most convenient, cleared the ground round about it, that there might be no impediment in my way, in case of an attack in the night, either from the water or the land; for I discovered by this time, that this small isthmus, from its remote situation and fruitfulness, was resorted to by bears and wolves. Having prepared myself in the best manner I could, I charged my gun and proceeded to reconnoitre my camp and the adjacent grounds; when I discovered that the peninsula and grove, at the distance of about two hundred yards from my encampment, on the land side, were invested by a Cypress swamp, covered with water, which below was joined to the shore of the little lake, and above to the marshes surrounding the lagoon, so that I was confined to an islet exceedingly circumscribed, and I found there was no other retreat for me, in case of an attack, but by either ascending one of the large Oaks, or pushing off with my boat.

It was by this time dusk, and the alligators had nearly ceased their roar, when I was again alarmed by a tumultuous noise that seemed to be in my harbour, and therefore engaged my immediate attention. Returning to my camp I found it undisturbed, and then continued on to the extreme point of the promontory, where I saw a scene, new and surprising, which at first threw my senses into such a tumult, that it was some time before I could comprehend what was the matter; however, I soon accounted for the prodigious assemblage of crocodiles at this place, which exceeded every thing of the kind I had ever heard of.

How shall I express myself so as to convey an adequate idea of it to the reader, and at the same time avoid raising suspicion of my want of veracity. Should I say, that the river (in this place) from shore to shore, and perhaps near half a mile above and below me, appeared to be one solid bank of fish, of various kinds, pushing through this narrow pass of St. Juans into the little lake, on their return down the river, and that the alligators were in such incredible numbers, and so close together from shore to shore, that it would have been easy to have walked across on their heads, had the animals been harmless. What expressions can sufficiently declare the shocking scene that for some minutes continued, whilst this mighty army of fish were forcing the pass? During this attempt, thousands, I may say hundreds of thousands of them were caught and swallowed by the devouring alligators. I have seen an alligator take up out of the water several great fish at a time, and just squeeze them betwixt his jaws, while the tails of the great trout flapped about his eyes and lips, ere he had swallowed them. The horrid noise of their closing jaws, their plunging amidst the broken banks of fish, and rising with their prey some feet upright above the water, the floods of water and blood rushing out of their mouths, and the clouds of vapour issuing from their wide nostrils, were truly frightful. This scene continued at intervals during the night, as the fish came to the pass. After this sight, shocking and tremendous as it was, I found myself somewhat easier and more reconciled to my situation, being convinced that their extraordinary assemblage here, was owing to this annual feast of fish, and that they were so well employed in their own element, that I had little occasion to fear their paying me a visit.

FROM *Downriver: A Yellowstone Journey*

Dean Krakel

OCTOBER TEN

*I*n a chilling mist, I carry the raft down a long hill to the river's edge below the town of Gardiner, Montana. Magpies squabble and flap among the junipers as I work and occasionally make teasing passes at the dog. Curious ravens croak overhead, wings swishing. Cottonwood leaves have already browned and blown away. When the clouds lift I expect to see snow on the Absarokas. Soon, winter. The river looks cold, unfamiliar, and fast.

It takes thirty minutes to pump up the raft, a gray Campways Searider, fourteen feet long, seven feet wide, a slightly pointed, upraised snout, and a rounded stern—my home for the next five hundred miles. I secure the rowing frame to the raft with nylon straps run through D-rings and clip nine-foot oars to pins starboard and port. A cane canoe seat with a folding back serves as a chair. Baggage goes in the stern, covered with a green tarp, and lashed down with rope— many strange hard lumps and bumps and points beneath canvas. Too much stuff for one, I think, but nothing goes back up the hill.

Finished, I check off a list inside my head. All the boating paraphernalia's been packed. I've groceries, cartridges and dog food, wool mitts, hip boots, overcoat and scarf, and a new English hunting cap.

Good-byes have been said. This morning I saw Alisa and Dean to school.

Rocking in a pool, the raft gives a savage tug at its leash. Time to go.

I coax Stryder, my hundred pound part collie part golden retriever, into the bow, take a last quick look around, a deep breath and shove off.

The current grabs the boat with more force than I'd anticipated and it takes one moment too long to scramble aboard. We're sucked left when we should be right, sent careening among rocks on the river's shallow side. A blast of ice water catches us broadside. The downstream oar stubs its blade on a rock, wrenches off the pin and out of my hand. While I'm struggling to shove the oar back on its pin, Stryder decides to abandon ship. Dropping the good oar I catch him by the collar, pin him to the floor with my feet.

By the time I've both oars in hand, we're washing sluggishly beneath the Gardiner Bridge, coasting the rollers out of town.

Somebody standing on the bank waves and points and yells, unheard above the Yellowstone's roar. I wave back and begin bailing water. Stryder shakes himself dry in my face, climbs forward, and sits looking downstream, nose in the air. And who cares what a landlubber might have to say anyway, ehhh? I warm up by rowing, ferrying back and forth, spinning to the left and right, getting reacquainted with moving water.

These first miles can be rough. In June, during flood, twenty thousand cubic feet of water a second snarl past the banks, water the color of creamed coffee boiling with debris—carrying whole trees and pieces, dead elk, broken bits of Styrofoam coolers, outhouses, boards, and corral posts. Ten-foot waves broad as a whale's back. A tenth that volume carries us now; exposed rocks hiss by like shark's fins, dark boulders lurk inches beneath the surface. The raft bottom occasionally scrapes gravel. Startled trout flee our shadow.

We're running west on a straight course between high dirt banks covered with sagebrush and autumn grass, jagged peaks of the Gallatin Range poking up to the south and west, steep Absaroka foothills east and north. Some houses' backsides up on the bank. Light flashing from the cars on U.S. 89.

Like water, civilization has followed the course of least resistance through the Yellowstone Valley. Animals first, migrating, wandering. Men following in their tracks. Then horsemen and wagons. The railroad. Towns. Blacktop roads.

Three plastic McKensie boats glide past willows on either side, somber guides at the oars, unsmiling clients casting from the bows.

On the Corwin Springs Bridge a red-haired kid in a yellow raincoat lofts a fish as long as his arm.

Corwin Springs was once known as Cinnabar, for Cinnabar Peak. For a decade Cinnabar was the end of the rail line for tourists en route to Yellowstone Park; from here they'd embark on the Grand Tour by stagecoach ("A strange vehicle," remarked one of Yellowstone's earliest tourists, the Earl of Dunraven, "mostly composed of leather. It was decorated with decayed leather; the sides were leather curtains; the top was leather; it was hung upon leather straps and thongs of the same material dangled from the roof."). Cinnabar Lodge boasted its own power plant, an irrigated golf course, hotspring bathhouse and a pine plank dance floor that accommodated a hundred couples. Calamity Jane hawked her autobiography *Beautiful White Devil of the Yellowstone* at the train station out front, and Specimen Smith stumped around selling "Specimens From Out of the Park."

"It is illegal to sell specimens from the park," an army officer told him. "Sign says 'From Out of the Park,'" quipped Specimen. When the railroad pushed upriver to Gardiner, making that town the park's north entrance, it put an end to Cinnabar's tourist dreams and the town died.

Sonny Brogan bought the lodge in the 1960s and turned the grounds into a pasture for his elk. In July Brogan cuts off the antlers of his bulls, sells the velvet to Koreans for forty dollars an ounce. The Koreans pass it on, either powdered or in round buttons as an aphrodisiac.

In the mid 1960s two freaked out characters murdered a hitchhiker near Cinnabar, cut out his heart during a thunderstorm as an offering to whatever demons possessed them, and threw the body into the Yellowstone. Two weeks later they were arrested in Haight Ashbury snacking on fingers. So mention cult and that, Charlie Manson, and Jim Jones are what people hereabouts think of; that's why they're wary of Ma Prophet's Church Universal and Triumphant buying the Malcolm Forbes ranch for $7 million and moving here from L.A.

At a press conference church members introduced themselves to the community, fifty ranchers standing in the Forbes tin barn, hats held in rough hands, white foreheads shining in the light cast from a television as students in a video ran around supermarket aisles dressed up like Uncle Sam shouting slogans. They'd come to Montana fleeing the holocaust towards which the rest of the nation was sliding, said Elizabeth Clare Prophet. Her people dreamed only of peace. The Great White Brotherhood's new home on the range, a golden Camelot by the river: a little Jesus, a little Buddha, a little Big Sur psychology—soul mates and twin flames, expanded consciousness, survivalism, astrology, mantra, and chants.

"It's nice to be here," said a member over the microphone, "you've got really great vibrations in this country."

For a time there was talk in Gardiner of forming a vigilante. The local preachers banded together, and the school principal banned church members' children. "Hell," said Brogan, "I might join." But in the end, like a lot of other valley residents, he sold.

Up on Cedar Creek Bill Dexter sits in a lawn chair out front of his shack, watching the river, stroking that long gray beard like some old billy goat guru. Bill hauls his water out of the creek. Hasn't shaved in sixty years nor bathed in ten. Walks everywhere he goes, carries a Ruger Blackhawk forty-four—"en kin damn shore shoot'er too." Keeps a year's supply of flour, coffee, and beans in fifty-gallon drums. Can't work hard or get around in the hills, can't run a trapline like he used to do. These days Bill spends a lot of his time jus settin', meditatin', wonderin' perhaps why his woman left him for Hawaii so long ago.

Pretty Dick Randell started the state's first dude ranch—the OTO—on Cedar Creek in the 1900s, constructed a road going from here to there that crossed the creek thirteen times in two miles. Last spring vandals broke into the old cabin and sawed the antlers off all the stuffed elk heads in the den. Sold them, I suppose.

At the canyon's head I drop the oars in calm water and drift, check the load, tighten all the straps, zip and tie the life vest, kick off the hip boots, and lecture the dog about jumping out—"don't try that stunt here." In the next five miles the river drops four hundred feet. A gentle enough grade if you're walking it. But rivers move differently under gravity's influence than we. Given the slightest excuse, water boils and pours, backs up and around, falls over and through—an endless mixing of current within current, motion within motion. Given the proper volume and speed, water alone will create waves as it ricochets off bends and banks and piles onto itself. It is rocks that create rapids, that determine constriction, pace, and configuration. An incline of twenty feet in a mile will give any water a voice; a drop of fifty feet among rocks will make it roar. Ahead, the dark lava rock walls of Dome Mountain part, revealing the narrow-cut canyon of Yankee Jim.

The smell of deep water rises from down there, a green smell, a fish and moss smell. An upriver breeze blows cool against my face. An echo like a distant storm. I nearly drowned in the river once. It was my first river trip, first time in a canoe: Dick Greeves and I with the mad gleam of St. Louis in our eyes. Dick had said that a float trip would change my perspective, and it certainly did. As our bow dropped over that first lip I turned and asked what we should do, referring to bow-pry, cross-draw, or j-stroke. I'd read all the books. "Best technique," said Dick, "is going to be to try and save our ass." Though we managed to do that, we lost some other things, among them the reason for going on. That was four years ago. Still, it's hard not to feel a foreboding sense of déjà vu.

Oaring into the mainstream I concentrate on what's ahead, the remembered route playing over and over, like a mantra, in my head. A tree on top of a rock eight feet above the surface, deposited during high water, marks the point of no return.

Rowing hard upstream on the river's left side, feeling the river's power trembling up through the blades into my hands, I try to stay in the main flow until I'm fifty yards above the first drop. Three-fourths of the river funnels over a ledge and erupts into foam and a large, erratic standing wave clapping backward over a hole that could hold a bus. Now I move left, hugging the shore, trying to stay off the rocks, straining at the oars. "Row! Row! Row!" I say aloud. There's no room for error. Banks blur as we drop down a smooth tongue into the first wave, bow-shattered crest drumming the raft like rain, wetting me to the chest, taking away my breath. Oars buck and jerk in my hands. We're lifted, then dropped, lifted again, and deposited in a long, calm, jade-colored pool. Turbulent boils percolate all around. Standing, I look downriver to the second drop, straining to see if there's anything I haven't seen before, didn't notice from the road, fighting back sudden doubts. Is there enough water to get through? What rocks are showing?

The river parts around a room-sized boulder, drops from sight. Foam flickers into the air like dragon's breath. Stryder stands with his front feet on the bow, nose pointed downstream, tail wagging. Rowing to the right, I line us up, then turn the raft sideways, raise the oars, and drift until we're hovering on the edge. Now I spin the bow first and tuck the oars in. The slot is so narrow I won't be able to use the oars until we're in the waves at the bottom. I lean forward, braced to drop the blades and pull as soon as we hit bottom. For an instant we hang on the lip, crashing whitewater filling the air, then fall in a sleek roller coaster rush over great hump-backed waves into the canyon's heart. Here the waves diminish, and we float silently on still water, all of the Yellowstone condensed by canyon walls into one turbulent pool thirty yards wide. A boil explodes from the surface, rears above my head, quivering like a block of Jell-O, collapses.

The canyon's named for Yankee Jim George, an ambitious, white-haired, wild-bearded Dutchman who anticipated making a living off tourists and miners and blasted a toll road across the rock on the mountain's south side in 1880. Five years later the Northern Pacific brought its line from Livingston to Cinnabar and put him out of business. Yankee Jim greeted each daily train with a shaking fist.

While staying at Cinnabar Lodge in 1903, Theodore Roosevelt sent a messenger downriver to summon Yankee Jim. He wanted to meet the cantankerous old cuss. Yankee Jim sent the messenger back with these words for the president: "You know where I live, Teddy."

Roosevelt was returning from Yellowstone Park where he'd had a bully good time showing off for his friend, the naturalist John Burroughs, rounding up elk badlands style. The president had amused the troops at Norris Station by trying out their skis on April snowdrifts. He stopped long enough in Gardiner to dedicate the cornerstone of park engineer Hiram Chittenden's stone-arch gateway. Roosevelt found it marvelous that "bits of the old wilderness scenery and the old wilderness life are to be kept unspoiled for the benefit of our children's children . . . no nation facing the unhealthy softening and re-laxation of fibre that tends to accompany civilization can afford to neglect anything that will develop hardihood, resolution, and the scorn of discomfort and danger."

From Cinnabar, Roosevelt sped west in his presidential car to Yosemite and a camping trip with John Muir. Muir was fighting desperately to keep Gifford Pinchot's dam out of his beloved Hetch Hetchy Valley and hoped "to do some forest good in freely talking around the campfire" with the president.

160

Drifting around a narrow bend we surprise five otters all trying to cluster around a dead sucker on top of a midriver rock, too intent on running their hands over their slick catch to notice the boat. There's only room on the rock for four otters and the fish. The one left out swims around until he finds a niche, climbs on, and forces another off.

"Hello," I say, and they sit upright, wrinkling noses upthrust. All dive, dark shadows passing beneath the boat.

In the last set of waves a trout as long as my arm and as deep through the chest as the oar blade swims upriver just off the bow. Separated by a trough we rise and fall together three times and then he's gone.

Now the Yellowstone bends due north, a course it will maintain for the next fifty miles. A gentle, fast current, stretching out to feel its banks after the canyon's constriction, splitting into its first definite channels around small willow islands and gravel bars. To the south, Electric Peak in the Gallatins turns blue with distance. The peak was named by a member of the Hayden Survey whose hair stood on end as he approached the summit. A few years later John Muir advised the weak of spirit to climb it during their park visit and get a charge. The ruins of some twenty ancient redwood forests buried one atop the other in ash have been discovered near the peak, each forest maturing and flourishing and then being smothered by volcanic eruptions thousands of years apart. The unique thing is that some of the trees are still standing . . . and there's petrified little birds in them singing petrified little songs just like Jim Bridger said. Yes!

The Absarokas are to the east, my right, dark peaks paralleling our course ten miles way, freshly whitened summits above lush stands of timber, like green velvet, seamed by ravines, avalanche chutes, and wild drainages. Mountain men called them the Yellowstone Range, appropriately enough. To the miners and early settlers they became the Snowies. Captain W. A. Jones, the first white man to cross them by what has become Sylvan Pass, tried to christen them the Sierra Shoshone. Finally, in 1879, they were officially named in honor of the Crow, whose name for themselves is Apsaruke. The old men say the word refers to a large bird no longer seen. In sign talk the people made a bird symbol with upraised palms touching heel to heel. French explorers mistranslated all of this into "*Gens de corbeaux*"—Crow. The

Crow name for white men was *Beta-awk-a-wah-cha*, sits-on-the-water, because they first saw them in a canoe.

We float past Mol Heron Creek, Slip 'n Slide, Joe Brown, and Tom Miner. It's almost dark by the time I pull us in to camp at an island at the mouth of Six Mile. Stryder plays with sticks while I unload. The sky is clearing, but out of habit I pitch the tent, build a fire, cook up some beans, and eat them with a warm tortilla.

My face is warm with sunburn, arm muscles ache.

The river turns to molten gold after sunset. A night wind sighs downriver, and house lights come on, twinkling like stars against the mountains. Honking geese fly past, low and fast, going upriver.

Up before dawn in pink light. Cold enough to form ice on the still pools at the edge of the river. Over a petty, sputtering fire I make coffee and cook breakfast, sit on a log scratching Stryder behind the ears, watching the sunrise over Emigrant Peak. A bald eagle skims upriver and coasts to a stop in a pine. Seven crows cross the river, cawing, wings flashing. Cattle bawl.

I scour the breakfast dishes with river sand, swirl rinse water as if panning gold, toss it into the current. Frost on dead leaves. Frost on the raft. I don gloves to shove off. Stryder, unsure about going with me this morning, waits on shore until the last moment, makes a leap, slips on the slick rubber, and takes a swim. Shafts of light break over the mountains through the cottonwoods turning water vapor into steam. Yellow cottonwood leaves drift alongside the boat, clinging to its sides.

Jim Bridger wintered on Emigrant Creek with a band of Crow in 1844. "Thirty year have I been knocking about these mountains," I can almost hear him say, "from Missoura's head as far south as the starving Gila. I've trapped a heap, and many a hundred pack of beaver I've traded in my time, waugh! What has come of it, and what's the dollars as ought to be in my possible? What's the ind of this I say? Is a man to be hunted by Injuns all his days? Many's the time I've said I'd strike for Taos and trap a squaw, for this child's getting old, and feels like wanting a woman's face about his lodge for the balance of his days; but when it comes to catching the old traps, I've the smallest kind of heart, I have . . . but beaver's bound to rise, I say, and hayar's a coon knows whar to lay his hand on a dozen pack right handy, and then he'll take the Taos trail."

I have often wondered, and history doesn't tell if Jim spent his winter with one of the "coarse featured, sneaky looking, thick lipped, sharp nosed" young women, as described by an early trader, or one of the "hags who could be compared to nothing but witches or demons. Some of them of monstrous size, weighing 250 to 300 pounds, with naked breasts hanging halfway down to their knees. Barelegged, hair cut short and their faces smeared over with white clay . . ." Waugh!

Gold was discovered up Emigrant Gulch in 1863. Yellowstone City, as its three hundred residents christened it, became the first town in the entire seventy-thousand-square-mile basin. That first winter (the town lasted three) flour sold for a hundred dollars a sack, bacon a dollar a pound. Hanging was the penalty for murder, robbery, or insulting one of the town's fifteen women. There was supposed to be fifty million dollars in gold buried in the banks of Emigrant Gulch, but nothing much ever came of it, and nothing much is left: a few old buildings and sluiceboxes rotting up in the hills and ghost mines with names like King Solomon, Black Warrior, Morning Star, Bunker Hill, Iceberg, Shoo-Fly, and Avalanche.

Trailerhouses and condos are at the Emigrant's mouth now. The creek's dry, its mothering snowbanks used up, its water rained over hayfields all summer long. There are a half-dozen Land for Sale signs—another ranch's being subdivided to pay the inheritance tax, or being sold because the view's become a lot more golden than cattle. Some junked cars used for riprap have been pushed to the river's edge. The Church Universal and Triumphant owns most of this land. The small town of Emigrant will soon be called Glastenberry; Ma Prophet predicts a community of ten thousand.

In 1867 Nelson Story brought cattle in to feed the miners. The army detained him at Fort Kearney on the Bozeman Trail, telling him he couldn't go on without escort and they hadn't the manpower to provide him with one. But Story had brought something other than cattle from Texas—repeating rifles. He left the fort, and got through. The first crop of wheat was harvested in 1868. Though it sounds like a real estate developer's concoction, the early settlers called this place Paradise Valley.

During the Indian Wars, the residents periodically fled paradise in flatboats and mackinaws constructed at John Tomislin's mill on

Mill Creek. They were crude boats, roughly constructed, and in them the travelers suffered six weeks of blizzards and rocks and Wolf, Bear, and Buffalo rapids; were caught on sandbars and on snags; were bushwacked by outlaws, ambushed by Indians, and drowned.

"If it were not for the expectation of being fired into by savages every moment, the traveler would enjoy the trip hugely," wrote the fourteen-year-old son of Montana's territorial judge.

At Pine Creek the river takes the first downward tilt I've felt since leaving Yankee Jim. More channels, sharper bends, riffle dropping to pool, pool to riffle, a tapestry of mountains unwinding, golden cotton-woods and white Absarokas reflected in water. Mergansers patter downriver in front of the boat, Woody Woodpecker heads out-stretched, wings flapping. I surprise two whitetailed deer drinking, and stop for lunch.

Taking my fishing rod I walk upriver to where the river pools at the base of white bluffs, an underground stream sweating down its face. Rings of feeding fish dimple the surface. I traverse the bluffs carefully, trying not to dislodge pebbles, tie on a wooly worm, and cast. The bug sinks just below the surface, and I strip it in slowly through a foam-covered eddy. Reel in, cheap reel clacking. Cast again, feeling the line straighten out and spring forward, straighten out again. The bug lands with a plop. A fish streaks for it, bumps it, and turns away. Another fish grabs it, turns, and I set the hook and bring a whitefish to bay. In ten minutes I've netted three more. Some people kill whitefish and throw them away—trash fish—but hungry and unprejudiced, I put mine on the stringer.

A fishing guide I know was once fishing this pool, caught a fourteen-inch whitefish, tossed it back, and was shocked to see a trout rise and suck it down.

Back on the river we pass all the regular things, cottonwoods and willows, mountains, ranchettes and cabins, prefabs here and there—first, second, third, and fourth homes—cows getting a drink. Past Deep Creek, Trail, Bullis, and Suce.

In the afternoon we pass through a narrow cut between Wine-glass Peak and some cliffs to the east. The river's slowing down, pool-ing up before entering the town of Livingston. This place's name is Allenspur, a railroad siding, the proposed site for a three-hundred-foot-tall earthen-fill dam that would create a lake thirty miles long, inundating the entire stretch we've passed through today.

There have been plans to dam the river, of course, ever since the first farmer scorched a crop: for hydroelectricity; for flood control. Blueprints have come and gone. But nothing has seriously threatened the Yellowstone so much as coal.

How vast and valuable the Yellowstone's resources are. In 1832 it was beaver fur. In '68 it was gold. In '75, buffalo. In '82, the open range. A century later it's the river's misfortune to flow atop the largest strip-minable coal formation in the world.

Coal has always been a part of the Yellowstone's history. Early explorers mentioned black seams in the river's bank; fur traders and homesteaders used the coal for heat, railroads mined it for their engines. But interest remained low until 1970, when the Environmental Protection Agency decreed that the amount of sulfur particulate passed into the air through Eastern factory stacks must be reduced. Since coal in the West is low in sulfur and is more economical to obtain than Eastern coal, it was much cheaper for coal users to have Western coal shipped to them than it was to install the necessary stack scrubbers to remove the sulfur or to switch to alternative fuels, and it would be even cheaper to build power plants at the mine mouth and send the electricity direct.

No one in the Yellowstone Basin thought much about any of this until the publication in 1971 of a diminutive report entitled *The North Central Power Study*. The report predicted that by the year 2000, strip mines in the Yellowstone Basin would be providing coal to twenty-five mine-mouth power plants. Thousands of megawatts would hum toward Portland, Spokane, and Chicago. There would be coal gasification and petrochemical complexes, slurry pipelines, and a quarter-million increase in population. The whole of this development would be fed by the Yellowstone, mainstem and tributaries, either diverted into pipes or released as needed from dams. Allenspur was merely one of nineteen potential sites.

Two years later, draglines and power plant stacks were on horizons everywhere, and energy companies were talking about using the entire Tongue and Powder rivers. Nearly half of the Yellowstone's annual flow of eight million acre-feet was about to be tapped.

Though the Yellowstone is considered Montana's river by virtue of its main channel, it and its major tributaries, the Clark's Fork, Bighorn, Tongue, and Powder, all originate in Wyoming. Wyoming accounts for nearly half of the river's seventy-thousand-square-mile basin. And while this basin is river rich, it's water poor. Rainfall averages less than fourteen inches a year. Whoever controls the water here controls the wealth, not to mention the destiny of fellow citizens and numerous mute life-forms. Water is the basis of everyone's living—indeed, of everyone's life. Those who think themselves unaffected by it are only insulated. Peruse any basin newspaper and you'll find the Yellowstone mentioned somewhere in bold print. Too much water, or the lack of it, determines local temperament and economy. Ranchers and farmers suffering from drought buy few new pickups and do little shopping in town. If winter storms bring the elk down early, it fills native paunches as well as wallets. Even the man pulling your car out of a ditch with a wrecker says, "Yeah, that spring storm was a bummer but just think of what it did for the snowpack," not to mention his business.

And yet laws concerning water were so lax as to be virtually nonexistent before 1973. Until then you could still establish a water right on a stream or river by simply staking a claim and putting said water to a beneficial use. First in line, first in right. Use it or lose it. The predominant philosophy of water users is that water flowing downstream is water going to waste. Though it's technically illegal to do so, these water rights had been traded and sold back and forth for a hundred years. And industries establishing their rights on the lower Yellowstone said while it was true they were taking most of the water, they were using it for the most good.

In 1973 a panicked Montana legislature passed a Water Use Act that, among other things, placed a moratorium on industrial use of the Yellowstone's water until some studies were done and a public hearing held. The legislature wasn't as concerned with keeping the river from drying up as much as they were with trying to determine who owned how much of what.

Faced with losing their water supply, Montana cities and towns, irrigating districts, and government agencies all filed claims on a piece of the Yellowstone. Wyoming wanted to devote its share to energy. North Dakota demanded that the Missouri be kept full. The Crow said they owned development rights on the Bighorn by virtue of treaty. Two Yellowstones couldn't have provided enough water.

A public hearing lasted two months and produced five thousand pages of testimony, pro and con. Crusty third-generation ranchers said the country had all been wilderness and wild rivers once and not worth a damn until the white man came. Developers argued for development. Think of the jobs! The cash flow! An Iowa farmer wrote a letter wondering what was to happen to his corn. Jack Hemingway flew out from Sun Valley, Idaho, and said a few words on behalf of trout. All the networks flew in to watch, and for a time you could catch the story on TV.

Amidst all the uproar one man stood out, a white-haired spokesman for the Montana Department of Fish, Wildlife, and Parks, James A. Posewitz. Posewitz said that a river exists for itself. It's alive, it creates and nourishes life. By flowing downstream the Yellowstone was doing just as God intended. It wasn't going to waste. Posewitz spoke for the voiceless and voteless users, of the fluctuations in water levels and temperatures that triggered trout to spawn. Of the difference that a few inches make to a paddlefish trying to swim upriver. Lowering the Yellowstone would make goose nests more vulnerable to predators. A river has the right to the use of its own water.

Indecision prevailed until 1979, when Montana's Board of National Resources and Conservation granted the river a pleasant but tenuous victory in the form of a 5.5 million acre-foot instream reservation.

You don't hear much about the river's fate now, but the issue's only dormant. Our needs for water only increase. And out in the pine and gumbo hills draglines and derricks keep on gnawing into the earth, turning our history into fuel and fuel into our history, lighting our lights, turning us on.

Going down a side channel I come on a fisherman sitting on the bank eating lunch and drinking a can of Bulldog Ale.

"Hello," I say and he hello's me back. I hover in his eddy and visit.

"Catchin' anything?" he asks.

When I tell him I'm not fishing, he shrugs. He's about seventy, white-haired beneath a red ball cap, and wearing a half-dozen sweaters of various colors in various states of disrepair under a much-stained fishing vest, black wool pants, and tennis shoes. He smells of willow and campfire and dank beaver pond and trout blood and liniment and old chew. He tells me he's fished every day of his life since retirement from the military. He used to run out from town when he was younger. Now he rides a bike. The largest trout he's ever caught weighed ten pounds.

He informs me that the pool I'm about to enter is named for the whorehouse that once flourished nearby ("Pity," he says, "pity"),

167

makes me a gift of three trout (no catch and release man this), tells me to beware the experts, and juts his chin good-bye.

I drop down a small run to the head of a long calm where two fishermen work, their McKensie boat snugged to shore. One stands waist deep in the river, casting long, powerful casts to the channel's other side, letting his weighted streamer tap against the concrete riprap and slide down into the current. The friend watches, arms folded across chest-high waders, puffing on a pipe. I hold back on the oars waiting for acknowledgement. The man turns, wades further down, and begins casting again. I oar ahead.

"Damn you," he screams above the water's roar, "you're going over my fish."

The river has begun bending east, the Great Bend as it's called. It was somewhere along here that William Clark struck the Yellowstone in July 1805. Clark was descending the river to a Missouri rendezvous with Lewis. As they returned from the Pacific they'd separated on the Beaverhead and were exploring homeward by different routes, returning downriver without the prehistorics they'd expected to find but loaded down with wonders nevertheless.

Clark had eight men with him, the woman Sacajawea (wife of Charbonneau, mother of sixteen-month-old Baptiste), his black slave York, and eighty head of horses. He'd wanted to build canoes the moment they struck the Yellowstone but thought the current too rough for skin boats and none of the cottonwoods along the banks sufficiently large for dugouts. The party proceeded overland to the mouth of the Shields River, which they named for John Shields, a member of the group, and made camp.

Sixty-four years after Clark passed the Great Bend, Amos Benson established a trading post, saloon, and stage stop, and three years after that, tourists began passing through on their way to Yellowstone Park. Bill Lee built a wretched little ferry that they used at considerable risk.

In 1883 the Northern Pacific Railroad build a supply depot a few miles up from Benson's Landing, named it for a railroad trustee, surveyed it, platted it, and put it on the map: Livingston, Montana—elevation forty-nine hundred feet. By the time the first Northern Pacific construction crew arrived, the town had five hundred citizens, two hotels, two restaurants, two watchmakers, two wholesale liquor dealers, two meat markets, two drug stores, six general mercantiles, a newspaper, and thirty saloons. Twenty thousand cattle and two hundred thousand sheep had summered in the vicinity, and the harvest had been thirty thousand bushels of grain and ten thousand bushels of potatoes. Calamity Jane was in town.

She'd been a scout for the army (disguised as a man) and said she'd been saved by a cold from dying with Custer at the Little Bighorn. She'd ridden for the Pony Express in the Dakotas, and would have killed Jack McCall when he murdered Wild Bill but in the excitement had left her guns at home. At the age of fifty she was described in the *Livingston Enterprise* as having "a deeply lined, scowling, sun-tanned face . . . with the leather-clad legs of a thirty-year-old cowpuncher." The reporter had found her at home smoking a cigar and doing dishes.

"I'm a rough woman, jedge," she told the court in her Ma Kettle voice when they awarded custody of her children to her husband, "but these kids allus have had a square deal from me. I ain't no saint, and yet I might be worse; I've nursed this man that's gettin' this divorce and I've saved his worthless life once; the law ain't givin' me a square deal—it never gives a woman a square deal no how."

Livingston itself sits like an island on the smooth buffalo plains, with serpentine Yellowstone curves shimmering up through the cottonwood leaves, blunt northern butt of the Absarokas, Mount Cowan, and Livingston Peak rising to the south, Crazy Mountains to the northeast, Bridgers to the northwest.

Most of Main Street was destroyed by a fire in 1924 but here and there are two-story, false-fronted brick buildings with painted advertisements for Coca-Cola or Yellowstone Sport Cigars ("Every puff a pleasure") on their sides. Though no one's used them in forty years, three's still hitching rings in the concrete sidewalk outside the Mint Bar. The population's twelve thousand now. There's three fewer bars than when the train arrived.

We float past the lumberyard, a cement plant that's been pouring its cement on the banks for years, an island covered by houses, a bridge with a canoe wrapped around an abutment, past a golf course—duffers blasting balls—two bridges, a sewage pipe, and, finally, past town.

Past Dry Creek, Billman, Fleshman, and Ferry. Clear water, blue water, white water, green water and all the tones in-between; riffles and deep pools, sand and gravel beaches, slight bluffs and short grass hills bright with unfinished construction, mountains turning vague with evening shadow.

Where Benson had his landing, we flush three geese standing on a sandbar spit. In the deep whirling eddy where the victims of Bill Lee's ferry drowned, a mallard drake squawks up. A fisherman lofts a big fish for me to see.

Exploring a stray channel I see a pink-skinned woman watching me from the bank. A tipi rises above the willowbrush, metal stovepipe sticking out the top. A man comes plunging out of the brush, jumps into the river off my bow, bounces up to the surface and runs onto the beach.

"We're having a good time," she says, "are you?"

"Yes," I say. Then I'm swept out of their life and into the mainstream.

A mile further and I make camp on a small island. Bake my fish with a potato and call it a night.

FROM *Heart* OF *Darkness*

Joseph Conrad

We stopped, and the silence driven away by the stamping of our feet flowed back again from the recesses of the land. The great wall of vegetation, an exuberant and entangled mass of trunks, branches, leaves, boughs, festoons, motionless in the moonlight, was like a rioting invasion of soundless life, a rolling wave of plants, piled up, crested, ready to topple over the creek, to sweep every little man of us out of his little existence. And it moved not. A deadened burst of mighty splashes and snorts reached us from afar, as though an ichthyosaurus had been taking a bath of glitter in the great river. . . .

'Going up that river was like traveling back to the earliest beginnings of the world, when vegetation rioted on the earth and the big trees were kings. An empty stream, a great silence, an impenetrable forest. The air was warm, thick, heavy, sluggish. There was no joy on the brilliance of sunshine. The long stretches of the waterway ran on, deserted, into the gloom of over-shadowed distances. On silvery sandbanks hippos and alligators sunned themselves side by side. The broadening waters flowed through a mob of wooded islands; you lost your way on that river as you would in a desert, and butted all day long against shoals, trying to find the channel, till you thought yourself bewitched and cut off for ever from everything you had known once—somewhere—far away—in another existence perhaps. There were moments when one's past came back to one, as it will sometimes when you have not a moment to spare to yourself; but it came in the shape of an unrestful and noisy dream, remembered with wonder amongst the overwhelming realities of this strange world of plants, and water, and silence. And this stillness of life did not in the least resemble a peace. It was the stillness of an implacable force brooding over an inscrutable intention. It looked at you with a vengeful aspect. I got used to it afterwards; I did not see it anymore; I had no time. I had to keep guessing at the channel; I had to discern, mostly by inspiration, the signs of hidden banks; I watched for sunken stones; I was learning to clap my teeth before my heart flew out, when I shaved by a fluke some infernal sly old snag that would have ripped the life out of the tin-pot steamboat and drowned all the pilgrims; I had to keep a look-out for the signs of dead wood we could cut up in the night for next day's steaming. When you have to attend to things of that sort, to the mere incidents of the surface, the reality—the reality, I tell you—fades. The inner truth is hidden—luckily, luckily. But I felt it all the same; I felt often its mysterious stillness watching me at my monkey tricks, just as it watches you fellows performing on your respective tight-ropes for—what is it? half a crown a tumble—' . . .

Sometimes we came upon a station close by the bank, clinging to the skirts of the unknown, and the white men rushing out of a tumbledown hovel, with great gestures of joy and surprise and welcome, seemed very strange—had the appearance of being held there captive by a spell. The word "ivory" would ring in the air for a while—and on we went again into the silence, along empty reaches, round the still bends, between the high walls of our winding way, reverberating in hollow claps the ponderous beat of the stern-wheel. Trees, trees, millions of trees, massive, immense running up high; and at their foot, hugging the bank against the stream, crept the little begrimed steamboat, like a sluggish beetle crawling on the floor of a lofty portico. It made you feel very small, very lost, and yet it was not altogether depressing, that feeling. . . . The reaches opened before us and closed behind, as if the forest had stepped leisurely across the water to bar the way for our return. We penetrated deeper and deeper into the heart of darkness. It was very quiet there. At night sometimes the roll of drums behind the curtain of trees would run up the river and remain sustained faintly, as if hovering in the air high over our heads, till the first break of day. Whether it meant war, peace, or prayer, we could not tell. The dawns were heralded by the descent of a chill stillness; the woodcutters slept, their fires burned low; the snapping of a twig would make you start. We were wanderers on a prehistoric earth, on an earth that wore the aspect of an unknown planet. We could have fancied ourselves the first of men taking possession of an accursed inheritance, to be subdued at the cost of profound anguish and of excessive toil. But suddenly, as we struggled round a bend, there would be a glimpse of rush walls, of peaked grass roofs, a burst of yells, a whirl of black limbs, a mass of hands clapping, of feet stamping, of bodies swaying, of eyes rolling, under the droop of heavy and motionless foliage. The steamer toiled along slowly on the edge of a black and incomprehensible frenzy. The prehistoric man was cursing us, praying to us, welcoming us—who could tell? We were cut off from the comprehension of our surroundings; we glided past like phantoms, wondering and secretly appalled, as sane men would before an enthusiastic outbreak in a madhouse. We could not understand because we were too far and could not remember, because we were travelling in the night of first ages, of those ages that are gone, leaving hardly a sign—and no memories.

The earth seemed unearthly. We are accustomed to look upon the shackled form of a conquered monster, but there—there could you look at a thing monstrous and free. It was unearthly, and the men were—No, they were not inhuman. Well, you know, that was the worst of it—this suspicion of their not being inhuman. It would come slowly to one. They howled and leaped, and spun, and made horrid faces; but what thrilled you was just the thought of their humanity—like yours—the thought of your remote kinship with this wild and passionate uproar. Ugly. Yes, it was ugly enough; but if you were man enough you would admit to yourself that there was in you just the faintest trace of a response to the terrible frankness of that noise, a dim suspicion of there being a meaning in it which you—you so remote from the night of first ages—could comprehend. And why not? The mind of man is capable of anything—because everything is in it, all the past as well as all the future. What was there after all? Joy, fear, sorrow, devotion, valour, rage—who can tell?—but truth—truth stripped of its cloak of time. Let the fool gape and shudder—the man knows, and can look on without a wink.

TANNER TRAIL AND MESQUITE THICKETS

Ann Haymond Zwinger

The Tanner Trail reaches the river at Mile 68.6. Sid and Marie Davis, two soil geologists, and I walk down it to join a group of USGS geologists mapping recent deposits along the river between Lava Creek at Mile 65.2 and Unkar Delta at Mile 73. For those who work in the bottom of the Grand Canyon, there are only four ways to reach the river, not counting vehicle access, which exists only at Lees Ferry, Diamond Creek, and Pearce Ferry. The first is by boat, often the only way that many places on the river can be reached. A second is by helicopter, extravagantly expensive and limited in the places one can be put down. The third way is on foot, down a maintained trail. In nearly 300 miles of river there are only two well-kept and traveled trails: the Bright Angel and South Kaibab from the South Rim, both reaching the river at Mile 80, the latter continuing across the river to the North Rim as the North Kaibab Trail. The fourth way is via the more plentiful, unmaintained old mining trails: Tanner, Bass, Hermit, and Hance, most without water, all requiring a degree of trail finding. Take your choice: any way takes time and effort and, occasionally, risk.

The Tanner Trail begins at Lipan Point, about twenty miles east of Grand Canyon Village. The trail drops from 7,300 feet to 2,700 in nine miles, cantankerous, steep, occasionally obscure, usually difficult. Somewhere nearby, in September 1540, the first Europeans looked down between their toes into a gorge deeper than any they had ever seen. In that year Hopi Indians led García López de Cárdenas, heading an exploring party sent out by Francisco Vásquez de Coronado, to the rim of the canyon and, according to the account of the trip's recorder, Castañeda, who not only did not accompany Cárdenas but wrote from memory twenty years later, they "spent three days on this bank looking for a passage down to the river which looked from above as if the water was six feet across, although the Indians said it was half a league wide." The Hopis, who surely knew how to get down to the river, did not lead the explorers there, and the Spaniards' attempts to get themselves down were futile. Nor did Father Francisco Tómas Garcés fare any better. In the summer of 1776 Garcés looked down into "a deep passage . . . steep-sided like a man-made trough," and called it after its color: Río Colorado.

Seth Tanner, a Mormon prospector, developed this old Indian trail down to the river in 1882 and subsequently discovered copper and silver in the area. Later it connected with the Nankoweap Trail across the river, a route developed in 1882 for geological exploration under the direction of the head of the new U.S. Geological Survey, John Wesley Powell. The connection also provided ingress and egress for horse rustlers, who could cross the river at low water and usually took time in the seclusion of the canyon to do some imaginative brand doctoring. On this side of the river, the Tanner Trail meets the Beamer Trail, which wavers northward along the river and links with the Hopi Trail up the Little Colorado River. The Grand Canyon rattlesnake was first collected here, which makes the Tanner Trail its type location and makes me very judicious indeed about where I place my hands and feet.

By noon we reach the top of the Redwall Limestone where the view opens down to Tanner Beach across the river, lying like an open peach half, across to Tapeats Sandstone ledges and Cardenas Lava dark as the ashes of a doused campfire. The Redwall sharply curtails access to the canyon. Very few breaches exist through this formidable limestone front. Shales crumble into slopes, often slippery, with an angle of repose that usually permits one to ascend or descend with impunity. But the Redwall rises sheer, immutable, allowing no way up, no way down, no way across. Only where a fault has shifted, only where a major stream has cut, do breaks form, and the Tanner Trail makes use of one of these.

The high impromptu steps chopped into the limestones are no problem for a six-footer's long legs, but a five-footer must endure a continual thud and jar. The alternative is unthinkable—going down on the seat of my pants—although the precedent to do so was set by adventurer-lecturer Burton Holmes, who took the difficult parts of the Hance Trail in that position in 1898.

The last few miles of the trail cross the pulverized slopes of Bright Angel Shale and Dox Formation, named (for heaven's sake) after Miss Virginia Dox from Cincinnati, Ohio, the first lady visitor that William Bass guided to the bottom of the Grand Canyon. The layers of brick red sandstone, siltstone and mudstone of the Dox Formation, part of the Grand Canyon Supergroup deposited a billion years ago, erode easily, giving the landscape an open, rolling character very different from the narrow, limestone-walled canyon upstream, both in lithology and color, fully fitting Van Dyke's description of "raspberry-red color, tempered with a what-not of mauve, heliotrope, and violet." Sediments flowing in from the west formed deltas, floodplains, and tidal flats, which indurated into these fine-grained sedimentary rocks thinly laid deposits of a restful sea, lined with shadows as precise as the staves of a musical score, ribboned layers, an elegant alteration of quiet siltings and delicious lappings, crinkled water compressed, solidified, lithified. A loose fragment of shale the size of a quarter starts a stream of little stony pumpkin seed chips with a quiet rustling and whispering.

At the base of these toasted slopes the bone-dry bed of Tanner Creek shirks to the river. Here, on January 22, 1900, Robert Brewster Stanton, with more faith than good sense, entrusted all his exposed film to a prospector who promised to carry it out and mail it to Denver for developing. Stanton did not know, until March 1 when he reached Diamond Creek nearly 160 miles downstream, that his rolls of film had turned out beautifully.

On the beach across the river, I can see my two big blue river bags, which came down on the raft from Lees Ferry, stuffed with all I will know of home for the next few weeks, and reflect that sometimes it's easier to get my gear here than it is me. The river surface rumples with afternoon wind, a raven on beach patrol eats overhead against a deep blue sky. Tamarisk tarnishes like brass, giving on to autumn.

From Tanner Beach sun skims the top of the Palisades across the river, by seven o'clock puts a blush on the creamy walls. No wonder

Clarence Dutton called them "palisades" when he saw them in 1886. With their tightly packed vertical shadows they look exactly like a fence of stakes.

Camp on river right occupies a huge sandbar that fills the inner curve of the river. Upstream a small dune has piled up on the beach. A 1:3,000 aerial map, taken six years ago to the month, records the tamarisk and driftwood piles in precisely the same places, but the dune itself has migrated upstream about three hundred yards.

Some of the plants sparsely scattered across the sand still bloom—white evening primrose, pink skeleton plant, magenta windmills, tangerine mallows, brittlebush, ricegrass, and the camper's plague, camel thorn. It's the first time I've seen this recent invader in numbers, and I would not be grieved were it the last. It grows in brakes waist to shoulder high, and its inch-long, needle-sharp spines make it a misery to walk through. It can pure ruin a beach for camping. It arrived in the general proliferation of riparian vegetation since dam closure, which brought many introduced species into these riverside areas. Although introduced exotics may not compete well with established native plants, their ability to colonize swiftly gives them an advantage when disturbance weakens native plant populations. The thousands of people coursing through the canyon aid in dispersing camel thorn, while their tramping keeps it from forming barbed-wire thickets. Two other troublesome plants have recently invaded: peppergrass, a mustard that spreads rapidly by underground roots, and Ravenna grass, an ornamental that the park uses in landscaping.

Walking inland, I slog up a coppice dune studded with a fair stand of arrowweed. Heaps of sand collar their stems, the dune still mobile and meddling with its inhabitants. Although dune soils drain well, they hold lenses of deep moisture in suspension by capillary action. In fact, dunes supply better habitats than those offered by saline soils or unstable talus. Annuals may dominate briefly after a rainy period, but over the long term perennials like arrowweed have best solved the challenges of drifting sand, with long, anchoring root systems that can undergo periodical burial and leaves able to endure intense reflected heat, covered with silky hairs that help curtail water loss. Many spiders and lizards prefer a loose sandy habitat into which they can burrow easily to avoid heat and desiccation, and omnivorous species that feed on detritus find it on the dune's unstable slip face where windblown debris accumulates.

Arrowweed illustrates its name with straight stems of uniform diameter, a bare shaft also used in basketry. It flowers frequently throughout the year with thimble-sized clusters of small lavender flower heads displayed against grayish leaves. Arrowweed, like another native plant, coyote willow, has multiplied rapidly on beaches since dam closure. All botanical surveys have noted it, beginning with that made by Lieutenant J. C. Ives, who found it along the banks as he boated up from the Gulf of California to Diamond Creek in 1858.

Arrowweed colonizes in somewhat drier habitats farther away from the water than willow and tamarisk. It reproduces by sending out runners from which new sprouts rise and hence forms thick, hedgelike clones. A fine duff of arrowweed leaves pave the sand, crunchy scraps of tan and gray overlaid with a plaid of narrow shadows. In the river-edge desert, organic input is so low and gets so quickly blown away that little collects to enrich the soil. Arrowweeds' dense growth pattern forms a windscreen so that leaves dropped on the ground are protected from wind and remain to disintegrate in place.

At the upper end of the beach, I begin a sketch and give up, in danger of becoming the core of a sand dune myself. Sand streams along the ground like a tan smoke and lays a film on my sketchpad. My pen grits on the paper and the ink dries before it touches the page. Gusting from downstream, wind corrugates the sand. A peppering of darker, heavier sand on the upstream face of the ripples visually exaggerates the contour. Sand grains that lift this easily range between 0.15 to 0.27 millimeters—the diameter of a fine drafting-pencil lead.

The sound of the wind changes from a freight train barreling through a tunnel of canyon walls to the stentorian breathing of some horror-movie monster. Fingers of wind scribble across the river, leaving graffiti on its surface. Slots of calm contain lozenges of blue sky outlined in tan, ripples as Renoir painted them. Another gust crosshatches the ripples, faceting them finer, and I remember the meticulous color notes Raymond Cogswell made for the photographs he took on the trip with his brother-in-law, Julius Stone, noting that "waves in mild rapids and riffles have a decided lilac tint, intensified by the mud color of the water." A blast hits shore, grabs a piece of beach and catapults it up into the air, then swirls it across the water like a sand-colored wraith, a ghost of sandbars past.

On my way back to camp I skirt a coyote willow thicket. Coyote willows have very narrow leaves with a strong midvein, much narrower-leaved than any other willow along the river, grayed with fine hairs in proportion to the aridity of their habitat. Like arrowweed, coyote willow clones by means of creeping rootstocks, a more effective means of reproducing than by seeds, for willow seeds are short-lived and must instantly land in a hospitable habitat, sprout quickly, and survive both flooding and desiccation, a formidable list of requirements for a tiny seed in a big desert river canyon.

Pinecone galls tip some of the willow branches, aberrant growths that look uncannily like miniature pinecones, caused by a tiny midge, *Rhabdophaga strobiloides*. In early spring the midges' first generation of the year produces galls on male willow catkins. The second generation attacks the leaf buds, causing this multiplication of miniature bud leaves, forming these distinctive galls. The cycle begins when a female lays an egg on a willow bud and the salivary enzymes she inserts during egg laying provoke the plant to proliferate tissue to isolate the newly hatched larva. This legless white comma of a larva may look totally nondescript—no eyes, no nose, no face—but when it plugs into the plant's vascular system, it becomes a sophisticated manipulator: it stimulates the plant's cells, both mechanically, through its feeding, and chemically, through its saliva, causing the tissues upon which the larva sups to differentiate from tissues in the rest of the plant. Within a couple of days all plant cells involved with nourishing the larva withdraw from the plant's normal growth cycle and usurp nourishment from the rest of the plant. Controlled now by the minute gourmand, their sole purpose is to feed and shelter the greedy little freeloader.

Gall makers, usually minute midges and wasps, are plentiful along the river, as their various designs: nubbins on hackberry leaves and furry balls on saltbush stems, red peppercorns on willow leaves, stem swellings on rabbitbrush, and fringed balls on sagebrush stalks, little nurseries of intricate sizes and shapes, housing oblivious sucklings against a treacherous and uncertain world.

One of camp duties is to settle, purify, and pump water for drinking and cooking. Boiling uses large amounts of fuel and generates a lot of heat on a warm day. Chlorox adds nothing to the taste of the water, although it kills most germs. Since filtering removes giardia and salmonella, a pump provides an efficient way to purify our water.

River water sits in big buckets overnight to settle out the silt. Upstream storms caused both the Paria and the Little Colorado to flood recently, spewing mud into the river, and this morning silt lies over an inch thick in the bottom of the buckets and tints the water pink. The little pump shudders and leaks with the effort of forcing Colorado River gravy through. When I remove the filter to clean it, a quarter-inch of velvety-fine silt coats it.

I spend half an hour alternately pumping and cleaning. You use water *very* judiciously when you have to replace what you use. Turning on a faucet and letting the water run while you brush your teeth seems an incomprehensible and flagrant waste of the rim-world. Down here it's "Water, water every where. Nor any drop to drink."

On the downstream side of Tanner Creek, archaeological sites around twenty-one hundred years old wreath a big dune. The crest of the dune is a popular campsite. This morning a National Park Service work crew stabilizes the loose sandy slopes that lead up to the campsite, an area heavily disturbed and eroded from overuse. The angle of repose of the dune sand lies at about a 25 percent angle. When the slope reaches 30 percent, which happens when footsteps momentarily steepen it, sand begins to avalanche. To control this erosion the crew embeds two-foot logs connected by cables into the slope. Logs and cables are not yet buried in the sand but, when hidden, will scarcely show and will provide a directed and firmer path for the hundreds of people who traipse up the dune's unstable slope. Crews have done their work so skillfully that most people are not aware that, for instance, popular camping beaches like those at Nankoweap and Cardenas have already been considerably stabilized, nor that the simple and ingenious "planting" of dead shrubs to block unsightly multiple paths has allowed them to recover.

Setting steps like this and providing other visitor guides are controversial. Some people feel that the Park Service unnecessarily tampers with the natural landscape. Uncontroversial is the fact that these devices help to stabilize and focus the traffic of 18,000 to 20,000 visitors per year to specific areas strengthened to withstand it.

A huge, half-moon cobble bar downstream supplies the dune with its sand. During high predam flows, the river probably covered the cobble bar, filling the spaces between the imbricated cobbles with wilts and sands. The stones, like those in most rocky river beaches, overlap one another like shingles, all tilting downstream. The bar sits high enough to have escaped inundation during the high flows of 1983–84, when only a tiny channel snaked in along the foot of the dune, but it was obviously overtopped in predam times, for the river has cut away the river terraces that once covered it, leaving twenty- and thirty-foot terrace walls that give valuable insight into Anasazi settlement patterns and land use, as well as how the terrain along the river has changed over the last few thousand years.

The walls of the terraces, sliced through by drainages, display a neat alternation of rusty red and beige layers. Wind-carried and water-carried deposits usually lie in discrete layers whose area can be mapped. Eolian sands are more uniform in grain size since the smaller grains have been blown out. Alternately sent downstream or momen- tarily stored in a sandbar, sand is the most plentiful sediment in the river ecosystem, moving through in the sequence of deposition and scour. Water-carried deposits may be both alluvial, brought in by the river, or colluvial, washed down from hillsides above. They are finer, often velvety, silt. Wet silt adheres to your skin, while coarser eolian sands feel like sandpaper and brush off cleanly. The extent and place- ment of these deposits has significance in management decisions for the Colorado River.

Layering of the two kinds of textures, colluvium enriched with minerals alternating with porous, well-drained sandy soils, made good agricultural soil for prehistoric farmers. A reliable correlation exists between Kayenta Anasazi occupation of A.D. 1050–1150 and one of these alluvial units, a layer geologists call the "striped layer" for its clear alternation of pale tan layers brought in by river flow and red layers sloshed down off the hillsides. These distinctive Roman-striped layers lie above the old high-water line of mesquite and cat's-claw acacia, held in a terrace estimated to have developed over a 400-to- 500-year period of deposition.

If this area was farmed, and it undoubtedly was, it profited by being enriched with influxes of sediment during spring floods. But over time, salts accumulated as rocks broke down, their contents of sea salt dissolved and percolated into the soil by rainwater, concen- trated by high evapotranspiration rates. After the river overflowed and renewed the land, it could be farmed again. Interspersed with the layers of alluvium are thin lines of charcoal, likely from burning na- tive vegetation to clear the land and perhaps crop stubble burning. Carbon dates on this charcoal also correlate well with periods of Anasazi occupation.

At the foot of the terrace, the cobble bar stretches to the river. Midway an island of tamarisk casts a parsimonious shade that a light breeze constantly rearranges. I eat lunch here, directly across the river from an eye-stopper graben in which a large section of the earth's crust dropped between two fault lines, "drop" being a relative term since the slippage required millennia. Grabens are often huge landforms, too large to see in their entirety, but this one is seeable in one glance. Named the Basalt Graben, its wedge shape makes it look like the keystone of a gargantuan masonry arch. Faulting, which began after the dark Cardenas lavas flowed out 1.1 billion years ago, displaced strata on the downstream side about seventeen hundred feet. The Basalt Canyon Fault brought the black basalt down to abut against the neatly layered red Dox. The Butte Fault forms the upstream side of the graben, the same fault visible a few miles upstream in Kwagunt and Nankoweap Canyons. This stunning panorama is a gift of the river that cut through it and made it manifest.

From a distance the cobble bar looks flat but as I continue to walk across it, I find it corrugated as a washboard. Silt cracks reticulate a narrow channel recently muddy. Drying slowly, the edges of the individual plates curl upward, splitting between layers. A big cottonwood log lies far up from the river, lofted in by a predam flood. Cobbles and pebbles stabilize and shade the sand, and between them grow bristly little sprouts all under four inches high, the river version of a rock garden. A Plimsoll line of tenuous green algae scribes many of the translucent quartz pebbles.

Some of the stones are beautifully rounded, those between one and two inches long the most whole and symmetrical. Above that size, they still betray their original irregular form with odd angles and hollows. Below that size they are generally shattered. It is as if between one and two inches the integrity of the rock and the abrasive power of the river reach eloquent equilibrium in a harmonious ratio of surface to volume, creating the perfect oval. Wrapped in autumn sunshine, I give thanks for river edges and the light that sparks off the ripples and a row of near-perfect river cobbles that the river once carried in its pocket.

The next day I wander up an arroyo, enticed by what's beyond a huge chunk of conglomerate that nearly stoppers its mouth. Nothing much grows in the flat gravel base of the arroyo, freshly washed and plaited with little sharp-edged, inch-deep channels. Masses of river gravel cemented by calcium carbonate band the creek walls, and chunks of it lie in the creek bed, a local phenomenon, a continuation of the well-cemented gravel along the left bank of the river since Kwagunt Creek. The pebbles, probably relic deposits from the Pleistocene, may be up to thirty thousand years old. When the Colorado River ran an estimated seventy-five to eighty feet higher, these gravels dropped on top of an impervious Dox Sandstone layer. Water percolating through the ground leached out the minerals that cemented the hodgepodge together.

Gray lines crisscross maroon layers of Dox as if the wall were tiled and grouted. These marked changes in rock color, often associated with rock fractures, sometimes limn the cracks or freckle the rock with "reduction spots" where ferrous oxide, the red iron ore contained in the rock, loses a molecule and is "reduced" to ferric oxide. Ferric oxide is grayish green, while ferrous is rusty red to burgundy. Farther up, thin cards of Dox Shale pave the slope—note cards, playing cards, calling cards, potato chips of shale holding at a steep angle of repose, some ripple-marked and mud-cracked, floodplain deposits that filtered down a billion years ago. Shallow, regular ripple marks scallop the larger slabs, docile fossil waves on peaceful fossil shores. I pace the shallow sea, walking the time between, reflecting on the kind of fossil I'd like to be. I guess I'd like my bones to be replaced by some vivid chert, a red ulna or radius, or maybe preserved as the track of a strange lug-soled creature locked in the sandstone—how did it walk, what did it eat, and did it love the sunshine? I step in the wrong place and the slope disappears beneath my feet in a clatter of stony imprecations.

Only the slightest of air movements nudges a sweetbush stem or tickles a brittlebush leaf. A small checkered butterfly samples summer's late bloomers. Dozens of grasshoppers clatter and ratchet, Chinese firecrackers in an Arizona desert. Bee flies zip between open flowers, all small tickings in this spread of timeless landscape, where the second hand moves but once a century. Chalky gray brittlebushes stand out dramatically against the dark shales. Brittlebush, *Encelia farinosa*, was named for Christopher Encel, a German naturalist; *farinosa* refers to the pale gray, mealy covering on its leaves and stems, an adaptation to prevent water loss. The stems secrete a fragrant resin that explains the Mexican name of "incensio." Prehistoric Indians chewed the resin and coated their bodies with its numbing sap to relieve pain.

Brittlebush twigs match the gray of the leaves, until I pass one small bush whose twigs shine amber and an uncharacteristic glitter coats the gritty sandstone beneath, the honeydew of hundreds of aphids that encrust the tip ends of the stems and cover the undersides of the leaves. Most cluster on the veins of young leaves, pinheads of off-white fuzz with horsehair legs, threadlike beaks plunged into plant tissue from which they siphon the plant's phloem, an arrangement at least 300 million years old. They eschew the tiny brand new, just unfurled leaves but crowd those an inch down from the tip, in the end affecting the whole plant since photosynthates must be shunted from growth areas to infested areas.

This flocking of aphids results from parthenogenetic reproduction. Females produce the year's first young without fertilization and continue to do so until some trigger occurs—a shift in the weather, shortening day length—or the plant stops providing nourishment. Then males hatch, mating occurs, producing offspring capable of wintering over.

When I dislocate an aphid from its chosen vein, it looks like some Lilliputian lunar vehicle under my hand lens. It stalks its way to the leaf margin, tests the abyss, and stops. Its characteristic cornicles, which stick out like twin tail pipes from the end of the abdomen, may have developed for defense, for they secrete a sticky substance that dabs a predator or parasite on the head and clogs up its mouthparts. Most aphids also emit alarm pheromones from their cornicles, a powerful message to which the rest of the colony reacts on the instant, dropping off the plant en masse. Oddly, since pheromones tend to be very specific communicators, the aphid alarm pheromone also energizes any tending ants.

Plant sap, when processed through the aphid's gut, becomes a more complex substance called honeydew, a sugary, energy-rich liquid of surplus ingested sap plus excess sugars and waste materials, which may come close to fulfilling the complete dietary needs of attending ants. Aphids produce copious amounts of honeydew, up to 133 percent of their body weight in an hour. If the sugary stuff collects on their bodies, it can mold and fungal infection may wipe out a whole colony. When an ant worker, which requires liquid food, palpates an aphid, the aphid produces a drop of honeydew that the ant imbibes.

The third party to this mutualistic arrangement is the brittlebush itself, which manipulates the aphids by speeding up or slowing down its productivity, and stimuli from the leaf determine whether an aphid prefers the shaded or the sunny side. Although in the long run aphids are not beneficial to plants, there may be a quid pro quo: if ants tend a plant's aphids, they may prevent other plant chewers and siphoners from attacking.

Despite the infestation, the brittlebushes look amazingly healthy. If they weren't, the aphids would have gotten the message and left. In my rim-world garden, aphids on my peonies and columbines offend me. Out here, where I have the time to observe, I appreciate how these little clockwork creatures perform their intricate, nefarious business in the most efficient aphid way possible.

The mouth of Basalt Canyon looks as if a road grader growled through and never came back to clean up the mess. Rocks pile in untidy heaps. Plants bend every which way, whacked crooked by recent storm flow in the canyon. A white cabbage butterfly dotters past, followed by its equally erratic shadow. I start up the canyon, dressed in sheer indolence with not one whit of foreboding about how the day will end, simply relishing the sunshine and "October's bright blue weather."

As the canyon cuts through the fault that bounds the downstream end of the garden, rosy sandstones give way to black basalt. The Cardenas Lava was discovered and named for exposures in this canyon. The resistant basalt rises almost vertically, and Basalt Canyon has a darker, more rigorous aspect quite unlike the scoop-shaped canyons and tributaries cut in softer rock. The rill of Basalt Creek gradually becomes a rivulet that trickles into a neatly woven, four-strand braid. It may only drizzle today but the high-water salt lines on the walls verify that when it flashes it runs feet deep, reams out the narrow places, scoops suck holes in the sand around the monstrous boulders it can't budge, and flings rough clasts in flagrant furrows.

Salt crusts every surface and outlines every crack and crunches crisply underfoot. Narrow lines of salt thread the walls, widening into raised welts that rub off at a touch. The basalt exudes so much salt that some segments of the wall are completely spiderwebbed by it. A hundred feet farther, an iron salt colors the rivulets brilliant rusty orange and leaves a fuzzy, flocculent surface deposit up to a quarter-inch thick, a soft and mushy burnt orange carpet. Pure iron is not soluble in water, and what colors the water orange is probably a salt such as ferric or ferrous phosphate. Where the coating thins to a skin, it turns the water surface as iridescent as an oil slick.

I walk upward until a high, curving travertine wall, hung with pennants of dark algae, glimmers with water and momentarily blocks passage. Here at the bottom of the canyon all is in shadow, but sun blazes the upper walls a ruddy cinnamon. A rust-red dragonfly and a tiny blue butterfly patrol. A big paper wasp, iridescent blue-black with henna wings, landing gear dangling, hums by. The time it has taken to get here marks this as the turnabout if I am to get back by five o'clock, as I said I would.

When I get back to the mouth of Basalt Creek I turn left, up-river. As I round the beach two ducks lift off, quacking. A small channel separates an island from shore, and in the quieter waters waterfowl land and feed. Ahead the beach ends in a five-foot drop directly into deep water—no rocks stick up, no ledges shelve out of the water to walk on or hold onto. I have no choice but to clamber up, batting through a thicket I can't see the end of. I bushwhack through a dense apron of tamarisk thicket, a horrid mass of dead trunks and thick branches interwoven like a steel mesh. A deadfall of branches hides channels gouged out by old flows. More than once my foot goes through and branches lock around my leg like a bear trap. When I pause to get my breath I'm conscious that blood drizzles down both legs. So much for wearing shorts.

Ahead and above the tamarisk grow the old high-water-line mesquites, a no-man's-land of interlocked trunks and barbed branches. The slope, a sliding slithering pile of shale, gives me nothing to grab onto except mesquite branches full of thorns that rake my shoulders like tiger's claws. I gingerly use thumb and forefinger to grasp each spiky branch and put it aside with great care, as slow as crawling through coils of barbed wire. I manage only a few feet before I give up. Only the mindless devotion to getting back when I said I would drives me forward.

I break the mesquite screen and surge back into the tamarisk, then through to the arrowweed, not the friendly open stems of our beach but a palisade of tall, tensile shrubs. Once, near eye level I spot a katydid the size and color of an arrowweed leaf. Ninety years ago, when I left this morning, the sight of a katydid this close would have riveted my attention. But not this afternoon. Without a second thought I bat it out of the way. It soars to another stem a foot away, unbound by what trammels me.

The light dims faster than makes sense. I occupy a high-anxiety nightmare in which I can never get to where I'm going, everything takes twice as long as it should, I forgot my airline ticket, I have no suitcase, no clothes, no money, and my flight is being called. After what seems hours of pushing and shoving, getting swatted and lashed, the breakthrough of the last screen comes so suddenly that the merciful beach opening below stuns me. In the deepening darkness I recognize the tail end of our beach, an endless quarter-mile from camp. I begin to jog, hitching along like a poorly articulated puppet. Ahead shrubs turn into people. I lift my arm in greeting. It hurts.

Enough scratches crisscross my shins for a dozen games of tick-tacktoe. Disinfectant stings unmercifully. I feel flagellated, flayed alive, splinters of bones strung together by bits of sinew and shreds of muscle, an ancient stylite of the desert, doomed to spend the remainder of my days bound to a mesquite tree, holding my unsaintly symbol, a bottle of iodine.

I worm my way into my sleeping bag exhausted, yearning for sleep to soothe. But sleep does not come. Tonight this canyon is too much—too much wind, too much river, too much sand, too many thorns, too many puzzles, too far to reach, too beyond to find.

FROM *Missouri River Journals*

John James Audubon

May 17, 1843, Wednesday . . . We have seen floating eight Buffaloes, one Antelope, and one Deer; how great the destruction of these animals must be during high freshets! The cause of their being drowned in such extraordinary numbers might not astonish one acquainted with the habits of these animals, but to one who is not, it may be well enough for me to describe it. Some few hundred miles above us, the river becomes confined between high bluffs or cliffs, many of which are nearly perpendicular, and therefore extremely difficult to ascend. When the Buffaloes have leaped or tumbled down from either side of the stream, they swim with ease across, but on reaching these walls, as it were, the poor animals try in vain to climb them, and becoming exhausted by falling back some dozens of times, give up the ghost, and float down the turbid stream; their bodies have been known to pass, swollen and putrid, the city of St. Louis. The most extraordinary part of the history of these drowned Buffaloes is, that the different tribes of Indians on the shores, are ever on the look-out for them, and no matter how putrid their flesh may be, provided the hump proves at all fat, they swim to them, drag them on shore, and cut them to pieces; after which they cook and eat this loathsome and abominable flesh, even to the marrow found in the bones. In some instances this has been done when the whole of the hair had fallen off, from the rottenness of the Buffalo. Ah! Mr. Catlin, I am now sorry to see and to read your accounts of the Indians *you* saw—how very different they must have been from any that I have seen! Whilst we were on the top of the high hills which we climbed this morning, and looked towards the valley beneath us, including the river, we were undetermined as to whether we saw as much land dry as land overflowed; the immense flat prairie on the east side of the river looked not unlike a lake of great expanse, and immediately beneath us the last freshet had left upwards of perhaps two or three hundred acres covered by water, with numbers of water fowl on it, but so difficult of access as to render our wishes to kill Ducks quite out of the question. From the tops of the hills we saw only a continual succession of other lakes, of the same form and nature; and although the soil was of a fair, or even good, quality, the grass grew in tufts, separated from each other, and as it grows green in one spot, it dies and turns brown in another. We saw here no "carpeted prairies," no "velvety distant landscape;" and if these things are to be seen, why, the sooner we reach them the better. . . .

May 18, Thursday . . . Our good captain called us all up at a quarter before four this fair morning, to tell us that four barges had arrived from Fort Pierre, and that we might write a few letters, which Mr. Laidlow, one of the partners, would take to St. Louis for us. I was introduced to that gentleman and also to Major Dripps, the Indian agent. I wrote four short letters, which I put in an envelope addressed to the Messieurs Chouteau & Co., of St. Louis, who will post them, and we have hopes that some may reach their destination. The names of these four boats are *War Eagle, White Cloud, Crow-feather,* and *Redfish.* We went on board one of them, and found it comfortable enough. They had ten thousand Buffalo robes on the four boats; the men live entirely on Buffalo meat and pemmican. They told us that about a hundred miles above us the Buffalo were by thousands, that the prairies were covered with dead calves, and the shores lined with dead of all sorts; that Antelopes were there also, and a great number of Wolves, etc.; therefore we shall see them after a while. . . .

May 20, Saturday . . . Three White Wolves were seen this morning, and after a while we saw a fourth, of the brindled kind, which was trotting leisurely on, about 150 yards distant from the bank, where he had probably been feeding on some carrion or other. A shot from a rifle was quite enough to make him turn off up the river again, but farther from us, at a full gallop; after a time he stopped again, when the noise of our steam pipe started him, and we soon lost sight of him in the bushes. We saw three Deer in the flat of one of the prairies, and just before our dinner we saw, rather indistinctly, a number of Buffaloes, making their way across the hills about two miles distant; after which, however, we saw their heavy tracks in a well and deep cut line across the said hills. Therefore we are now in what is pronounced to be the "Buffalo country," and may expect to see more of the animals to-morrow. . . .

May 23, Tuesday . . . The wind blew from the south this morning and rather stiffly. We rose early, and walked about this famous Cedar Island, where we stopped to cut large red cedars [*Juniperus virginianus*] for one and a half hours; we started at half-past five, breakfasted rather before six, and were on the lookout for our hunters. *Hunters!* Only two of them had ever been on a Buffalo hunt before. One was lost almost in sight of the river. They only walked two or three miles, and camped. Poor Squires' first experience was a very rough one; for, although they made a good fire at first, it never was tended afterwards, and his pillow was formed of a buck's horn accidentally picked up near the place. Our Sioux Indian helped himself to another, and they all felt chilly and damp. They had forgotten to take any spirits with them, and their condition was miserable. As the orb of day rose as red as blood, the party started, each taking a different direction. But the wind was unfavorable; it blew up, not down the river, and the Buffaloes, Wolves, Antelopes, and indeed every animal possessed of the sense of smell, had scent of them in time to avoid them. There happened however to be attached to this party two good and true men, that may be called hunters. One was Michaux; the other a friend of his, whose name I do not know. It happened, by hook or by crook, that these two managed to kill four Buffaloes; but one of them was drowned, as it took to the river after being shot. Only a few pieces from a young bull, and its tongue, were brought on board, most of the men being too lazy, or too far off, to cut out even the tongues of the others; and thus it is that thousands multiplied by thousands of Buffaloes are murdered in senseless play, and their enormous carcasses are suffered to be the prey of the Wolf, the Raven and the Buzzard. . . .

Sunday, May 28 . . . Both shores were dotted by groups of Buffaloes as far as the eye could reach, and although many were near the banks they kept on feeding quietly till we nearly approached them; those at the distance of half a mile never ceased their avocations. A Gray Wolf was seen swimming across our bows, and some dozens of shots were sent at the beast, which made it open its mouth and raise its head, but it never stopped swimming away from us, as fast as possible; after a while it reached a sand-bar, and immediately afterwards first trotted, and then galloped off. Three Buffaloes also crossed ahead of us, but at some distance; they all reached the shore, and scrambled up the bank. We have run better this morning than for three or four days, and if fortunate enough may reach Fort Pierre sometime to-morrow. The prairies appear better now, the grass looks green, and probably the poor Buffaloes will soon regain their flesh. We have seen more than 2,000 this morning up to this moment—twelve o'clock. . . .

June 7, Wednesday . . . We reached Fort Clark and the Mandan Villages at half-past seven this morning. Great guns were fired from the fort and from the *Omega*, as our captain took the guns from the *Trapper* at Fort Pierre. The site of this fort appears a good one, though it is placed considerably below the Mandan Village. We saw some small spots cultivated, where corn, pumpkins, and beans are grown. The fort and village are situated on the high bank, rising somewhat to the elevation of a hill. The Mandan mud huts are very far from looking poetical, although Mr. Catlin has tried to render them so by placing them in regular rows, and all of the same size and form, which is by no means the case. But different travellers have different eyes! We saw more Indians than at any previous time since leaving St. Louis; and it is possible that there are a hundred huts, made of mud, all looking like so many potato winter-houses in the Eastern States. As soon as we were near the shore, every article that could conveniently be carried off was placed under lock and key, and our division door was made fast, as well as those of our own rooms. Even the axes and poles were put by. Our captain told us that last year they stole his cap and his shot-pouch and horn, and that it was through the interference of the first chief that he recovered his cap and horn; but that a squaw had his leather belt, and would not give it up. The appearance of these poor, miserable devils, as we approached the shore, was wretched enough. There they stood in the pelting rain and keen wind, covered with Buffalo robes, red blankets, and the like, some partially and most curiously besmeared with mud; and as they came on board, and we shook hands with each of them, I felt a clamminess that rendered the ceremony most repulsive. Their legs and naked feet were covered with mud. They looked at me with apparent curiosity, perhaps on account of my beard, which produced the same effect at Fort Pierre. They all looked very poor; and our captain says they are the *ne plus ultra* of thieves. It is said there are nearly three thousand men, women, and children that, during winter, cram themselves into these miserable hovels. . . .

June 9, Friday . . . I went up to the top of the hills, bounding the beautiful prairie, by which we had stopped to repair something about the engine. We gathered some handsome lupines, of two different species, and many other curious plants. From this elevated spot we could see the wilderness to an immense distance; the Missouri looked as if only a brook, and our steamer a very small one indeed. At this juncture we saw two men running along the shore upwards, and I supposed they were in pursuit. Meantime, gazing around, we saw a large lake, where we are told that Ducks, Geese, and Swans breed in great numbers; this we intend also to visit when we come down. At this moment I heard the report of a gun from the point where the men had been seen, and when we reached the steamboat, we were told that a Buffalo had been killed. From the deck I saw a man swimming round the animal; he got on its side, and floated down the stream with it. The captain sent a parcel of men with a rope; the swimmer fastened this round the neck of the Buffalo, and with his assistance, for he now swam all the way, the poor beast was brought alongside; and as the tackle had been previously fixed, it was hauled up on the fore deck. Sprague took its measurements with me, which are as follows: length from nose to root of tail, 8 feet; height of fore shoulder to hoof, 4 ft. 9½ in.; height at the rump to hoof, 4 ft. 2 in. The head was cut off, as well as one fore and one hind foot. The head is so full of symmetry, and so beautiful that I shall have a drawing of it to-morrow, as well as careful ones of the feet. Whilst the butchers were at work, I was highly interested to see one of our Indians cutting out the milk-bag of the cow and eating it, quite fresh and raw, in pieces somewhat larger than a hen's egg. One of the stomachs was partially washed in a bucket of water, and an Indian swallowed a large portion of this. Mr. Chardon brought the remainder on the upper deck and ate it un-cleaned. I had a piece well cleaned and tasted it; to my utter astonish-ment, it was very good, but the idea was repulsive to me; besides which, I am not a meat-eater, as you know, except when other provisions fail. The animal was in good condition; and the whole carcass was cut up and dispersed among the men below, reserving the nicer portions for the cabin. This was accomplished with great rapidity; the blood was washed away in a trice, and half an hour afterwards no one would have known that a Buffalo had been dressed on deck. . . .

June 11, Sunday . . . This day has been tolerably fine, though windy. We have seen an abundance of game, a great number of Elks, common Virginian Deer, Mountain Rams in two places, and a fine flock of Sharp-tailed Grouse, that, when they flew off from the ground near us, looked very much like large Meadow Larks. They were on a prairie bordering a large patch of Artemisia, which in the distance presents the appearance of acres of cabbages. We have seen many Wolves and some Buffaloes. One young bull stood on the brink of a bluff, looking at the boat steadfastly for full five minutes; and as we neared the spot, he waved his tail, and moved off briskly. On another occasion, a young bull that had just landed at the foot of a very steep bluff was slaughtered without difficulty; two shots were fired at it, and the poor thing was killed by a rifle bullet. I was sorry, for we did not stop for it, and its happy life was needlessly ended. I saw near that spot a large hawk, and also a very small Tamias, or Ground Squirrel. Harris saw a Spermophile, of what species none of us could tell. We have seen many Elks swimming the river, and they look almost the size of a well-grown mule. They stared at us, were fired at, at an enormous distance, it is true, and yet stood still. These animals are abundant beyond belief hereabouts. We have seen much remarkably handsome scenery, but nothing at all comparing with Catlin's descriptions; his book must, after all, be altogether a humbug. Poor devil! I pity him from the bottom of my soul; had he studied, and kept up to the old French proverb that says, "Bon renommé vaut mieux que ceinture doré," he might have become an "honest man"—the quintessence of God's works. . . .

. . . A heavy shower put off running a race; but we are to have a regular Buffalo hunt, where I must act only as a spectator; for, alas! I am now too near seventy to run and load whilst going at full gallop. . . .

June 16, Sunday . . . All was arranged, and at half-past three this afternoon we were traveling towards Fort Union. But hours previous to this, and before our scanty dinner, Owen had seen another bull, and Harris and Bell joined us in the hunt. The bull was shot at by McKenzie, who stopped its career, but as friend Harris pursued it with two of the hunters and finished it I was about to return, and thought sport over for the day. However, at this stage of the proceedings Owen discovered another bull making his way slowly over the prairie towards us. I was the only one who had balls, and would gladly have claimed the privilege of running him, but fearing I might make out badly on my slower steed, and so lose meat which we really needed, I handed my gun and balls to Owen McKenzie, and Bell and I went to an eminence to view the chase. Owen approached the bull, which continued to advance, and was now less than a quarter of a mile distant; either it did not see, or did not heed him, and they came directly towards each other, until they were about seventy or eighty yards apart, when the Buffalo started at a good run, and Owen's mare, which had already had two hard runs this morning, had great difficulty in preserving her distance. Owen, perceiving this, breathed her a minute, and then applying the whip was soon within shooting distance, and fired a shot which visibly checked the progress of the bull, and enabled Owen to soon be alongside of him, when the contents of the second barrel were discharged into the lungs, passing through the shoulder blade. This brought him to a stand. Bell and I now started at full speed, and as soon as we were within speaking distance, called to Owen not to shoot again. The bull did not appear to be much exhausted, but he was so stiffened by the shot on the shoulder that he could not turn quickly, and taking advantage of this we approached him; as we came near he worked himself slowly round to face us, and then made a lunge at us; we then stopped on one side and commenced discharging our pistols with little or no effect, except to increase his fury with every shot. His appearance was now one to inspire terror had we not felt satisfied of our ability to avoid him. However, even so, I came very near being overtaken by him. Through my own imprudence, I placed myself directly in front of him, and as he advanced I fired at his head, and then ran *ahead* of him, instead of veering to one side, not supposing that he was able to overtake me; but turning my head over my shoulder, I saw to my horror, Mr. Bull within three feet of me, prepared to give me a taste of his horns. The next instant I turned sharply off, and the Buffalo being unable to turn quickly enough to follow me, Bell took the gun from Owen and shot him directly behind the shoulder blade. He tottered for a moment, with an increased jet of blood from the mouth and nostrils, fell forward on his horns, then rolled over on his side, and was dead. He was a very old animal, in poor case, and only part of him was worth taking to the fort. Provost, Squires, and Basil were left at the camp preparing for their departure after Otter and Beaver as decided. We left them eight or nine catfish and a quantity of meat, of which they took care to secure the best, namely the boss or hump. On our home-ward way we saw several Antelopes, some quite in the prairie, others far away on the hills, but all of them on the alert. Owen tried unsuc-cessfully to approach several of them at different times. At one place where two were seen he dismounted, and went round a small hill (for these animals when startled or suddenly alarmed always make to these places), and we hoped would have had a shot; but alas! no! One of the Antelopes ran off to the top of another hill, and the other stood looking at him, and us perhaps, till Owen (who had been re-mounted) galloped off towards us. My surprise was great when I saw the other Antelope following him at a good pace (but not by bounds or leaps, as I had been told by a former traveller they sometimes did), until it either smelt him, or found out he was no friend, and turning round galloped speedily off to join the one on the lookout. We saw seven or eight Grouse, and Bell killed one on the ground. We saw a Sandhill Crane about two years old, looking quite majestic in a grassy bottom, but it flew away before we were near enough to get a shot. We passed a fine pond or small lake but no bird was there. We saw several parcels of Ducks in sundry places, all of which no doubt had young near. When we turned the corner of the great prairie we found Owen's mare close by us. She had run away while he was after An-telopes. We tied her to a log to be ready for him when he should reach the spot. He had to walk about three miles before he did this. However, to one as young and alert as Owen, such things are nothing. Once they were not to me. . . .

July 21, Friday . . . We were up at sunrise, and had our coffee, after which Lafleur a mulatto, Harris, and Bell went off after An-telopes, for we cared no more about bulls; where the cows are, we can-not tell. Cows run faster than bulls, yearlings faster than cows, and calves faster than any of these. Squires felt sore, and his side was very black, so we took our guns and went after Black-breasted Lark Buntings, of which we saw many, but could not near them. I found a nest of them, however, with five eggs. The nest is planted in the ground, deep enough to sink the edges of it. It is formed of dried fine grasses and roots, without any lining of hair or wool. By and by we saw Harris sitting on a high hill about one mile off, and joined him; he said the bulls they had killed last evening were close by, and I offered to go and see the bones, for I expected that the Wolves had devoured it during the night. We travelled on, and Squires returned to the camp. After about two miles of walking against a delightful strong breeze, we reached the animals; Ravens or Buzzards had worked at the eyes, but only one Wolf, apparently, had been there. They were bloated, and smelt quite unpleasant. We returned to the camp and saw a Wolf cross our path, and an Antelope looking at us. We determined to stop and try to bring him to us; I lay on my back and threw my legs up, kicking first one and then the other foot, and sure enough the Antelope walked towards us, slowly and carefully, however. In about twenty minutes he had come two or three hundred yards; he was a superb male, and I looked at him for some minutes; when about sixty yards off I could see his eyes, and being loaded with buck-shot pulled the trigger without rising from my awkward position. Off he went; Harris fired, but he only ran the faster for some hundred yards, when he turned, looked at us again, and was off. When we reached camp we found Bell there; he had shot three times at Antelopes without killing; Lafleur had also returned, and had broken the foreleg of one, but an Antelope can run fast enough with three legs, and he saw no more of it. We now broke camp, arranged the horses and turned our heads towards the Missouri, and in four and three-quarter hours reached the landing. On entering the wood we again broke branches of service-berries, and carried a great quantity over the river. I much enjoyed the trip; we had our supper, and soon to bed in our hot room, where Sprague says the thermometer has been at 99° most of the day. I noticed it was warm when walking. I must not forget to notice some things which happened on our return. First, as we came near Fox River, we thought of the horns of our bulls, and Mr. Culbertson, who knows the country like a book, drove us first to Bell's, who knocked the horns off, then to Harris's, which was served in the same manner; this bull had been eaten entirely except the head, and a good portion of mine had been devoured also; it lay immediately under "Audubon's Bluff" (the name Mr. Culbertson gave the ridge on which I stood to see the chase), and we could see it when nearly a mile distant. Bell's horns were the handsomest and largest, mine next best, and Harris's the smallest, but we are all contented. Mr. Culbertson tells me that

Harris and Bell have done wonders, for persons who have never shot at Buffaloes from on horseback. Harris had a fall too, during his second chase, and was bruised in the manner of Squires, but not so badly. I have but little doubt that Squires killed his bull, as he says he shot it three times, and Mr. Culbertson's must have died also. What a terrible destruction of life, as it were for nothing, or next to it, as the tongues only were brought in, and the flesh of these fine animals were left to beasts and birds of prey, or to rot on the spots where they fell. The prairies are literally *covered* with the skulls of the victims, and the roads the Buffalo make in crossing the prairies have all the appearance of heavy wagon tracks. . . .

August 4, Friday . . . We soon saw that the weather was becoming cloudy, and we were anxious to reach a camping-place; but we continued to cross ranges of hills, and hoped to see a large herd of Buffaloes. The weather was hot "out of mind," and we continued till, reaching a fine hill, we saw in a beautiful valley below us seventy to eighty head, feeding peacefully in groups and singly, as might happen. The bulls were mixed in with the cows, and we saw one or two calves. Many bulls were at various distances from the main group, but as we advanced towards them they galloped off and joined the others. When the chase began it was curious to see how much swifter the cows were than the bulls, and how soon they divided themselves into parties of seven or eight, exerting themselves to escape from their murderous pursuers. All in vain, however; off went the guns and down went the cows, or stood bleeding through the nose, mouth, or bullet holes. Mr. C. killed three, and Harris one in about half an hour. We had quite enough, and the slaughter was ended. We had driven up to the nearest-fallen cow, and approached close to her, and found that she was not dead, but trying to rise to her feet. I cannot bear to see an animal suffer unnecessarily, so begged one of the men to take my knife and stab her to the heart, which was done. The animals were cut up and skinned, with considerable fatigue. To skin bulls and cows and cut up their bodies is no joke, even to such as are constantly in the habit of doing it. Whilst Mr. Culbertson and the rest had gone to cut up another at some distance, I remained on guard to save the meat from the Wolves, but none came before my companions returned. We found the last cow quite dead. As we were busy about her the rain fell in torrents, and I found my blanket *capote* of great service. It was now nearly sundown, and we made up our minds to camp close by, although there was no water for our horses, neither any wood. Harris and I began collecting Buffalo-dung from all around, whilst the others attended to various other affairs. The meat was all unloaded and spread on the ground, the horses made fast, the fire burned freely, pieces of liver were soon cooked and devoured, coffee drunk in abundance, and we went to rest. . . .

August 5, Saturday . . . Provost tells me that Buffaloes become so very poor during hard winters, when the snows cover the ground to the depth of two or three feet, that they lose their hair, become covered with scabs, on which the Magpies feed, and the poor beasts die by hundreds. One can hardly conceive how it happens, notwithstanding these many deaths and the immense numbers that are murdered almost daily on these boundless wastes called prairies, besides the hosts that are drowned in the freshets, and the hundreds of young calves who die in early spring, so many are yet to be found. Daily we see so many that we hardly notice them more than the cattle in our pastures about our homes. But this cannot last; even now there is a perceptible difference in the size of the herds, and before many years the Buffalo, like the Great Auk, will have disappeared; surely this should not be permitted. . . .

ALONG THE DELTA

John Hildebrand

The wind blew from the southwest, from the sea, tilting the river into a billowy expanse of whitecaps. I kept the bow windward to quarter the waves so they swept past without shipping much water over the gunwales. Sometimes a large swell heaved the front of the canoe out of the water and then dropped it into the lurch with a splash. I would sooner run Five Finger Rapids in a bathtub than face the lower Yukon on a breezy day. Rainwater collected in pools in my lap and streamed down my back until my lower half was soaked. Hugging the shore, I searched for a level landing. But sheer rock cliffs ran down to the water on the right bank, and the river was too wide and wind tossed for me to consider crossing to the leeward bank. Besides, I could barely see through the rain to the dismal far shore.

Tacking around a blind point, I landed on a pocket beach strewn with foam and driftwood. There is a great sense of relief at making landfall in rough weather, when each mile has been hard won. Quickly, I unpacked the tent and looked around for a smooth spot to erect it. Then I hesitated—fresh tracks led out of the bordering woods and made a transit of the beach. I'd seen plenty of black bear tracks before, but these were larger and more formidably spaced. Pressed into the soft yellow clay, each print was as wide across as the length of my boots and topped with five toes and radiating claw points just now filling with rain. The tracks belonged to a brown bear, a coastal grizzly, and they left no less an impression on me than on the wet beach. Faced with a choice of terrors, I debated whether to take my chances with the storm-tossed river or camp here and face a sleepless night.

The river was an uncertainty, but the bearish nightmare was already fully formed in my brain: A sharp snort as claws rend the tent. A great, dish-faced profile sways overhead, so near I smell the close, rancid breath. The beaded eyes are set close together; the silver fur on its humped back glistens in the moonlight. I reach for the shotgun at my side, but the mechanism jams. I open my mouth to cry out but cannot. The bear pulls me from the sleeping bag into a terrible embrace as the dream dissolves around me.

I repacked the tent and launched back into the whitecapped waves.

Landing finally in a tiny grotto formed by projecting rock spurs, I set the tent on a narrow shelf of broken shale. It looked like a place for votive candles and miraculous springs. Out of the wind and safe from night-wandering bears, I fell into a deep, dreamless sleep. For two days I remained storm-bound on that ledge, protected from the storm and sealed off from the rest of the world. When I stuck my head outside the tent on the second day, I seemed to be in the middle of a cloud. The far bank was lost in fog, and the river's surface lay broken into gray waves like overlapping tiles on a slate roof.

The notes from my journal give some hint of my mood:

August 8. Still raining. Wind from the south. I am curled in a fetal position in my sleeping bag, head tucked under the covers, listening to the rain's patter and the steady lashing of waves against the shore. Finished last of whiskey yesterday, a small thing but one of those pleasures that civilize a camping trip. Did nothing today but memorize the tent's stitchery.

I boiled water over the small kerosene stove for tea and to keep the tent warm. Wet clothes were strewn everywhere. Some were trying to dry and others I used to plug the tent's leaky corners where pools of rainwater had formed. My journal entries were becoming more cryptic and full of complaints. I had reached that dangerous point on a long journey when things break down, when the essential organization on which you depend turns to chaos. Dishes are put away dirty, clothes don't dry out, meals are simplified to a few soggy crackers and tea. Mistakes wait to happen because your mind is set not on the tasks at hand but on getting home. I started making wish lists: dry clothes, a warm bed, a drink with ice. A few books remained to read, most having been given away on the journey in small payment for some kindness. Encased in my sodden sleeping bag, knees drawn to my chest, I reread a paperback *Odyssey* with a new sympathy for the shipwrecked Odysseus—"poor fellow, kept from his friends, all this while in trouble and sorrow, in that island covered with trees, and nothing but the waves all about it, in the very middle of the sea."

In the afternoon the fog lifted enough to provide clearance between the river and cloud ceiling. I bailed out my canoe and started again. The Yukon reaches its southernmost point at Roundabout Mountain, near the abandoned settlement of Ohagamiut, having looped back to nearly the latitude it started at in Whitehorse. Rounding the horn, the canoe began to pitch and yawl in heavy chop. The wind had shifted and I found myself plowing north into stinging drizzle and the teeth of a thirty-knot gale. The river yawned three miles across where it swallowed an island. By ducking into side channels, I could run out of the wind until the slough rejoined the main channel and cast me back into the maelstrom. Shivering wet, my teeth chattering, I was determined now to motor on toward the next village. It was a fateful decision because soon I was too weak and thick-headed to think about putting up a tent in this wind. When my strength gave out, I would just tie up along shore and lie down in the rain for a long sleep. Each deserted bend in the river brought a new disappointment. I had nearly decided to moor the canoe to a cutbank and crawl into the alders when I saw a pair of strange lights burning ahead in the sky. They were the headlights of an airplane flying low beneath the clouds, descending upon the landing strip at Marshall.

I took a room above the store in Marshall. Few villages on the lower river have places for a visitor to stay, so it seemed great luck to find one here. The heat wouldn't come on, but I thawed out with a hot shower, my first since Tanana, and crawled exhausted between the sheets. About six o'clock I heard the downstairs door slam as the storeowner left and his teenage replacement arrived. Immediately she put a love song on the record player, something current and insipid. She must have been heartsick, or maybe the record changer was broken, but she played that dreary song over and over again until the lyrics were etched in my brain. Even after she locked up for the night and went home, the words kept returning like a bad dream.

I awoke in the morning to barking dogs and the whine of two-stroke engines—the sounds of village life. Looking out a rain-streaked window, I saw a man puttering down a muddy road on his motorbike, a rifle slung across his back. Marshall sits at the base of Pilcher Mountain on a high ledge over the Yukon. Beyond the back yard clutter of woodpiles, oil cans, and clotheslines flying in the gale, the river lay puckered into whitecaps beneath a slate gray sky.

The storeowner, a stocky, pleasant Eskimo named Leslie Hunter, drove me around the village in his pickup truck. Splashing down the road, Hunter pointed out the new fish-processing plant. "Lots of fish this year," he said, "but not much money." We passed a boarded-up hotel, bleached white as a whalebone, a remnant of Marshall's past as a fledgling gold camp. Two prospectors discovered gold on nearby Wilson Creek in 1913 and named the creek for the current president and the townsite for his running mate, Thomas Marshall, who had campaigned under the bromide, "What this country needs is a good five-cent cigar." The stampede to Marshall was the last major gold rush on the Yukon. Most of the village, however, seemed only a few years old. Set on barren tundra, the prefabricated housing in poster-paint colors gave Marshall the look of one of those instant Wyoming strip-mining towns. Hunter's grandfather had come from Pennsylvania to be the mining camp's first postmaster, but just as his grandson now favors the Eskimo side of the family, so had Marshall changed complexions over the years.

The truck rocked in the wind as we parked above a beach littered with tethered skiffs and miserable-looking dogs curled in the mud. I asked Leslie Hunter if any of the old miners had stayed on in Marshall. There were a few, he said. One had just died at eighty-three, still chipping away at his claims. He'd hired a pilot to drop him at his cabin forty miles back in the hills. When the pilot flew back a month later to check on him, he found only a burnt cabin and some charred bones in the doorway. The prospector had stockpiled Molotov cocktails for bear protection because his eyesight was too poor for aiming a rifle, and the consensus was that the gasoline bombs, not the bears, got him in the end.

Hunter told me there was another old-timer who lived just up the road, and he dropped me at Gene Tetinek's cottage. Tetinek answered the door in a plaid wool shirt and bedroom slippers, a shock of white hair falling across his forehead. Stacks of newspapers and bundled magazines lay on the floor. He sat back in an easy chair and filled his pipe from a tobacco tin. A photograph of the paddle-wheeler *Nenana* hung on the wall. We listened to the weather forecast over the

Nome radio station, first in English and then in Yupik Eskimo; another storm was spiraling up the coast from the Aleutians.

When I told Tetinek of my travels, he seemed unimpressed. I had arrived too late, he said, to see the real North. Old-timers were always telling me that.

"Used to be if you wanted to settle someplace, all you had to do was throw up a log cabin, and that was that. Not anymore. The country's changed."

In the summer of 1934, Tetinek was cutting cordwood in Fort Yukon when he got the itch to travel. He paid five dollars for a flimsy ratting canoe and set off down the Yukon, reaching Marshall just as gold hit thirty-five dollars an ounce on the open market. He was offered a job in one of the mines, but turned it down to spend the winter outside. Hiring on as a deck hand on the steamboat *Nenana*, he retraced his route upriver, hopped a freight to the railhead at Seward, and then took a steamship to Seattle, where he hitchhiked the last leg home to Cleveland. Tetinek returned to the America of the National Recovery Act, a country of soup kitchens and bread lines. The depression was in full swing, so he never even bothered looking for work. The next summer he returned to Marshall to operate a hydraulic hose in the Willow Creek mine. The hose shot stream water from the nozzle with enough ballistic force to strip the soil down to gold-bearing bedrock. When the gold mines shut down after the war, he operated a trading post until retiring.

I asked him why, with the price of gold so high, the large mines hadn't started up again.

"It isn't the price of gold, it's the price of everything else. Especially freight, if something breaks down and you need to have it shipped up. Last year I ordered a boat from Seattle, and the freight cost more than the boat!"

Once a year Tetinek flew to Anchorage for a change of pace, but when I asked why he didn't move there permanently, it was clear he'd soured on the city.

"What would I do there? You need a car to get anywhere. If you have a snow tractor, you need a permit."

One thing bothered me about Tetinek's story. I had seen a ratting canoe in a museum in Fort Yukon. Built of canvas stretched over a spruce frame, they are employed in the spring for hunting muskrat and look as tippy as a pea pod.

"Where did you stow your supplies?"

205

"Supplies?" The tone of his voice implied my own needs were extravagant. "Plenty of room for a sleeping bag, a rifle, some grub. What *more* could you possibly need?"

Before I checked out of my room above the store, Leslie Hunter warned me of three bad spots between Marshall and St. Marys, "stretches where the wind blows one way and the river goes the other." He had no map and so depended upon his words and the urgency of his gestures to convey the downriver landmarks, the islands and bends that I was to watch for. But I didn't pay much attention: I was in too big a hurry to leave during what appeared to be a lull in the storm. Immediately after leaving Marshall, I crossed a half mile of open water to a long island that broke the wind blowing off the main channel. I had completely forgotten about the first of the bad spots until, rounding the lee of the island, I stumbled into it. The wind was blowing a terrific gale. The waves broke with a sigh, lifting the canoe so that it teetered on the crest of a wave before plunging into the sea green trough. The major problem of small-boat navigation in heavy swells is keeping boat and waves on a parallel course. I would quarter the smaller waves, then align the bow to meet the oncoming rollers. Five inches of freeboard were all that separated me from the river. Yet as long as the waves didn't come from the side, breaking over the gunwales, the canoe would ride out the chop. Each roller rushing headlong toward the canoe seemed fated to swamp it, but each time the crest fell short, the little boat riding over the wave instead of beneath it.

The Yukon's course became more erratic, describing corkscrews and oxbow turns, as it cut away at the headlands. Changing direction, the river moved in and out of the wind, and for long stretches at a time I had smooth sailing. The second bad spot was Dogtooth Bend, a several-mile loop around a cuspid of tundra. At the bend, the channel I was following intersected with an even larger channel, and the waves, instead of charging at the bow, suddenly swept down from the stern. The canoe surfed forward on the crest of a wave heading for shore. Unable to change course for fear of presenting the boat sideways to the swells, I watched helplessly as the backs of green rollers rushed past to break in a line on the beach. Between waves, the prop scraped sand and kicked out of the water with an awful whine. Then the outboard stalled. The canoe lurched sideways and began to ship water. With no power or steerage, there was nothing I could do but tilt the engine up and paddle to keep the bow straight as the waves deposited me ashore.

The far end of the beach was not pounded nearly so hard by the surf. Lining the canoe to the sheltered end, I cast off again. The rain had stopped, and a sickly yellow light shone below the clouds. I turned into a leeward slough where the alder banks drew close, and the wind's tumult died as suddenly as if a window had been shut. A red fox trotted along the shore, tail unfurled like a pennant. For miles I followed this interior passage before stopping on a damp sandbar for the evening.

The edge of the sandbar was muddy, and as I carried gear ashore from the canoe my rubber boots pulled from the mire with a sucking noise. I shared the sandbar with an enormous spruce log propped up on its roots and pointing downriver. Scoured from a riverbank by spring ice, its branches sheared off to nubs, the great log had rafted downstream in floodwater to be stranded here, smooth and polished. Its trunk sheltered my tent from the wind and its roots made resinous kindling for my fire.

Walking down to the river to wash my dinner dishes, I found that I wasn't alone. Voices and soft laughter carried faintly from a fish camp at the end of the slough, and somehow this discovery made me feel more forlorn. When you travel alone, it's not the strangeness of places that tugs at your heart but the way things are the same. The voices spoke in Yupik, but I could make out the peculiar cadences of family talk, the small jokes and affections. The few risky moments I'd recently had on the river only sharpened my sense of isolation. One of the most human of fears, I think, must be of dying alone. After a close call, we want someone to share our relief; we want to matter, not in any general way, but to someone in particular. I was tired of being a floater. When I could see past the bitterness of my failed marriage, I had to admit that, in balance, the good memories outweighed the bad. And, since memories were all I had at the moment, I wanted to cherish them. Crawling into the tent, I began a long-postponed letter to my ex-wife. I meant to finally clear the air between us, so it was really a good-by letter, but since we hadn't spoken civilly in two years it was a hello, as well.

The sky cleared the next morning. The sun felt warm against my back as I loaded the canoe and headed down the slough toward the main channel. Nobody was home at the fish camp except for a husky pup tethered to a stake.

The Yukon spread out windless and benign, a deeper shade of blue than the sky. Fishing boats bobbed in the distance—the truest measure of good weather. The rough water and bad weather behind me, I felt expansive, no longer in a hurry. The end of the trip seemed in sight. With the proper attitude, I thought, one could make a bargain with the river, stay on its good side.

I trolled up to a shovel-nosed skiff. An Eskimo fisherman and his son, perhaps the voices I'd heard the night before, were untangling a burbot from their net. The burbot had the head of a toad and body of an eel and glared malignantly from the bottom of the boat as it expired.

How far, I asked, to Pilot Station.

"You're almost there. You'll see it right around the next bend."

The Yukon formed a T as it bent sharply to the southwest and the Chuilnak River entered from the east. Racing around the bend, I saw the blue-roofed houses of Pilot Station in a saddle between two hills. The village could not have been more than a mile away, so I steered a direct course for it, cutting diagonally across the river.

Then everything went wrong.

A blast of wind caught me as I cleared the bend. Funneled down the narrow flume of the channel, the wind curled the river back on itself. Billowy waves loomed ahead like a range of green hills dusted with snow. Too late, I remembered Leslie Hunter's warning about the final bad stretch of river. It was here.

If I headed straight for shore, the waves would smash the canoe broadside and capsize it, so I had no choice but to steer straight into the green wall of water. The first swell lifted the bow into the air, the horizon tilted, and the canoe slid down the long valley of the wave. Climbing the next crest, I tried to count the oncoming rollers, wondering how they would break, trying to read the one that would finally crash over the bow and swamp the boat.

The sensation was of being propelled forward by a mob, a noise roaring in my ears, unable to stop or turn but only keep pace and stay alert. The shore lay a quarter-mile swim in either direction, but it might as well have been half an ocean away. If I capsized, silt would fill my pockets and boots and I would do the Australian crawl in slow motion to the bottom.

Seagulls careened overhead. Safe on two counts, the gulls pivoted their small white heads to see if I had any fish in the boat or if perhaps I was a fish. At first I felt a perverse thrill as the canoe smacked into a wave and still emerged upright. But knowing that I was almost certainly going to drown soon filled me with rage. At the fisherman for not warning me. At the river for letting me come this far only to drown in plain sight of blue-roofed houses. But mostly at myself for being so careless, so stupid as to ruin a perfectly good life by throwing it away. Shouting into the wind, I prayed the most basic prayer: Save me. Spare my life.

A roller swept the canoe up, then slammed it down into the hollow so hard that the gas tank nearly jumped into my lap. Between one terrible crest and the onslaught of another, I began veering ever so slightly toward the right bank, then straightening the bow before the next roller hit. Slowly, I edged farther from the foamy peaks until the canoe slipped into the sidewash. Then suddenly I was out of it, in calm water, the village shining ahead.

"I saw you in trouble out there," a young fisherman said as I hauled the canoe out of the river. He was bailing the bilge water from his skiff with a plastic pail. "But there was nothing I could do. You have to cross directly in front of the village to avoid those big waves. Lots of people drown where you crossed. It's a real bad spot."

On wobbly legs, I walked up to the beach past the Russian church and up a hill to the little post office to mail the letter I'd written the night before. The mail plane had just arrived, and I had to wait in line while the mail was sorted. But it was a pleasant wait. People joked about the delay and enjoyed the sunshine. Standing there, among strangers, I found myself smiling too and thought: How amazing all of this is—simply being alive! I was elated because my life had been handed back to me when it seemed almost certainly lost. I felt the wind in my hair and noticed that my red baseball cap was gone, the one drunken Lonnie had given me long ago in Circle. It must have blown off in mid-river and was now drifting to rest somewhere in the delta.

THE BEST RAINBOW TROUT FISHING

Ernest Hemingway

THE TORONTO STAR WEEKLY,
AUGUST 28, 1920

Rainbow trout fishing is as different from brook fishing as prize fighting is from boxing. The rainbow is called *Salmo iridescens* by those mysterious people who name the fish we catch and has recently been introduced into Canadian waters. At present the best rainbow trout fishing in the world is in the rapids of the Canadian Soo.

There the rainbow have been taken as large as fourteen pounds from canoes that are guided through the rapids and halted at the pools by Ojibway and Chippewa boatmen. It is a wild and nerve-frazzling sport and the odds are in favor of the big trout who tear off thirty or forty yards of line at a rush and then will sulk at the base of a big rock and refuse to be stirred into action by the pumping of a stout fly rod aided by a fluent monologue of Ojibwayian profanity. Sometimes it takes two hours to land a really big rainbow under those circumstances.

The Soo affords great fishing. But it is a wild nightmare kind of fishing that is second only in strenuousness to angling for tuna off Catalina Island. Most of the trout too take a spinner and refuse a fly and to the 99 per cent pure fly fisherman, there are no one hundred per centers, that is a big drawback.

Of course the rainbow trout of the Soo will take a fly but it is rough handling them in that tremendous volume of water on the light tackle a fly fisherman loves. It is dangerous wading in the spots that can be waded, too, for a mis-step will take the angler over his head in the rapids. A canoe is a necessity to fish the very best water.

Altogether it is a rough, tough, mauling game, lacking in the meditative qualities of the Izaak Walton school of angling. What would make a fitting Valhalla for the good fisherman when he dies would be a regular trout river with plenty of rainbow trout in it jumping crazy for the fly.

There is such a one not forty miles from the Soo called the— well, called the river. It is about as wide as a river should be and a little deeper than a river ought to be and to get the proper picture you want to imagine in rapid succession the following fade-ins:

A high pine covered bluff that rises steep up out of the shadows. A short sand slope down to the river and a quick elbow turn with a little flood wood jammed in the bend and then a pool.

A pool where the moselle colored water sweeps into a dark swirl and expanse that is blue-brown with depth and fifty feet across.

There is the setting.

The action is supplied by two figures that slog into the picture up the trail along the river bank with loads on their backs that would tire a pack horse. These loads are pitched over the heads onto the patch of ferns by the edge of the deep pool. That is incorrect. Really the figures lurch a little forward and the tump line loosens and the pack slumps onto the ground. Men don't pitch loads at the end of an eight mile hike.

One of the figures looks up and notes the bluff is flattened on top and that there is a good place to put a tent. The other is lying on his back and looking straight up in the air. The first reaches over and picks up a grasshopper that is stiff with the fall of the evening dew and tosses him into the pool.

The hopper floats spraddle legged on the water of the pool an instant, an eddy catches him and then there is a yard long flash of flame, and a trout as long as our forearm has shot into the air and the hopper has disappeared.

"Did you see that?" gasped the man who had tossed in the grasshopper.

It was a useless question, for the other, who a moment before would have served as a model for a study entitled "Utter Fatigue," was jerking his fly rod out of the case and holding a leader in his mouth.

We decided on a McGinty and a Royal Coachman for the flies and at the second cast there was a swirl like the explosion of a depth bomb, the line went taut and the rainbow shot two feet out of water. He tore down the pool and the line went out until the core of the reel showed. He jumped and each time he shot into the air we lowered the tip and prayed. Finally he jumped and the line went slack and Jacques reeled in. We thought he was gone and then he jumped right under our faces. He had shot upstream towards us so fast that it looked as though he were off.

When I finally netted him and rushed him up the bank and could feel his huge strength in the tremendous muscular jerks he made when I held him flat against the bank, it was almost dark. He measured twenty-six inches and weighed nine pounds and seven ounces.

That is rainbow trout fishing.

The rainbow takes the fly more willingly than he does bait. The McGinty, a fly that looks like a yellow jacket, is the best. It should be tied on a number eight or ten hook.

The smaller flies get more strikes but are too small to hold the really big fish. The rainbow trout will live in the same streams with brook trout but they are found in different kinds of places. Brook trout will be forced into the shady holes under the bank and where alders hang over the banks, and the rainbow will dominate the clear pools and the fast shallows.

Magazine writers and magazine covers to the contrary the brook or speckled trout does not leap out of water after he has been hooked. Given plenty of line he will fight a deep rushing fight. Of course if you hold the fish too tight he will be forced by the rush of the current to flop on top of the water.

But the rainbow always leaps on a slack or tight line. His leaps are not mere flops, either, but actual jumps out of and parallel with the water of from a foot to five feet. A five-foot jump by any fish sounds improbable, but it is true.

If you don't believe it tie onto one in fast water and try and force him. Maybe if he is a five-pounder he will throw me down and only jump four feet eleven inches.

Fishing the Rhone Canal

Ernest Hemingway

THE TORONTO DAILY STAR,
JUNE 10, 1922

Geneva, Switzerland.—In the afternoon a breeze blows up the Rhone valley from Lake Geneva. Then you fish up-stream with the breeze at your back, the sun on the back of your neck, the tall white mountains on both sides of the green valley and the fly dropping very fine and far off on the surface and under the edge of the banks of the little stream, called the Rhone canal, that is barely a yard wide, and flows swift and still.

Once I caught a trout that way. He must have been surprised at the strange fly and he probably struck from bravado, but the hook set and he jumped into the air twice and zigged nobly back and forth toward every patch of weed at the current bottom until I slid him up the side of the bank.

He was such a fine trout that I had to keep unwrapping him to take a look and finally the day got so hot that I sat under a pine tree on the back of the stream and unwrapped the trout entirely and ate a paper-bag full of cherries I had and read the trout-dampened *Daily Mail*. It was a hot day, but I could look out across the green, slow valley past the line of trees that marked the course of the Rhone and watch a waterfall coming down the brown face of the mountain. The fall came out of a glacier that reached down toward a little town with four grey houses and three grey churches that was planted on the side of the mountain and looked solid, the waterfall, that is, until you saw it was moving. Then it looked cool and flickering, and I wondered who lived in the four houses and who went to the three churches with the sharp stone spires.

Now if you wait until the sun gets down behind the big shoulder of the Savoie Alps where France joins on to Switzerland, the wind changes in the Rhone valley and a cool breeze comes down from the mountains and blows down stream toward the Lake of Geneva. When this breeze comes and the sun is going down, great shadows come out from the mountains, the cows with their manypitched bells begin to be driven along the road, and you fish down the stream.

There are a few flies over the water and every little while some big trout rises and goes "plop" where a tree hangs over the water. You can hear the "plop" and look back of you up the stream and see the circles on the water where the fish jumped. Then is the time to rewrap the trout in Lord Northcliffe's latest speech reported verbatim, the reported imminent demise of the coalition, the thrilling story of the joking earl and the serious widow, and, saving the [Horatio] Bottomley [fraud] case to read on the train going home, put the trout filled paper in your jacket pocket. There are great trout in the Canal du Rhone, and it is when the sun has dropped back of the mountains and you can fish down the stream with the evening breeze that they can be taken.

Fishing slowly down the edge of the stream avoiding the willow trees near the water and the pines that run along the upper edge of what was once the old canal bank with your back cast, you drop the fly on to the water at every likely looking spot. If you are lucky, sooner or later there will be a swirl or a double swirl where the trout strikes and misses and strikes again, and then the old deathless thrill of the plunge of the rod and the irregular plunging, circling, cutting up stream and shooting into the air fight the big trout puts up, no matter what country he may be in. It is a clear stream and there is no excuse for losing him when he is once hooked, so you tire him by working him against the current and then, when he shows a flash of white belly, slide him up against the bank and snake him up with a hand on the leader.

It is a good walk in to Aigle. There are horse chestnut trees along the road with their flowers that look like wax candles and the air is warm from the heat the earth absorbed from the sun. The road is white and dusty, and I thought of Napoleon's grand army, marching along it through the white dust on the way to the St. Bernard pass and Italy. Napoleon's batman may have gotten up at sun up before the camp and sneaked a trout or two out of the Rhone canal for the Little Corporal's breakfast. And before Napoleon, the Romans came along the valley and built this road and some Helvetian in the road gang probably used to sneak away from the camp in the evening to try for a big one in one of the pools under the willows. In the Roman days the trout perhaps weren't as shy.

So I went along the straight white road to Aigle through the evening and wondered about the grand army and the Romans and the Huns that traveled light and fast, and yet must have had time to try the stream along towards daylight, and very soon I was in Aigle, which is a very good place to be. I have never seen the town of Aigle, it straggles up the hillside, but there is a cafe across the station that has a galloping gold horse on top, a great wisteria vine as thick through as a young tree that branches out and shades the porch with hanging bunches of purple flowers that bees go in and out of all day long and that glisten after a rain; green tables with green chairs, and seventeen per cent dark beer. The beer comes foaming out in great glass mugs that hold a quart and cost forty centimes, and the barmaid smiles and asks about your luck.

Trains are always at least two hours apart in Aigle, and those waiting in the station buffet, this cafe with the golden horse and the wisteria hung porch is a station buffet, mind you, wish they would never come.

TROUT FISHING IN EUROPE

Ernest Hemingway

THE TORONTO STAR WEEKLY,
NOVEMBER 17, 1923

Bill Jones went to visit a French financier who lives near Deauville and has a private trout stream. The financier was very fat. His stream was very thin.

"Ah, Monsieur Zshones, I will show you the fishing." The financier purred over the coffee. "You have the trout in Canada, is it not? But here! Here we have the really charming trout fishing of Normandy. I will show you. Rest yourself content. You will see it."

The financier was a very literal man. His idea of showing Bill the fishing was for Bill to watch and the financier to fish. They started out. It was a trying sight.

If undressed and put back on the shelf piece by piece the financier would have stocked a sporting goods store. Placed end to end his collection of flies would have reached from Keokuk, Illinois, to Paris, Ontario. The price of his rod would have made a substantial dent in the interallied debt or served to foment a central American revolution.

The financier flung a pretty poisonous fly, too. At the end of two hours one trout had been caught. The financier was elated. The trout was a beauty, fully five and a half inches long and perfectly proportioned. The only trouble with him was some funny black spots along his sides and belly.

"I don't believe he's healthy," Bill said doubtfully.

"Healthy? You don't think he's healthy? That lovely trout? Why, he's a wonder. Did you not see the terrific fight he made before I netted him?" The financier was enraged. The beautiful trout lay in his large, fat hand.

"But what are those black spots?" Bill asked.

"Those spots? Oh, absolutely nothing. Perhaps worms. Who can say? All of our trout here have them at this season. But do not be afraid of that, Monsieur Zshones. Wait until you taste this beautiful trout for your breakfast!"

It was probably the proximity to Deauville that spoiled the financier's trout stream. Deauville is supposed to be a sort of combination of Fifth Avenue, Atlantic City, and Sodom and Gomorrah. In reality it is a watering place that has become so famous that the really smart people no longer go to it and the others hold a competitive spending contest and mistake each other for duchesses, dukes, prominent pugilists, Greek millionaires and the Dolly sisters.

The real trout fishing of Europe is in Spain, Germany and Switzerland. Spain has probably the best fishing of all in Galicia. But the Germans and the Swiss are right behind.

In Germany the great difficulty is to get permission to fish. All the fishing water is rented by the year to individuals. If you want to fish you have first to get permission of the man who has rented the fishing. Then you go back to the township and get a permission, and then you finally get the permission of the owner of the land.

If you have only two weeks to fish, it will probably take about all of it to get these different permissions. A much easier way is simply to carry a rod with you and fish when you see a good stream. If anyone complains, begin handing out marks. If the complaints keep up, keep handing out marks. If this policy is pursued far enough the complaints will eventually cease and you will be allowed to continue fishing.

If, on the other hand, your supply of marks runs out before the complaints cease you will probably go either to jail or the hospital. It is a good plan, on this account, to have a dollar bill secreted somewhere in your clothes. Produce the dollar bill. It is ten to one your assailant will fall to his knees in an attitude of extreme thanksgiving and on arising break all existing records to the nearest, deepest and wooliest German hand knitted sock, the south German's savings bank.

Following this method of obtaining fishing permits, we fished all through the Black Forest. With rucksacks and flyrods, we hiked across country, sticking to the high ridges and the rolling crests of the hills, sometimes through deep pine timber, sometimes coming out into a clearing and farmyards and again going, for miles, without seeing a soul except occasional wild looking berry pickers. We never knew where we were. But we were never lost because at any time we could cut down from the high country into a valley and know we would hit a stream. Sooner or later every stream flowed into a river and a river meant a town.

At night we stopped in little inns or gasthofs. Some of these were so far from civilization that the innkeepers did not know the mark was rapidly becoming worthless and continued to charge the old German prices. At one place, room and board, in Canadian money, were less than ten cents a day.

One day we started from Triberg and toiled up a long, steadily ascending hill road until we were on top of the high country and could look out at the Black Forest rolling away from us in every direction. Away off across country we could see a range of hills, and we figured that at their base must flow a river. We cut across the high, bare country, dipping down into valleys and walking through woods, cool and dim as a cathedral on the hot August day. Finally we hit the upper end of the valley at the foot of the hills we had seen.

In it flowed a lovely trout stream and there was not a farmhouse in sight. I jointed up the rod, and while Mrs. Hemingway sat under a tree on the hillside and kept watch both ways up the valley, caught four real trout. They averaged about three-quarters of a pound apiece. Then we moved down the valley. The stream broadened out and Herself took the rod while I found a look-out post.

She caught six in about an hour, and two of them I had to come down and net for her. She had hooked a big one, and after he was triumphantly netted we looked up to see an old German in peasant clothes watching us from the road.

"Gut tag," I said.

"Tag," he said. "Have you good fishing?"

"Yes. Very good."

"Good," he said. "It is good to have somebody fishing." And went hiking along the road.

In contrast to him were the farmers in Ober-Prechtal, where we had obtained full fishing permits, who came down and chased us away from the stream with pitchforks because we were Auslanders.

In Switzerland I discovered two valuable things about trout fishing. The first was while I was fishing a stream that parallels the Rhone river and that was swollen and grey with snow water. Flies were useless, and I was fishing with a big gob of worms. A fine, juicy-looking bait. But I wasn't getting any trout or even any strikes.

An old Italian who had a farm up the valley was walking behind me while I fished. As there was nothing doing in a stream I knew from experience was full of trout, it got more and more irritating. Somebody just back of you while you are fishing is as bad as someone looking over your shoulder while you write a letter to your girl. Finally I sat down and waited for the Italian to go away. He sat down, too.

He was an old man, with a face like a leather water bottle.

"Well, Papa, no fish to-day," I said.

"Not for you," he said solemnly.

"Why not for me? For you, maybe?" I said.

"Oh yes," he said, not smiling. "For me trout always. Not for you. You don't know how to fish with worms." And spat into the stream.

This touched a tender spot, a boyhood spent within forty miles of the Soo, hoisting out trout with a cane pole and all the worms the hook would hold.

"You're so old you know everything. You are probably a rich man from your knowledge of fishworms," I said.

This bagged him.

"Give me the rod," he said.

He took it from me, cleaned off the fine wriggling gob of trout food, and selected one medium-sized angleworm from my box. This he threaded a little way on the number 10 hook, and let about three-fourths of the worm wave free.

"Now that's a worm," he said with satisfaction.

He reeled the line up till there was only six feet of leader out and dropped the free swinging worm into a pool where the stream swirled under the bank. There was nothing doing. He pulled it slowly out and dropped it in a little lower down. The tip of the rod twisted.

He lowered it just a trifle. Then it shot down in a jerk, and he struck and horsed out a 15-inch trout and sent him back over his head in a telephone pole swing.

I fell on him while he was still flopping.

The old Italian handed me the rod. "There, young one. That is the way to use a worm. Let him be free to move like a worm. The trout will take the free end and then suck him all in, hook and all. I have fished this stream for twenty years and I know. More than one worm scares the fish. It must be natural."

"Come, use the rod and fish now," I urged him.

"No. No. I only fish at night," he smiled. "It is much too expensive to get a permit."

But by my watching for the river guard while he fished and our using the rod alternately until each caught a fish, we fished all day and caught 18 trout. The old Italian knew all the holes, and only fished where there were big ones. We used a free wriggling worm, and the 18 trout averaged a pound and a half apiece.

He also showed me how to use grubs. Grubs are only good in clear water, but are a deadly bait. You can find them in any rotten tree or sawlog, and the Swiss and Swiss-Italians keep them in grub boxes. Flat pieces of wood bored full of auger holes with a sliding metal top. The grub will live as well in his hole in the wood as in the log and is one of the greatest hot weather baits known. Trout will take a grub when they will take nothing else in the low water days of August.

The Swiss, too, have a wonderful way of cooking trout. They boil them in a liquor made of wine vinegar, bay leaves, and a dash of red pepper. Not too much of any of the ingredients in the boiling water, and cook until the trout turns blue. It preserves the true trout flavor better than almost any way of cooking. The meat stays firm and pink and delicate. Then they serve them with drawn butter. They drink the clear Sion wine when they eat them.

It is not a well-known dish at the hotels. You have to go back in the country to get trout cooked that way. You come up from the stream to a chalet and ask them if they know how to cook blue trout. If they don't you walk on a way. If they do, you sit down on the porch with the goats and the children and wait. Your nose will tell you when the trout are boiling. Then after a little while you will hear a pop. That is the Sion being uncorked. Then the woman of the chalet will come to the door and say, "It is prepared, Monsieur."

Then you can go away and I will do the rest myself.

$\mathcal{M}$IDNIGHT'S $\mathcal{R}$IVERS

Harry Middleton

$\mathscr{E}$ven when I am not in the high country, when the business of getting a living keeps me away from the rush and rhythm of bright mountain rivers and trout, wild country keeps me company. Rivers move freely in mind and memory, rivers that I have known and many that I have only heard of, read about, visited through the books and the stories of other anglers. I have generously stirred all these rivers into my imagination. Even if I never experience any of them first-hand, if I never fish the wild rivers of Alaska or Idaho, New Zealand or Labrador, it is important that such rivers, such wild country, exists. There is solace even in the dream of such places, such water, such fish. There is more than a touch of magic in wildness: just the possibility of it nourishes the spirit.

Many a time have I merely closed my eyes at the end of yet another troublesome day and soaked my bruised psyche in wild water, rivers remembered and rivers imagined. Rivers course through my dreams, rivers cold and fast, rivers well-known and rivers nameless, rivers that seem like ribbons of blue water twisting through wide valleys, narrow rivers folded in layers of darkening shadows, rivers that have eroded down deep into a mountain's belly, sculpted the land, peeled back the planet's history exposing the texture of time itself. Rivers and sunlight, mountains and fish: they are always there, rising up out of exhaustion, a sudden rush of sound and motion, a Wagnerian assault of light and shadow, hissing water, pounding rapids, chilly mountain winds easing inexorably into a requiem of distant rapids, a fish's silent rise, the splash of blue-green water over the backs of wet black stones.

These dreams of rivers and wild river country, of trout, often take me by surprise, producing mysterious, comic ballets of clonic spasms, a puppetry of haphazard muscular shakes and shivers as sleep takes hold, as dreams rise, pillaging memory, fashioning worlds not of fact but of desire.

More and more these days my dreams are of rivers, of wild water, water that carries me away.

Last night there was such a dream, a dream of a bright river, a river boiling with trout.

Before last night I had not dreamed of rivers and mountains for a long time. Of late, there seems to be time for little save work, the hamster wheel of responsibility and obligation. I lost my job a year ago. Not an uncommon thing in America these days. It happens to more than two thousand Americans each day, every day. I used to work for Southern Progress Corporation, which is a wholly owned subsidiary of the Time-Warner Corporation. Southern Progress is a publisher of regional magazines. Its most famous magazine is *Southern Living*, which has been touted as the world's most successful regional magazine. Its readers adore it because each month the magazine leads them on a wonderful journey through fairyland—through a South, not as it was or as it is, but as they imagine it to be, a place of perpetual sunshine and happiness, a place of endless prosperity and good times, a never-never land of beauty and harmony, a land free of violence and prejudice, hatred and ignorance, poverty and suicide, a land that generates nothing but opportunity, success, great recipes, bountiful gardens, luxurious homes, bright and shiny people caught in the generous embrace of success and good news. Few magazines can whip up an image as can *Southern Living*.

I polished the image as hard as anyone. Indeed, my friend, the CEO of Southern Progress, told me I was the best polisher he had. My problem was that I kept finding cracks in the image. I raised my voice, said that there was trouble in fairyland, that the South, since it was full of human beings, was heir to all kinds of human woes, things that recipes and new wallpaper couldn't fix, despair and heartache that a window full of geraniums and a weekend at Disneyland could not mend. I kept dragging in bad news, a South marked by the tragedy and comedy of the human condition. On the morning of the day that I lost my job, I was in my friend the CEO's office giving him a fly-fishing lesson. That afternoon he told me to pack up and get out, thus adding further evidence to my theory that anyone who takes up the fly-fishing life is asking for trouble and is certain to get it. My friend the CEO smiled and laughed as he told me I was through, told me it was nothing personal and loaded me down with compliments. He kept the little instruction fly rod I had made for him.

My friend the CEO did what he thought was best for Southern Progress. Too, I believe my friend the CEO really believed I would be able to walk out the door and find another job. Recession and unemployment and hard times are alien notions to him. After all, the company's magazines assure him that prosperity is everywhere, that it is as deep and wide and plentiful as Southern sunshine.

Outside my friend the CEO's door, beyond the merry, cheerful borders of fairyland, life is even more miserable and ridiculous than usual. There is little work. Even in the best of times, writers and editors are never in high demand. These days, however, there is no demand at all. The value of writers and editors has shrunk to nearly zero. This is what a magazine publisher in New York City recently told me: "Last week I could buy writers and editors at a dime a dozen. This week I can buy a legion of them for a box of donuts and a pot of lukewarm coffee."

My job went. My obligations, however, stayed. Because I am a writer and an editor, I have few marketable skills and talents. I finally got lucky, though, and found work shelving groceries at the supermarket down the mountain. Meanwhile, as the country's economy continued to sour, fall apart, so did mine. I sold my canoes, my shotguns, nearly all my camping gear. Not enough. I added another job repairing shoes, replacing worn-out soles, sold my books, emptied my savings, gave up trying to pay for health insurance. Not enough. I got another job riding the back of county garbage truck no. 2, sold whatever was left.

Everything but three fly rods and two reels, the old blue sleeping bag, my beat-up backpack. My days begin at eight in the morning and end after midnight. Because I have not been able to shake my awful addiction to writing, I write from midnight until four in the morning.

From four until seven I sleep. Sometimes I dream.

When dreams come, as they did last night, they are of the high country and mountain rivers and wild trout.

Last night's river was nameless: only a wide bend, a shoal of fast water, a series of dark pools giving way downstream to rapids. There was warm sunlight coming in wide veins off the surface of the river. I could feel it against my arms and neck, my face. A cool wind blew among oaks and hickories. The river moved through a pinched-in mountain canyon dominated by dark, hulking, mineral-stained bluffs. The canyon's stone walls seemed to undulate with moving shadows. Above and below the dark pools the river was silver, marked by flashes and bursts of sunlight.

I was there, asleep in the blue sleeping bag along the bank, near the wide bend where the river was shallow and hissed as it moved over the shoal of dark stones. I was soaked in warm sunlight, dreaming a dream within a dream. And the bright waters pressed downstream, time's silver, coiled, two-headed arrow, life's medium, motion given depth and character and fat with indifferent fish hanging in the currents, life with jaws open and belly empty.

The dream emptied me out of the blue sleeping bag, demanded participation as well as observation. I could feel the pull of the river against my thighs, the sweet invitation to let go, the urgent appeal to give in, let the river wash me away, carry me downstream into undiscovered country—that distant margin where there was no plain distinction between land and water, sunlight and shadow, form, time, and motion.

One thing about my dreams of rivers—I never fall. I worked the water, walking slowly upstream, moving effortlessly along the edges of the dark pools, into the fast, shallow water, sunlight glinting off the green fly rod's ferrules. For some reason I was barefoot: the moss-backed stones felt as though they were encased in some sort of amniotic membrane. I have no explanation for why I was barefoot in the icy water except that there is an edged honesty to dreams: they are never less ridiculous than the life that goes on and on above the dream line.

This is not to say that dreams cannot refashion life, usually for the better. In last night's dream my casts were heartbreakingly perfect, my presentation uncorrupted allurement. There was wind, but no wind knots; tricky current, but no difficulty with drag; there were magical hatches, but no pressure to match them. As I recall, I spent the entire dream fishing a single Griffith's Gnat. Its appeal never frayed. In short, there was never, as there is in an angler's waking hours, any conscious thinking about fishing, only fishing itself: emotions, feelings, sensations, instinct, rather than technique and theory. The fishing was close, the trout easily released. Each fish seemed to hold in the translucent water for a long moment before vanishing, dissolving back into water and light, a light that flashed with the purity and intensity of summer lightning.

Hawks rose on warm winds. From the thick woods, where the shadows were cold and black, came a thrush's plaintive song. There were dimples of broken water on the pool above me. Rings of dark water moving in ever-widening circles until they broke softly against the riverbank. Fish moving. Rainbow trout on the river. Salmon pounding the water. Cutthroat wrinkling through the middle depths. Suspicious, heavy-bodied, rapacious, slack-jawed brown trout on the bottom waiting for the light's decline, night's cloak of anonymity. Brook trout thrashing at the surface so that the pools looked like cauldrons not of boiling water but of roiling wild fish.

The dream and river were one, inexorably joined, so that they seemed to go on and on, even after both spit me out before dawn, cast me into that slow waking that is like a diver with the bends trying to recover from a binge of having gone too fast, too far, too deep, of not wanting the drunk to end, not wanting to resurface at all.

Each night, before pushing away from the typewriter, falling into bed, I open the window at the far end of the room. The cold air that gathers at the edge of morning is a good alarm clock. I wake in the room's dull cold light, the dream still glowing in my head, a hedge against hard times, whatever the day brings. I can feel myself smiling at my good fortune, the good fortune of having wisely invested so much time in wild country, so many, many years in the pursuit of trout and the bright, fast rivers they live in, demand, the good fortune of filling my memories and imagination with wildness, memories that sustain me, good times or bad, that will nourish me whether or not I ever fish again, will illuminate me whether I ever again feel the press of wild country or am left only with its mark on my skin, its legacy in my blood, its spirit moving like bright wild rivers through my mind.

FROM THE JOURNALS OF THE LEWIS & CLARK EXPEDITION

Meriwether Lewis

June 13th, 1805

This morning we set out about sunrise after taking breakfast off our venison and fish. We again ascended the hills of the river and gained the level country. Fearing that the river bore to the south, and that I might pass the Falls if they existed between this and the snowy mountains, I altered my course nearly to the south and proceeded through the plain. I sent Fields on my right and Drouilliard and Gibson on my left, with orders to kill some meat and join me at the river, where I should halt for dinner.

I had proceeded on this course about two miles with Goodrich at some distance behind me, when my ears were saluted with the agreeable sound of a fall of water, and advancing a little further, I saw the spray rise above the plain like a column of smoke, which would frequently disappear again in an instant, caused, I presume, by the wind which blew pretty hard from the S.W. I did not, however, lose my direction to this point, which soon began to make a roaring too tremendous to be mistaken for any cause short of the Great Falls of the Missouri. Here I arrived about 12 o'clock, having traveled, by estimate, about 15 miles. I hurried down the hill, which was about 200 feet high and difficult of access, to gaze on this sublimely grand spectacle.

I took my position on the top of some rocks about 20 feet high opposite the center of the Falls. This chain of rocks appears once to have formed a part of those over which the waters tumbled, but in the course of time has been separated from it to the distance of 150 yards, lying parallel to it, and an abutment against which the water, after falling over the precipice, beats with great fury. This barrier extends on the right to the perpendicular cliff which forms that border of the river, but to the distance of 120 yards next to the cliff it is but a few feet above the level of the water, and here the water in very high tides appears to pass in a channel of 40 yards next to the higher part of the ledge of rocks. On the left, it extends within 80 or 90 yards of the larboard cliff, which is also perpendicular. Between this abrupt extremity of the ledge of rocks and the perpendicular bluff, the whole body of water passes with incredible swiftness.

Immediately at the cascade, the river is about 300 yards wide. About 90 or 100 yards of this, next the larboard bluff, is a smooth even sheet of water falling over a precipice of at least 80 feet; the remaining part, about 200 yards wide, on my right, forms the grandest sight I ever beheld. The height of the fall is the same as the other, but the irregular and somewhat projecting rocks below receive the water in its passage down, and break it into a perfect white foam which assumes a thousand forms in a moment, sometimes flying up in jets of sparkling foam to the height of fifteen or twenty feet, which are scarcely formed before large rolling bodies of the same beaten and foaming water are thrown over and conceal them. In short, the rocks seem to be most happily fixed to present a sheet of the whitest beaten froth for 200 yards in length and about 80 feet perpendicular.

The water, after descending, strikes against the abutment before mentioned, or that on which I stand, and seems to reverberate, and being met by the more impetuous current, they roll and swell into half-formed billows of great height which rise and again disappear in an instant. The abutment of rock defends a handsome little bottom of about three acres which is diversified and agreeably shaded with some cottonwood trees.

In the lower extremity of the bottom there is a very thick grove of the same kind of trees which are small. In this wood, there are several Indian lodges formed of sticks. A few small cedar grow near the ledge of rocks where I rest. Below the point of these rocks, at a small distance, the river is divided by a large rock which rises several feet above the water, and extends downward with the stream for about 20 yards. About a mile before the water arrives at the pitch, it descends very rapidly, and is confined on the larboard side by a perpendicular cliff of about 100 feet. On the starboard side it is also perpendicular for about three hundred yards above the pitch, where it is then broken by the discharge of a small ravine, down which the buffalo have a large beaten road to the water, for it is but in very few places that these animals can obtain water near this place, owing to the steep and inaccessible banks. I see several skeletons of the buffalo lying in the edge of the water near the starboard bluff which I presume have been swept down by the current and precipitated over this tremendous fall.

About 300 yards below me, there is another abutment of solid rock with a perpendicular face and about 60 feet high, which projects from the starboard side at right angles to the distance of 134 yards, and terminates the lower part nearly of the bottom before mentioned, there being a passage around the end of this abutment, between it and the river, of about 20 yards. Here the river again assumes its usual width, soon spreading to near 300 yards but still continuing its rapidity. From the reflection of the sun on the spray or mist which arises from these Falls, there is a beautiful rainbow produced which adds not a little to the beauty of this majestically grand scenery.

After writing this imperfect description, I again viewed the Falls, and was so much disgusted with the imperfect idea which it conveyed of the scene, that I determined to draw my pen across it and begin again; but then reflected that I could not perhaps succeed better than penning the first impressions of the mind. I wished for the pencil of Salvator Rosa, a Titian, or the pen of [James] Thomson, that I might be enabled to give to the enlightened world some just idea of this truly magnificent and sublimely grand object which has, from the commencement of time, been concealed from the view of civilized man. But this was fruitless and vain. I most sincerely regretted that I had not brought a camera obscura with me, by the assistance of which even I could have hoped to have done better, but alas, this was also out of my reach.

I therefore, with the assistance of my pen only, endeavored to trace some of the stronger features of this scene by the assistance of which, and my recollection aided by some able pencil, I hope still to give to the world some faint idea of an object which at this moment fills me with such pleasure and astonishment; and which of its kind, I will venture to assert, is second to but one in the known world.

I retired to the shade of a tree, where I determined to fix my camp for the present, and dispatch a man in the morning to inform Captain Clark and the party of my success in finding the Falls, and settle in their minds all further doubts as to the Missouri. The hunters now arrived, loaded with excellent buffalo meat, and informed me that they had killed three very fat [buffalo] cows about ¾ of a mile from hence. I directed them, after they had refreshed themselves, to go back and butcher them and bring another load of meat each to our camp, determining to employ those who remained with me in drying meat for the party against their arrival. In about two hours, or at 4 o'clock P.M., they set out on this duty, and I walked down the river about three miles to discover, if possible, some place to which the canoes might arrive, or at which they might be drawn on shore in order to be taken by land above the falls, but returned without effecting either of these objectives.

The river was one continued scene of rapids and cascades, which I readily perceived could not be encountered with our canoes, and the cliffs still retained their perpendicular structure, and were from 150 to 200 feet high. In short, the river appears here to have worn a channel in the process of time through a solid rock.

On my return, I found the party at camp. They had butchered the buffalo and brought in some more meat, as I had directed. Goodrich had caught half a dozen very fine trout and a number of both species of the white fish. These trout (caught in the Falls) are from sixteen to twenty-three inches in length, precisely resemble our mountain or speckled trout in form and the position of their fins, but the specks on these are of a deep black instead of the red or gold color of those common to the U. States. These are furnished long sharp teeth on the palate and tongue, and have generally a small dash of red on each side behind the front ventral fins. The flesh is of a pale yellowish red or, when in good order, of a rose red.

I am induced to believe that the brown, the white, and the grizzly bear of this country are the same species, only differing in color from age or more probably from the same natural cause that many other animals of the same family differ in color. One of those which we killed yesterday was of a cream-colored white, while the other in company with it was of the common bay or reddish brown, which seems to be the most usual color of them. The white one appeared from its talons and teeth to be the youngest; it was smaller than the other, and although a monstrous beast, we supposed that it had not yet attained its growth, and that it was a little upwards of two years old. The young cubs which we have killed have always been of a brownish-white, but none of them as white as that we killed yesterday. One other that we killed some time since had a white stripe or list of about eleven inches wide entirely around his body just behind the shoulders, and was much darker than these bear usually are.

My fare is really sumptuous this evening: Buffalo's humps, tongue, and marrowbones, fine trout, parched meat, pepper and salt, and a good appetite. The last is not considered the least of the luxuries.

$\mathscr{T}$HE $\mathscr{W}$ILLAMETTE

Kathleen Dean Moore

$\mathscr{I}$ *wanted my daughter to lie in the tent, pressed between her brother and her father, breathing the air that flows from the Willamette River at night, dense with the smell of wet willows and river algae. I wanted her to inhale the smoke of a driftwood fire in air too thick to carry any sound but the rushing of the river and the croak of a heron, startled to find itself so far from home. I wanted the chemical smell of the tent to mix with the breath of warm wet wool and flood through her mind, until the river ran in her veins and she could not help but come home again. That is why, on the weekend before my daughter left for Greece, I made sure that the family went river-camping on the Willamette.*

My daughter comes from a long line of people with strong homing instincts. My daughter's grandmother, my mother, was born in a river town, Thornaby-on-Tees, Yorkshire, in a brick house three blocks from the North Sea. Although she breathed the seaweed wind, she never walked on the beach below the limestone cliff at the end of her street. Warning signs and long coils of barbed wire protected the homeland against German invasion and kept my mother away from the sea.

Her father was one of the few men left at home in England during World War One. He was a ships' model builder who carved little wooden warships, patterns for the shipyards at Sunderland. Sometimes he brought his work home. My mother's strongest memory of England was the fragrance of fresh cedar curling under his plane and falling in long coils on the kitchen table. As he worked the wood, my grandfather sang Scottish folk songs—*You take the high road and I'll take the low road*—and the Navy hymn, *for those who perish on the sea*.

One night, my grandfather took my mother into the city to see where the zeppelins had firebombed the streetcar barns. Under cover of darkness, the zeppelins had moved slowly, silently, upriver to the shipyards, following the lights of the ships on the Tees. They dropped their bombs, turned, and ran back to the sea. After that, blackout was imposed, and the zeppelins, when they returned, followed moonlight reflected on the river. My mother thought how beautiful the river must have appeared to the German airmen, its surface ablaze in reflected light from exploding buildings, and how anxious they must have been to get back home.

After the war, the shipyards shut down and my grandfather—unemployed and uneasy—began to think about emigrating. He argued for America because it was the only country that printed "In God We Trust" on its money. My grandmother refused to leave home unless she could come back to Thornaby-on-Tees every four years for the rest of her life. When my grandfather made her that promise, she gave away everything that wouldn't fit in three tea chests and dressed her children in their best clothes for the trip to America. Their destination was Cleveland, where an uncle had an extra room.

From the day they arrived, the family saved everything they had for four years and then, every four years, spent everything they had saved to go back home. They traveled on the Cunard Line, second class. I have the picture postcards they sent back to America: yellowing photographs of oversized ships lined with tiny people wearing hats and waving. I also have ten teacups, one for every trip. They are decorated with painted ivy or pictures of the Queen. One says, *there'll always be an England*.

When I was first married, we lived in an apartment above a delicatessen in Cleveland. The apartment had a balcony overlooking a major arterial. Evenings, we sat on the balcony in lawn chairs and watched the city life flow out of Cleveland in heavy white cars. One night we drove into the city to see the oil slicks burning on the Cuyahoga River. We couldn't get close enough through the brickyards and factory gates to see the river. But we could see thick black clouds trapped in the rivercourse, glowing red underneath.

We began to think about leaving Cleveland. My husband argued for Oregon, because it had clean, cold rivers. So we moved to the

Willamette Valley and made our home here. But I returned to Cleveland every year at Christmastime.

I have a picture in my memory of the drive through darkness to the Portland airport, with white fog flowing down the Willamette River as if even the air ran to the sea. I have a picture of the airport in early morning darkness. People are crowded together with their coats on, some sleeping curled up in chairs, their belongings in piles beside them. Everyone is solicitous, subdued, uneasy, as I imagine people to have been in the harshly-lit tunnels under London during the War.

Fewer and fewer things drew me back to Cleveland each year, but still I went. At first there was the house I grew up in, and my mother and father and my two sisters, and the carols we always sang after supper. We sang slowly, in four-part harmony—deep, rich, thick Methodist chords. My mother chose the songs and gave us the pitch. *Winds through the Olive Trees, four verses.* And there were the English family foods—roast beef and Yorkshire pudding and decorated cookies between layers of wax paper in the roasting pan. We always took a picnic to the park in the snow, turning the picnic table on its side to shelter us from the wind coming off the lake. And always, there was the same joke about how the house was so full of people that we would have to cut off the back half of the Christmas tree and wedge it up against the wall.

But the house dropped out of the picture when my mother and father moved to a smaller place. My sisters got married and moved to bright new houses in the suburbs near Pittsburgh and Baltimore. Then my mother died. We couldn't pitch the songs. My father got sick. And so the rituals dropped away one by one, until there was nothing left at home except my father and the joke about half a Christmas tree. Finally, it seemed that the only reason to go home for Christmas was that someone needed to be there to hear my father tell the joke.

I know a biologist who studies the homing instinct in garter snakes. He says that garter snakes spend the winters clustered together in rock piles underground, ancestral wintering dens that may have been home to the snakes for a thousand years. In the spring, all the snakes crawl out and travel, maybe half a mile. Each one establishes a home base for the summer, a pile of leaves or the space under a fallen log. They travel out each day, but each night they make their way back home along the same trails. When biologists draw a snake's wanderings on a map of the land, the lines are thick, drawn back and forth, back and forth, like rays extending out from a home base. In the fall, the adults travel back to spend the winter with their relatives in their ancient family home.

Before they return to the den, the females give birth to a pile of lithe little snakes and then move on, leaving the babies to fend for themselves. The babies spend the winter, who knows where. But the next fall, the yearlings travel back unerringly to their ancestral home—a place they have never been. As they go home, they will pass over other dens that would be perfectly good places to spend the winter, not stopping until they get to the den that shelters their own elderly aunts and distant relations.

Scientists know so much about homing in animals: Bees orient to polarized light. Salamanders steer by lines of geomagnetic force. Garter snakes follow scent. Pigeons use the position of the sun. Songbirds follow the stars. They are all drawn to a place proved to be safe by the hard, undeniable fact of their own existence.

But who has studied the essential issue: What will draw our own children back home?

By the time we got all our camping gear stowed away in the driftboat, it was late afternoon. In the shadows of the riverside cottonwoods, the air was cold and sharp. So we drifted along the eastern bank of the river, glad for the warmth of the low light. We pulled up onto the gravel beach of an island thick with willows and set up the tent on a pocket of sand.

After supper, my daughter and I walked down the shore. We wore high black rubber boots and walked sometimes in, sometimes out of the water, the round rocks grinding and rolling under our feet. Far ahead, a beaver slapped its tail against the river. We talked quietly—about her visa, about loneliness, about how the skyline of the distant coast range seemed to glow in the dark.

Fog thickened the darkness, so even though it wasn't late, we turned back toward our supper fire. We didn't talk much on the way back, but we sang like we often do along the edge of a river, where the density of the air and the rush of the river make the music rich and satisfying. We sang the Irish Blessing—my daughter sang the soprano part—and we did fine, the river singing the bass line, the rocks crunching under our boots, until we got to the last blessing: May the rain fall softly on your fields. Then I couldn't do it any more. I sent my daughter back to the fire alone. I lay face down on the round rocks and cried until the steam from my lungs steeped down

*into the dried mud and algae, and the hot breath of the river rose steaming
and sweet around my face.*

Maybe the homing instinct is driven by traditions: hanging Christmas
stockings each year on nails pushed into the same little holes in the
mantel. Maybe it is driven by smells or tastes or sounds. But maybe
the homing instinct is driven only by fear. On the road, at dusk and
away from home, the foreboding, the oppression of undefined space,
can be unbearable. Pioneers knew this dread; they called it *Seeing the
elephant*. Starting out, the wide open spaces were glorious—the op-
portunities, the promise, the prairie, all fused with light streaming
down from towering clouds. Then suddenly the clouds became an elephant, a mastodon, and the openness turned ominous. The silence
trumpeted and the clouds stampeded. Dread blackened the edges of
the pioneers' vision. They saw the elephant and turned their wagons
around, hurrying through the dusty ruts back to St. Louis. They had
to go back. They had to get home.

The French existentialists knew that feeling: *la nausée*, existen-
tial dread. The pioneers—they, we—walk out into a world we think
makes sense. We think we understand what things are and how they
are related. We feel at home in the world. Suddenly, without a warning, the meaning breaks off the surface, and the truth about the world
is revealed: Nothing is essentially anything. The prairie gapes open—
"flabby, disorganized mass without meaning," Sartre said. Pioneers can
create meaning by their decisions, but those decisions will be baseless,
arbitrary, floating.

This discovery comes with a lurch, thick in your stomach, like
the feeling you get when you miss a step on the stairs. When the feeling comes over you, you have to go home, knowing that home doesn't
exist—not really, except as you have given meaning to a place by your
own decisions and memories.

*Robins singing woke me up in the morning, a whole flock of robins at
the edge of the Willamette. Each robin was turned full into the sun. I
climbed out of the tent and sat cross-legged on the gravel, my face turned
toward the warmth, my eyes closed, bathed in pink light. Soon my daughter, in long underwear and rubber boots, ducked out of the tent and walked
into the river to wash her face. She scooped up a pot of river water and carried it to the kitchen log to boil for tea. Crossing to the campbox, she rum-
maged around inside until she found matches, scratched a match against a*

stone, lit the stove, and set the teapot on the burner. Then she sat on the broad log in a wash of sunlight, pulling her knees up to her chest and tilting her face toward the light. Her hair, in the sun, was as yellow as last winter's ash leaves in windrows on the beach.

Scientists say that a wasp can leave its hole in the ground, fly from fruit to fruit, zigging and zagging half the day, and then fly straight home. A biologist once moved the three rocks that framed a wasp's hole and arranged them in the exact same pattern, but in a different place. The wasp landed between the rocks, right where its hole should have been, and wandered around, stupefied.

My three rocks are the Willamette River. Whenever I walked out of the airport, coming home from a visit to my father's house, I could smell the river, sprayed through sprinklers watering the lawn by the parking lot. The willow-touched water would wash away the fumes of stale coffee and jet fuel and flood me with relief. This is what I want for my daughter.

$\mathscr{S}$ACHEM $\mathscr{R}$IVER

Roderick Haig-Brown

$\mathscr{I}$ have told this story before in different ways, but it is the best fishing story I know and it touches one of the loveliest rivers I know.

In the summer of 1927 I went up to the northern end of Vancouver Island to work for the Wood and English Logging Company on Nimpkish Lake. I had heard, before I went, that the Nimpkish River had a run of tyee salmon probably at least the equal of the Campbell River run, and I made up my mind that I was going to get some fishing out of it. In 1927 I was away at the head of the lake all through September and missed the run, but in 1928 I was ready for it, with a brand-new Murdoch spinning rod, a good line and plenty of spoons that were supposed to be of the right kind.

My knowledge of the fishing was wretchedly slight. The tyees ran in September—that seemed fairly definite. Someone, a few years earlier, had caught a sixty-seven-pounder by trolling with a hand line inside the river. But, so the boys in camp told me, it was the height of folly to expect to catch such fish on rod and line: in the first place, no such fancy gear could possibly deceive them into taking hold; and if by some obscure chance an especially foolish fish were to impale itself on the hook, no possible good could come of it; rod, reel, line and everything else would be irreparably smashed or else taken right away in the first run.

Fishing for trout in the river and waiting for ducks on the tide flats at the mouth of the river during the previous year, I had learned a little about the water; but I didn't really know where to start in. Not

243

too far above tidewater, I thought; perhaps the first pool above. And that was where I went with my new rod and a big bright spoon on the last Sunday of August.

The pool I had chosen was very big, deep and fairly slow between high, steep banks. I found it difficult to fish and discouraging because I could not wade to cover it properly, and no fish showed to convince me that I was not wasting my time. As a matter of fact, I doubted if any were yet in the river, and my main purpose in coming down had been to size up the water before the fish came in rather than to catch fish. So in a little while I left the big pool and followed the river on down.

I came almost at once to a much more promising pool, one at the head of tidewater which I later named Lansdowne Pool. It was separated from the other pool by a wooded island and a short rapid. The main body of the river flowed on the east side of the island, under the bank that I was following, and stretching back from the pool on this side were several acres of cleared land with a primrose-yellow farmhouse set in a small orchard in the middle of them—something altogether unique in the Nimpkish watershed, but I knew the farm belonged to the Lansdowne family and I had met the two sons once or twice when I had been trout fishing up the river. I tried a few casts in the pool, but there was a deep eddy under my bank which made it difficult to reach the water properly, and I strongly suspected that the best lying place in the pool was under the steep rock bank on the far side. So once again, and very fortunately, I told myself, I was exploring rather than fishing and went on my way.

I had great hopes of the estuary of the river. I knew that at Campbell River the tyees were caught only in salt water and that, generally speaking, Pacific salmon were supposed to be impossible to catch once they had left salt water, though I knew also, from Cobb's *Pacific Salmon Fisheries*, that they were caught by anglers in the Willamette River. I supposed vaguely that my best hope might be to find some tidal pool where the fish rested before committing themselves to fresh water. On this Sunday of exploration the tide was fairly well in over the flats, and I could not follow the river channel as closely as I had hoped. But I could see that there was a short and narrow pool under the far bank some two hundred yards below Lansdowne Pool and a larger pool under a high-cut bank of blue clay a hundred yards down from that. Opposite this Blue Clay Pool was a small grassy islet, Sachem Island, then a shallow channel about forty yards wide, then a much more considerable island, the Indian Island, with several Indian smokehouses standing on it, separated from the bank I was following by a deep backwater.

A little below the Indian Island I met Ed Lansdowne. He was sixteen years old then and looked younger, dressed in a shirt and a pair of blue shorts, without shoes or stockings, his hair a tight cap of red curls above his sunburned face. I liked what I had seen of Ed up the river and I felt sure at once that he would prove a valuable con-spirator in this salmon-fishing project. He was not talkative or much given to asking questions, but the new rod caught his admiring eye and I told him what I was looking for. He was doubtful, but not discouraging.

"There was a policeman used to come over from the Bay and troll in the river with a hand line. He caught a few. Pete and some other guys come once in a while, but they fish outside."

He pointed downstream to where the Fishing Island, a low tri-angular island with more fishing shacks and net racks, split the tide and held the river in its channel.

"Beyond the Fishing Island—between there and Green Island— you can see the fish finning out there when the run's in. You see them all the way up the river too, past Sachem Island and as far up as our place."

"Do they seem to lie much in the pool opposite your place?" I asked.

"Sure, they lie there pretty good. We see them jumping and rolling—you can hear them all night sometimes. But, I don't think there's any in yet this year." He grinned. "Gee, I'd sure like to see you get one."

I told him I wanted to fish the pool the next Sunday. Did he think the fish would be in and could he get hold of a boat from some-where? He thought that the fish would surely be in and he knew of a boat he could probably get. So we made it a date.

I was down at the side of the pool well ahead of the appointed time, in spite of a five-mile walk from camp, and Ed was soon with me. He had not been able to get a boat, but he had a raft, a heavy thing of logs with planks spiked across them, which would float when the tide came in and which he thought we could maneuver enough to cover at least some of the good water. The fish were in all right. A big one jumped soon after I arrived, and others jumped at intervals all through the morning while we waited for the tide. From time to time

I waded out and tried to cast to where they were lying, but I had not yet learned to handle the big six-inch spoon very well and I knew I wasn't reaching them. So at last I sat down to wait with Ed and plan what we would do when the raft floated. Every five or ten minutes a fish jumped and the splash echoed back from the timbered hill opposite. They were huge fish, cleaner and brighter than I had dared hope, though some were bronze rather than silver; I tried to guess weights—thirty, I would say, forty-five. Then a great pig of a fish would come over in a short-bodied arc, and I would realize that if the last one had been forty-five this one must be seventy at least. And perhaps he was; the Nimpkish had yielded her ninety-pounders to the nets.

The tide came in at last, the raft floated and we pushed off. The surface of the pool was still and dark now, with only an easy current through it and a little ripple close under the foot of the rapids, which still ran white and strong and broken against the big boulders. I fished carefully and thoroughly and expectantly, working the big spoon very deep and slow; we covered the whole pool several times, but nothing touched the spoon. It wasn't easy to handle the heavy raft with only a paddle and pole over the deep water, but Ed did really well with it and worked at least as hard and enthusiastically as I did for a long while. We went up behind the island and found a deep still backwater fed by only a light riffle of water from the Canyon Pool, and once or twice we saw the shadows of big fish moving or lying near bottom. Ed, whose brother was a commercial troller, began to wonder if my spoon was working just right, and knowing little of how a spoon should work, I began to feel doubtful myself. Then Ed suggested that we might do better when the tide started to ebb, so we ran the raft back to the beach and waited. Ed went up to the house and came back with huckleberry wine and sandwiches.

"Do you really think we've got a chance to catch something?" he asked.

"Sure," I said, and I was sure. "The hand trollers catch fish, don't they? There's no difference in what we're doing."

"They mostly catch them out in the salt chuck."

"I know that. But there's no reason a fish should change so much just for coming up a mile or so on the tide. And anyway, they fish mostly in the salt chuck. You said so yourself."

The tide began to ebb at last, and we started to fish again. This time we took the raft straight across to the low rock face of the far bank and held there, for it seemed that we might have disturbed the pool too much by moving about in our first attempts. I worked the spoon through the water every way I knew, fast and slow, deep and shallow, steadily and in jerks, casting upstream and across and down. Still nothing took. I could see that Ed was getting a little restless and told him about a fisherman's faith in the last cast of the day—if you make enough of them, saying each time "just one more," you're sure to get something.

"You still think there's a chance?" Ed asked. "I don't."

"There's always a chance," I said. "I'm going to try it right through to dark. You stay with me, and if we get a fish, I'll send you up a Hardy trout rod from town next week."

So we kept fishing. I really had plenty of hope left in me. After all, I had fished the Frome with Greenhill every day for a solid week to catch my first Atlantic salmon and I knew something of how dour and moody nonfeeding fish can be. The tide was almost out of the pool now, and a hand troller came up, rowing right through the middle of it. That, I thought, wouldn't help any. I made a cast at a long angle upstream and fished it back to me deep down. I noticed that the sun was gone behind the hill and most of the pool was in shadow. Then the spoon came against something solid and heavy. I struck hard; the line ran out for fifteen or twenty yards, then went slack.

"That was it," I said. "But we'll get another."

We did. Two or three casts later I felt the spoon stop, brought the rod up and was into a fish that ran with wild strength straight up toward the rapids. I checked him as hard as I dared, because I had only sixty or seventy yards of line on the reel. There were about a dozen turns left on the reel when he came out in a beautiful jump not ten feet from the stern of the hand troller's boat.

"Let's get across," I said, "and finish him from the bank. He'll tangle in that guy's line if we don't."

Ed picked up the paddle and drove the raft across. I jumped overboard in three or four feet of water with the fish still on. But we had him. He ran again, several times, almost as strongly as the first time. Then he was swirling and fighting about twenty feet away, unable to tear loose from the strain I held on him but still too strong to give up. I walked back onto dry land, drawing him in, then went forward again into the water, shortening line. He came close, and I reached for his tail, gripped it and carried him ashore. He was a perfect fish, silver and clean, certainly a spring salmon, but he was hooked just ahead of the dorsal fin and weighed only twenty-one pounds.

"What do you think happened?" Ed asked. "Do you think we just snagged him?"

"No," I said. "He came at it; I'm sure of that. We can't prove it though—not till we get another one."

"Tonight?"

"No, you've earned that trout rod now. Next Sunday."

Ed had a boat the next Sunday. We fished the pool for a while without touching anything, then went down the river to see what we could find. I wanted a thirty-pounder, to meet the British Columbia angler's traditional but arbitrary distinction between tyee and spring salmon, and I wanted him hooked fairly and squarely in the mouth, so that I'd have an answer for the boys in camp who still insisted that there was nothing new about snagging salmon—anyone could do that.

There was some tide in and the water was quite smooth. Below Sachem Island we saw the little arrowhead ripples of a school of fish swimming up the river, and I cast across them from the boat. A big fish turned and had the spoon. I had spliced an extra length of backing onto my line since the previous Sunday, but he had all the old line and backing and a good part of the new out before I could bring him up to break the surface. He didn't exactly jump when he did come up, but for twenty or thirty seconds he stayed right at the surface and thrashed the water white. Suddenly he turned and came hard back for the boat, getting himself some slack line, but I soon picked that up, and he seemed well hooked. For about twenty minutes he fought this way, running close to the surface, turning when I put heavy pressure on him, running again and jumping occasionally. He made one more short run, which I held easily, then I told Ed to head in for the island, where we could tail him—we still had no gaff. Something made him run again, strongly and fiercely for forty or fifty yards. That seemed to finish him. He lay on the surface with little movement. I tried to lead him back to the boat, and he began to roll.

"Quick," I told Ed, "row out to him. I think I can get him right where he is."

Then the spoon came away. The fish was still rolling in the surface, his belly showing white. Ed drove the boat toward him, and I crouched, ready to grab any part of him I could reach. But as we got there, he righted himself and all we saw was his big, pale, shadowy form swimming slowly down through the clear water.

"Gosh," I said, "forty-five pounds anyway. And that's leaning over backward to be fair."

"Yes," Ed said. "Hooked in the mouth too. I could see."

"Seeing like that's no proof though."

"There's no proof he was forty-five pounds either."

We got what we wanted the next Sunday, a thirty-two-pound fish, bright and clean, hooked in the mouth and killed after a good fight in the shallow water between Sachem Island and the Indian Island. That was the last fish we killed that season. I had to go up to work in the camp at the head of the lake, and by the time I got back to the river again, it was October and a high freshet had drawn all the big fish on upstream to their spawning in Woss Lake and the Klaanche River. But at least we knew the game was worth trying; we had killed two fish, had narrowly missed getting a third, and had run several others, some of them in Lansdowne Pool. Next season, we promised ourselves, we would be really fishing, with proper equipment and at least some knowledge to start on.

It happened that September of 1929 found me with a broken elbow and a very slim bankbook after a bad summer of contract logging. As it turned out, that was a fairly convenient set of circumstances: I couldn't hire out on another job until the elbow was mended and I was within easy reach of the Nimpkish. The logical thing seemed to be to go there and combine business, pleasure and convalescence by catching what tyees I could and selling them.

The season started slowly. A few fish were in the river at the end of August, but Ed and I were busy cutting a winter's wood for Mrs. Lansdowne. When the wood was all split and piled in the woodshed, we began to fish. This year we were well off for boats. We had a small power boat, a good ten-foot dinghy and a canoe, so we could cover a lot of water in searching for fish. I caught the first tyee in Lansdowne Pool on September first, a fine fish of forty pounds, and after that we picked up fish fairly regularly all the way down the river from the pool and out in the salt water as well. There was a great run of big cohos in early September of that year, so we spent quite a lot of our time on them, using the little power boat to tow the dinghy and canoe over to Race Pass or wherever the fish were feeding. Pound for pound, the cohos outfought the big tyees, and fishing for them was certainly more remunerative than fishing for the tyees because they took so freely. But after the first few days I always stayed in or near the river; in spite of the quick-jumping fight of the cohos, there was something in the solid, heavy take of the tyees and the tremendous power of their first run that I could not resist. Besides that, there was the steady hope of a fifty- or sixty-pounder and all the attraction of fishing a river instead of salt water.

It is difficult to pick out the great days of that month of fishing—almost any day that one has the luck to kill a salmon of thirty or forty pounds is a great day. But there are some days and some fish that I remember more clearly than others. There was an evening at Sachem Island, with a flooding tide and sunset light smoothing the water until it seemed as still as a lake's surface on a windless evening. I had anchored the dinghy a little below the island and about forty yards over toward the right bank of the river. I could see schools of fish finning three or four hundred yards downstream, opposite the Fishing Island, and I knew that they would soon come up to pass me; so I waited, standing in the dinghy ready to cast. In a little while the first school came on, thirty or forty big fish, each one pushing his slender, arrowhead ripple ahead of him on the face of the still water. It was very quiet, and the crash of a great fish jumping somewhere up in the bend seemed to hang over the river long after its last echoes had died away. The fish were very close now, coming steadily but slowly. I swung the spoon back, then sent it out across them; it flew well for once, cutting the air with its edge, and dropped gently ten yards beyond the school and perhaps ten yards upstream of the leaders. I could see the outlines of the big bodies under the finning ripples and the tiny flashes of the spoon as I reeled it in, held only a few inches below the surface by a half-ounce lead. The leader of the school turned toward it and began to follow it, two or three feet behind the hook. I could see him clearly, and he was very big; and muscles tightened all through my arms, making my hands clumsy on the reel. A ripple moved, fast, from the near side of the school, and something hit with a jolt that dipped the rod hard down. I struck, and the still water was heaved by thirty or forty great smooth swirls as the school turned short away. The reel ran wildly, and I checked with all the strength of my fingers until my fish jumped twice about seventy yards away. He turned then and ran hard back for the boat, bored deep down, came out again in another jump, very high and very near the boat. Ten minutes later I gaffed a thirty-five-pounder.

Twice more the same thing happened. Once the fish threw the hook when he was halfway out on his first run; the other time I gaffed another thirty-pounder. The sky was still light, and I could see the colors of trees and grass; but it was almost dusk, and the surface of the water had that clear, dark shine that makes every movement of it seem oily and slow. Another school came up and another fish took. After my strike he was still for perhaps one full second, as fish often are, then he began to take out line, jumped in the first ten yards, jumped again a moment later and kept going. Something warned me to grab for the anchor line. The fish was still running. The anchor came free of the shallow and hung straight down in deep water. The river current and the start of the ebb carried the dinghy down, and the fish still ran, straight out for salt water. He jumped again, high and tumbling over, falling flat, ran a few yards and jumped again just as high. He was big and very silver, and I clamped down on the reel until he was towing the dinghy. Twice he checked, and I picked up on him until most of the line was back on the reel. But each time he ran again and jumped in his running with all the abandon of a coho and all the authority of his own forty-five-pound weight. I was outside the river mouth when he came alongside at last, completely played out so that I could slip the gaff under his gill cover and lift him into the dinghy. He was unlike any fish I had seen in the river before, beautifully clean and with a greenish sheen along his back, thick and deep as a good fish should be, yet gracefully shaped instead of hog fat as so many tyees are. No other tyee ever fought me that way.

I remember too a leaden-gray morning when the light made the water seem opaque and palely off-white. I was on the salt chuck below the river mouth, halfway down to the old breakwater, when a school showed near me, and I made a quick cast which immediately hooked a fish. He ran a few yards, and the spoon came back. I cast again, hooked another and fought him in frantic haste while the school kept showing near the boat. I killed him, a thirty-three-pounder, in six minutes and cast again as soon as he was in the boat. Another fish took, ran and sent the spoon back. Three times that happened, then I hooked and killed a thirty-nine-pounder. By the time he was in the boat, I had lost the school, but they, too, were bright, clean fish, newly arrived from the north and not yet rid of their salt-water ways.

At dusk salmon crowd into the river channel from all their nearby lying places. I was there one evening in late September, working the last stage of a long ebb tide. There were schools all around me in the narrow channel, and I had already touched several fish without hooking one of them. I made a careless cast that landed right in the middle of a school and saw the great swirls of frightened fish all around the spoon. I began to reel in disgustedly, holding the rod high to hurry the spoon. Thirty feet from the boat a fish took with a slash that broke water, jarring the rod almost to breaking. I saw a great, dark tail roll out in the swirl, let him take line and slipped the anchor. He made a heavy run, deep and strong. I made him work for line and brought him to the surface in a threshing break sixty or seventy yards away. He came in a little—or rather the tide and river drifted the boat up on him—but went away again and went down. He didn't sulk but swam strongly and heavily, and I couldn't lift him at all. Suddenly he came up fast, slashed the water with his great tail and went down again. I told myself that here was the sixty-pounder at last and I could afford to take things slowly, even if it was getting dark. When he came up near the boat, we were within a hundred yards of Green Island, drifting fast for the kelp bed. I reached for the gaff, but he was still swimming strongly three or four feet down in the water and ten or fifteen feet away from the boat. Nothing that I could do would bring him closer, and we drifted into the kelp bed that way. I thought it was all over then; the line would tangle on one of the heavy stems and give him his chance to tear away the hook. But he seemed afraid of the kelp. He turned deliberately away from two plants, tried to turn from a third and the movement let me lift him. On the surface he seemed helpless, floundering among the trailing ribbons while I floundered to bring the boat within gaffing reach. Three times I missed with the gaff, clumsily and inexcusably; then suddenly he was easy, and I had him, not sixty pounds, but forty-eight, a noble bronze color, so deep-bodied and hog-backed that for once I doubted the steelyards.

That was 1929. I missed the next two seasons, but in 1932 and 1933, Ed and I fished again. We were both of us wiser and better fishermen, and we fished carefully and thoroughly, keeping close records not only of every fish we killed but of every day we fished and every fish that moved to us at all. They were fine records, full of details of time and tide and light, of the condition of the fish, of the leads we used and the spoons, even of the angles of the casts that hooked fish—upstream, downstream or straight across. But we stored them in a house that burned down in 1934. There is less now to check my memory of those two seasons than the simple notes I kept of the earlier ones.

But we did learn certain things. We solved, in some measure, the difficulty of catching fish in Lansdowne Pool by finding that the best time in any day comes after the sun has gone behind the hill. Between that time and full darkness we were nearly always able to hook at least two fish. There were exceptions to this for which we could never properly account—September 2, 1932, was one of these. Ed went down to the pool at three-thirty in the afternoon. I followed him an hour later and found him fighting a thirty-five-pounder; he had another already in the canoe and had lost three others after short runs. Between that time and darkness we hooked and fought nine more big fish and lost at least as many more in the first or second run. The fish were almost the start of the run, and the pool was full of them. Time and again they took as the spoon hit the water. It was a No. 6 Superior, copper at first, changed to brass as the light failed, and fished with a ¾-ounce lead. At the head of the pool and just below the rapid there is a fast ripple three or four feet deep between the line of the main current and the light flow that comes in from the backwater behind the island. Holding the canoe in the backwater and dropping the spoon in the shallow ripple, we hooked fish after fish, and many times we saw the flash of their heavy bodies as they turned in striking. Ed hooked the biggest fish of the day, a forty-eight-pounder, in the main run. I knew somehow in the moment the fish took that he was heavier than the others and I drove the canoe hard to follow his run. He jumped once, still running, turned at the tail of the pool and started back. I had turned the canoe and was holding it well over toward the west bank, but he ran straight for the foot of the rapids, jumped there and swung over into the eddy.

"That's the end of him," I said. "He'll come back to us now."

He circled and did come back, and I put the gaff where I could reach it easily. Ed tried to lift him, but he swirled his great tail once near the surface, then ran again upstream through the strongest current. It was a moment before either of us realized what was happening; then Ed said, "He's going on, straight up for the Canyon Pool."

He jumped then, right among the rocks and the broken water, thirty or forty yards up in the rapid. Then he was quiet, and we couldn't see him or tell exactly where he was because the current held the line down. I pushed the canoe up along the west side of the river to the backwater, then swung out across the foot of the rapid and picked up the pole. Ed got his drowned line up out of the water, and we could see that the fish was at least fifty yards above us and still working slowly upstream.

"Heave the daylights out of him," I said. "It's about the only chance. Pick up your line fast when he comes down through."

Ed lifted with everything the rod had. The strain turned the fish across the current so that it caught the side of his body and threw him down, but as he came back, the line still ran out.

"Round a rock," I said and pushed the canoe in tight against the foot of the rapids.

Ed jumped out and started up, stumbling and slipping on the rocks but making time; he had to find which rock was holding the line and bring the rod round it. He was almost there when I saw the fish, hanging helplessly on his side, bounced by the current waves at the head of the pool. I picked up the gaff and began to edge the canoe toward him; then Ed was round the rock, and the fish was drifting down out of reach. Ed came back, half swimming, and piled into the canoe, and I gaffed the fish for him down at the tail of the pool again.

There were no other days in the pool like that one, but we caught fish often enough in the broad-daylight hours to keep us trying. And we caught fish down below, outside the river, in the channel by the Fishing Island, off Sachem Point, in daylight and dusk, on many different stages of tide. The biggest we killed weighed 52½ pounds, which is not really big for a tyee. We saw many jumping that were much larger and, perhaps once or twice, we hooked larger ones. There was one that I hooked below Sachem Island in the first hour of a big ebb tide. He took deep down in twenty feet of water and made his first run lazily downstream. We followed him almost carelessly in the boat. Suddenly he turned into the stream and really ran, still deep, straight up the main channel. I saw the hundred-yard mark slip away on the line.

"Get after him, Ed," I said. "I can't stop him."

Ed pulled hard on the oars, but for several seconds the line was still going out; then the fish turned and came slowly downstream toward us. I held hard, trying to lift him, but he came back to the boat still two or three fathoms down. Rowing steadily, Ed was little more than holding place against tide and river. The line started out again fast, cutting the water toward the channel between Sachem Island and the Indian Island.

"He'll break this time, sure," I said. "There can't be more than five feet of water in there."

But he didn't break. He took a hundred and twenty yards plus whatever distance Ed's rowing moved the boat and came slowly back near bottom all the way.

"Gosh," I said, "if he doesn't show soon, I'll begin to think he's big."

"You aren't bearing down on him. You never let one get away with that much line before."

"I never had one wanted it so badly."

Then the third run started up the channel between the Indian Island and the bank. It went on and on, stronger and faster than either of the others, yet Ed was rowing up hard in the slack water behind the island. The hundred-yard mark flashed out again; then the reel stopped running. I knew he was off, but neither of us would believe it until we saw the spoon come back to us, wobbling its stupid flashes in the green water.

FROM *Mississippi Solo*

Eddy Harris

1

The Mississippi River is laden with the burdens of a nation. Wide at St. Louis where I grew up, the river in my memory flows brown and heavy and slow, seemingly lazy but always busy with barges and tugs, always working—like my father—always traveling, always awesome and intimidating. I have watched this river since I was small, too young to realize that the burdens the Mississippi carries are more than barges loaded with grain and coal, that the river carries as well sins and salvation, dreams and adventure and destiny. As a child I feared this river and respected it more than I feared God. As an adult now I fear it even more.

I used to have nightmares filled with screams whenever I knew my family planned some excursion across the river and I'd have to go along. That old Veteran's Bridge seemed so weak and rickety. My imagination constructed a dilapidated and shaky span of old wooden slats, rotted and narrow and weak with no concrete support anywhere. The iron girders that held the poor thing up were ancient and rusty, orange and bumpy with oxidation where they should have been shiny and black. The bridge wavered in the wind and was ready to collapse as the car with my family in it approached, and then we would plunge through the air after crashing the brittle wooden guardrail and we'd dive toward the river. Everyone screamed but me. I held my ears every time and waited for the splash. It never came. I always awoke, always lived to dream the dream again and again, not only when asleep but even as we crossed the river.

The river was full of giant catfish and alligators, ice floes and trees that an often enraged and monster-like river had ripped from the shores along its path.

The Mississippi. Mighty, muddy, dangerous, rebellious, and yet a strong, fathering kind of river. The river captured my imagination when I was young and has never let go. Since I can remember I have wanted to be somehow a part of the river as much as I wanted to be a hero, strong and brave and relentless like the river, looming so large in the life and world around me that I could not be ignored or forgotten. I used to sit on the levee and watch the murkiness lumber down to the sea and I'd dream of the cities and towns the river had passed, the farms and fields and brides, the magic in the debris picked up here, deposited there, and the other rivers along the way: Ohio, Illinois, Arkansas, taking all on a beautiful voyage to the Gulf of Mexico and beyond. I wanted to go too. I wanted to dip first my toes in the water to test, then all of me, hanging onto whatever and floating along with it, letting the river drop me off wherever and pick me up later and take me on again. I didn't care where, I just wanted to go. But my parents wouldn't let me.

But now I am a man and my parents can't stop me. I stand at that magical age, thirty, when a man stops to take stock of his life and he reflects on all the young-man's dreams that won't come true. No climbs up Everest, no tryout with the Yankees, no great American novel. Instead, reality: wives and babies and mortgages, pensions, security and the faraway future. No great risks. No more falling down. No more skinned knees. No great failures. I wondered: is all this inevitable?

I've never minded looking stupid and I have no fear of failure. I decided to canoe down the Mississippi River and to find out what I was made of.

2

Once they have reached a certain age, dreamers are no longer held in high esteem. They are ridiculed instead, called loony and lazy, even by their friends. Especially by their friends!

Dreams are delicate and made of gossamer. They hang lightly on breezes and suspend as if from nothing. The slightest wind can tear them apart. My dream was buffeted by my friends. What the hell for? they asked me. What are you trying to prove? Why don't you just go over Niagara Falls in a barrel?

And this was from my friends. God, how that hurt. One friend even told me to take a bus, for God's sake. Instead of helping me fly, my friends were pulling me down, and laughing at me.

Putting a canoe into the headwaters of the Mississippi and aiming it for New Orleans is not something a man is supposed to do. It is not considered normal or sane. Perhaps it is the danger involved, or perhaps it is too much an act of desire and determination, an act of passion and volition, or simply too out of the ordinary.

For whatever reasons, my idea met with disapproval, and instead of childish jubilation I approached canoeing the river with doubt and sorrow—sorrow because the glory with which I first came upon this adventure was dashed by friends. Like Galileo before the Church, I was ready to relinquish my radical approaches and be normal.

But this dream of mine, still suspended on the breeze and delicate as ever, was just as real as those flimsy summer spider webs hanging in the air, and just as clinging. Once the webs attach themselves to you they are hard to get rid of. And so it was with my desire to ride the river.

3

A man blessed with a flood of ideas has the luxury to squander them, to sift through his wealth until he finds the right idea for the right occasion. He may lose a great many of them, but he can afford it.

When a man has only one great notion, it becomes all the more valuable, a jewel, a prized and noble possession. He cherishes it like a kid with his last stick of candy. He guards it, he secretes it away, taking it out every night at bedtime just to look at it, to hold it up to the light and ponder it and wonder just when to taste it at last, all the while being haunted by its existence and his burning desire to hurry up with it. An obsession.

For weeks I ached with the thought of doing the river. But I had no canoe. I had no camping gear. I had no money. The initial reaction from my friends had left me secretive and without allies to support even spiritually my idiotic plan. And pretty soon it would be too late to go. Already it was the first week of October and Minnesota, where I would start, had seen its first snowfall.

One friend came to mind and I turned to him not because he could help give birth to this dream I had, but because of all the people I knew, Robert would at least listen to me and not tell me I was crazy. He would not tell me to give it up.

He was an old man, and every time I went to see him I was sure it would be the last I'd see him alive. He's been my special friend since long before I can remember, more like an uncle than just some old man I knew and liked, the kind of friend who will always understand. He is always your last resort, when he should be your first. An old man from a long time ago when every problem could be solved with a couple of drinks and a couple of hours of talking—with him mostly listening. When you need good advice, the one to turn to is the one who listens well; the best talk, the best advice comes from yourself.

Robert and I used to drink sodas together, back when he tried to teach me music. About the time I was heading off for college, I graduated to beer. Tonight I would be doing advanced studies. Tonight, he did most of the talking.

A skinny black man with a head shaped like a peanut, Robert had very little hair and what hair he did have he wore cut so close to his scalp it looked more like razor stubble. He always wore a fedora, either grey or brown, even indoors.

Normally I would come to him and he'd be working on the transmission of his car or taking his stereo apart and putting it back together. He was always tinkering with something and there was junk lying all around. I'd come over and watch him and hint in roundabout fashion that something was bothering me and he'd tinker patiently with me and we'd take our time until we'd squeezed the problem out. Then we'd have a look at it and a drink.

But not today. Today he wanted to get right to it, as if he were in a hurry. Not that he had someplace to get to, but a different kind of hurry, as if he hadn't much time to waste anymore.

"Well, let's get to it," he said. And I knew this session was going to be different from all the others. If there was any advice or wisdom to offer, he was going to give it out straight and not have me scratch around until I found it.

"I haven't seen you in a long time," he said. "Something must be bothering you. What is it?"

I felt like a worm of a man who only calls his friends when he needs some favor. But more than that, I felt all the frustration that surged through Robert and made the squiggly vein in his temple twitch, frustration I was noticing for the first time.

I told him my plans, that I was going to do the river. I told him the obstacles that blocked me, that I still had no canoe, no gear, no money, and that everyone I knew had said it was impossible and stupid. And he said:

"Don't you listen to them. They got no imagination. They got no vision. And it makes them jealous because you do, and they'll try to stop you, try to change you. But don't you let them."

It was not advice. It was a command.

Robert had at one time been a wonderful tap dancer. His apartment was littered with photos and newspaper clippings and mementos of when he and his partner used to tear up the boards on the circuit. Their special routine: standing back to front, only inches apart and dancing in unison, so swiftly as to be a blur, their timing so exquisite that from head on you could see the movements of only one man. The big time called, movies, New York, but he never went. He never said why, but now I had a glimpse.

He turned instead to music, taught himself the trombone, played in local jazz bands and learned music so well that he did most of the arrangements for the bands he played in. Again there was a chance for the big time. Again he stayed in St. Louis.

He got married, had children, and settled into a normal job. The closest he got to music any more was teaching it to me. He used to give me trumpet lessons. The jobs he settled for were all a black man in those days could expect: shining shoes, being a custodian in office buildings and schools, mopping and polishing floors, cleaning desks and mending broken things.

He reached across the table and grabbed me. His fingers were long and bony, his hands strong from building things. He held me by the wrists and squeezed me hard.

"I know you can do it," he said. "I have confidence in you. Always have."

Canoeing? Writing?

His eyes gathered in the soft light around us and sparkled with a thousand secrets.

"And maybe there ain't nobody else who does," he whispered, "but we don't much care what they think about us no how. Do we?"

The old man licked his lips, his dry-looking tongue flicking out past his dentures, feeling the air and smacking his lips lightly as if he were tasting something. He wore an expression I took to be sadness, but maybe it was just fatigue or longing. Maybe it was the inevitable expression of commingled jealousy and exhortation an old man finds when he knows his time has come and gone and all he can do is pass the baton.

He pulls down a bottle of whiskey from the shelf and one glass. Before he comes to sit again he pauses and looking down at me he shifts the false teeth in his mouth and nods to himself with a satisfied smile. He grabs a second glass from the shelf and slides it across to me. Without a word, Robert was telling me plenty.

He leaned in close. His eyes squinted, studying me.

We sat quietly just like that for a moment. I squirmed in my seat until we drank. Our drinking is clean, without ceremony. No clinking of glasses, no toasts. Just eyes locked, his on mine, and the simultaneous raising of glasses to lips.

The whiskey burns. I emit a noise you might hear in a cartoon. Robert screws up his face as though suffering with each swallow. He clears his throat with a guttural, teeth-clenched "Aaah!"

When he finally speaks, he whispers.

"Are you afraid?"

"Well," I reply. "I'm no expert canoeist. I swim okay, but—"

"That's not what I mean."

"What else is there to be afraid of? Drowning? Freezing to death? Wild animals? Or just not being able to take it?"

"Well," he says. "If you get out and you can't take it, that sure is going to mess with your mind. How you deal with failure is just as important as the failure itself, but that's not what I'm talking about neither."

He reaches slowly for the bottle and he pours. This time, before we drink, he tilts his glass toward me.

"You're black too, you know," he says. His smile is cunning. "Or have you forgotten?"

"I haven't forgotten, but so what? What's that got to do with anything?"

He takes a long slow sip and sneaks a peek at me from over the rim of his glass.

"What is it you're wanting to do?"

"Canoe the Mississippi."

"From where?"

"From the beginning."

"And where's that?"

"In Minnesota."

"In Minnesota," he repeats. "Do you know how many black people there are in Minnesota? About six."

He takes another sip.

"And how far you planning to go?"

"New Orleans."

"Through the South," he said. He sips again. "From where there ain't no black folks to where they still don't like us much. I don't know about you, but I might be a little concerned about that."

Then I see the river. First as a blue line on a map. Then, as Robert talks on and I see myself out there, a black man alone and exposed and vulnerable, the blue line blurs and fragments until there is more than one Mississippi River. There is the river of legend, the Father of Waters. The river of steamboats and gamblers. The river flowing with the tears and sweat of slaves. I can hear the beating of Indian drums and the singing of slaves resting in the shade of plantation willows on the banks of the old man river. The river has come alive in my mind, the sights, sounds and smells of the river in my imagination.

But I know the river won't be like that, fur trappers in buckskin shirts, paddlewheelers piled high with bales of cotton, Indian canoes sliding silently. I know it won't be like that, but I don't know what to expect. If I had any idea before of how it might be, I don't now.

Robert says to me: "Did you ever stop to think that your friends might not want you to do this because it might be dangerous?"

"No, I never did. They just made fun of me."

"You know how friends are. Maybe it's their way of saying they don't want you to get hurt."

I hesitate. "Maybe." I'm not convinced.

"Maybe they don't want you to get shot by some redneck in the woods. Maybe they don't want you to fall in and drown. Or maybe they're trying to protect you from something else."

"What's that?"

"You see, everybody thinks his way is the right way. The Bible-bangers think God is the answer. A man with a wife and kids and a house and a good job, if he's happy with them all, he thinks that's where satisfaction comes from. Everybody thinks he knows what's best so when a friend comes by with a different way, especially a risky way, you want to save him. You see?"

"I see," I say, but I'm really confused. "But what about imagination and vision? What about jealousy?"

"Oh, I'm not saying they're not jealous. Envy is what fuels their convictions. When a man secretly wants what you have and maybe he's ashamed of it and maybe he knows he can never have it, that's when he goes out of his way most to make it seem worthless. Just like some men are reassured by other people's failure. That's where vision and imagination come in."

"Without vision and imagination," Robert says softly, "you never look for your own path to glory. And glory can mean Mount Everest or Nobel Prizes or a wife and kids and security. It can even be canoeing down the Mississippi. But it takes vision to see what shoes fit you and what shoes fit the other guy. And the thing to remember is: don't take it all so serious. Failure is horrible, but it's not the worst thing there is."

4

Robert, a weak old man with absolutely no power over me—with my bare hands I could snap him in two like a pencil between my fingers—and yet it was he who had the power to set me free. Old people and children, frailty and innocence: they seem so innocuous that we battle them laughing and unarmed, like David and Goliath. Then they beat us with magic.

I toppled from my perch of indignation and admitted to myself that maybe I was being foolish in wanting to do the river, maybe I was wrong. I still wanted to do it, but I was trying at least to see the objections.

I hadn't thought before of any genuine concern. When my friend Walter suggested I tow along behind me a second canoe—like a spare tire in case of emergency—I thought he was making fun of me. (The suggestion was a little crazy.) But now I could see Barbara's fear for my safety when she wanted me to pack a walkie-talkie—just in case.

264

And never before had I considered jealousy. I had figured any opposition was pettiness and spite. Now there existed the possibility that they'd love to dream such dreams, to take such journeys but could not and resented me because I could. Until I opened my mind to their motives I could never admit that there lurked within the darker corners of my soul my own jealousies and simpler longings, like when I hug a friend's wife or carry their baby or lie on the floor in the warmth and coziness of their home. Only then could I see the merits of their chosen style and admit that my style was part rebellion but also in part reassurance that my choices, risky and exciting and unconventional, were the right ones.

Because of an old man, I could approach my less-traveled roads more securely, less troubled and without the feeling that I am in some sort of competition. Without that extra burden, I opened up. I could admit my desires and acknowledge my deficiencies and fears. And suddenly friends came to the rescue, just as friends are supposed to do.

Enthusiasm becomes contagion. When Brian says, "Tremendous idea. Do it!" the feeling is one of jubilation; there is approval at last, the buttressing of those tender spots.

When Bobby C. reaches out in that quiet and soft voice that's almost a whisper and says, "You're going to make it. It just takes time, but I know you're going to make out," there is sadness at not having much to show for all the years of dreaming, the struggling and failing, and there is pressure to perform, to pull back up and try again and make people proud. And there is, of course, determination. *Damn right, I'll make it!*

And when Robinovich catches fire with my fever, it's as if I had known all the time that I'd make this journey. She gets so caught up in the excitement that she wants me to go as much as I want to go myself. She wants to go, too, but can't. She can, however, drive me up to Minnesota when the time comes and, wonder of wonders, she knows where I can borrow a canoe. If not for Robinovich. . . .

Late on a Friday night in mid-October, ten days after the first snow has fallen on Minneapolis, Robinovich and I left St. Louis and headed north for Lake Itasca, the river's source.

Armed with a purple rabbit's foot and a plastic Jesus, a St. Christopher and some miracle dirt from a shrine in Sanctuario de Chimayó in New Mexico, and for warmth a bottle of tequila, we were far too excited to be scared.

5

And there—Oh my God!—it is. Lake Itasca in all its pristine glory.

The air is as pure as the kiss from a child at bedtime and very cold and very clear, its sharp edges stinging my nose with every deep breath I take, but so sweet in its purity that I take breath after painful breath until my face hurts and my eyes water.

The sun hangs low in the southwest sky about to set behind ranges of trees stretching endlessly in every direction. As the sky sheds one layer of light and color for another hue, a darker hue edging toward purple, the air cools off even more. Any other time, any other day, I might be hopping around frowning and shouting and hating the cold. But not this day, for too much has gone into my getting here and far too much emanates *from* here, and cold though I am and chilled right through, I am as giddy as a child on champagne and just as excitedly foolish. I dance and jig and flit from here to there wearing no coat nor sweater. My flannel shirt is plenty warm for I am finally and emphatically here. Lake Itasca. And it is truly splendor and beauty.

Robinovich watches me, laughing at me. She is bundled up and ready for winter. She probably thinks I'm crazy, but she knows me well so it's all right. She knows I'm crazy. For the past few hours since we entered this land of green pine, blue skies and lakes, she has suffered through my oohs and aahs and other exclamations of delight as I absorbed the beauty of northern Minnesota.

"One," I'd shout, then, "there's one, and two and three . . ." as I tried to count the lakes we passed to see if really there are ten thousand in this state as the motto claims.

Ten thousand lakes, I don't know. But there are plenty and the land around all covered with tall timber, pine and birch trees white and speckled like dalmatians, and lakes everywhere that remind me of the north of Sweden. Winters here must be equally severe so it's no wonder this land was settled by Swedes. Nothing in this world could remind them so much of the beauty and harshness of their home.

Robinovich is still laughing. I laugh too just thinking about how funny I must appear. And what a sight we must have looked driving up here. Sporty red car with an eighteen-foot green canoe on top, in late autumn, in the cold and in the wind. Being shoved about on the highway by that wind and having to stop every so often to readjust the ropes that lashed canoe to car. Long after the season for recreational boats of size and strength. And here we were out with a canoe? No wonder we took our share of stares.

"Lake Itasca? In that thing?"

At Avon, a stone's throw of a town in either direction, the man pumping gas for us frowned in a most peculiar way at the very notion of it. He held his laughter very well, however, and spoke with a straight face, but I'm glad I didn't tell him the whole plan.

"It's a beautiful spot up there all right, but I don't know if I'd want to be out on the lake today. Why in the world did you pick this time of year to go canoeing?"

"Took me this long to round up the canoe. But it's not too cold, do you think?"

I was shivering in the wind while we talked. He looked at me like I was crazy.

"Better wait till tomorrow just the same," he advised. "Gonna get colder, but this wind should die down some by then."

He was right. The next day did turn colder. But it was cold enough right then and I went and huddled inside his little gas station and waited for him to finish pumping the gas. He didn't need my help out there.

It was a little station, one set of pumps. The whole setup came straight out of the old photos of the South. Small station big enough for maybe three cars at a time. Any more than that and they'd spill out into the street, which wouldn't have been any major crime, in this little town.

Inside there was little warmth, only a break from the wind. These Minnesotans must be tough, I figured, and when he came back in, I told him so. He smiled.

"Yeah, well," he said. "I guess you get used to anything."

He brushed off my comment casually, but I could see he took it as a compliment, with pride.

"You think this is cold," he said. "Wait till winter sets in. Freezing winds, snow up to your elbows and nothing but grey all around. Those who can't take it get on out. But it's like anything else; all depends on what you're used to."

Then he took down one of the maps he had for sale and unfolded it among the clutter of tools and tires and grime, and he showed me the route to the lake.

A small kindness, and at the time I thought nothing of it. He showed me the route, and I let him. I already knew the way, of course, but if he wanted to be helpful, who was I to spit on his generosity. Goodness takes two: giver and receiver. Besides, he might have known a shortcut. But he didn't.

On leaving Avon, my mind turned back to Robert and what he'd said about going from "where there ain't no black folks to where they still don't like us much." And I thought about being black.

For me, being black has never been such a big deal, more a physical characteristic rather like being tall: an identifier for the police and such. Part of my identity, but not who I am.

I do not intend to imply that I would be exactly the same person if I were not black—any more than if I were not tall—but I'll leave it to the existentialists to debate how I might have turned out if I'd been Chinese and short, or what other preoccupations I might have if I weren't losing my hair. As far as I have always been concerned, I'm who I am from the inside to the out, not the other way around. I never gave great importance to how people reacted to my being black or tall or bald. What mattered most was how I reacted—to all my assets and deficiencies.

But suddenly being black, as well as being tall, took on new meaning. Being tall because of the long journey ahead with me sitting cross-legged in a canoe. Being black because of how I would perceive and be perceived.

The gas station man in Avon had treated me just as I would have expected him to: with courtesy, kindness and respect. Was this how I was going to be treated all the way down the river, with kindness? If so, I wouldn't mind. But I'd be less than thrilled if I were looked on kindly because there were no other blacks around to set the tone, just as I'd be disappointed if people mistreated me because of their exposure to blacks. I would most like to witness some general goodness in the human soul pouring out to strangers, and barring that, I'd want people to give me a chance to make my own imprint on them—for good or for bad—and then their behavior toward me would be based on me. Too selfish? Too simplistic? Well maybe. But I hoped that's what the gas station man's behavior was a reflection of: my being a thoroughly charming and friendly fellow, and he was only reciprocating.

But still the haunting question: where are all the black folks?

I had seen one little black kid playing in front of a house along the road we traveled, but that was way back in Iowa. There must be some in Minnesota, but where were they?

And a better question: why weren't they?

It is perhaps startling to realize that there are places blacks don't much go to.

For obvious reasons, blacks don't lie on the beach much or hang out by the pool.

Blacks aren't often found cruising the bazaars in Bangkok, or sliding down the ski slopes. Finances could be a problem, but the travel magazines seem not to want blacks to travel, or think that blacks don't travel, or maybe just don't care. The advertisement photos rarely—extremely rarely—show blacks enjoying exotic holiday destinations. Why?

And why aren't there very many blacks in Minnesota? Too cold in winter? Safety in numbers? Small town conservatism and bigotry? More jobs in the major industrialized urban centers? Or are there some more subtle rules being worked?

I went to a wonderful bluegrass music festival in Park City, Utah, high up in the Uinta Mountains. Sunshine, spectacular scenery, fabulous musicians. I was the only black face there. Why? Because blacks don't want to listen to certain kinds of music? Because blacks don't like the mountains and crisp clean air? Or because blacks feel there are certain places where they don't belong, certain things they can and cannot do? Is the exclusion self-imposed or by hints both subtle and overt?

You don't find many blacks canoeing solo down the Mississippi River and camping out every night. Why not? Are there evils out there to greet them if they do?

I never thought the things I did were so remarkable. My getting to travel and see so much of the world I pinned on restlessness and good fortune. Good fortune, yes, but maybe more. Maybe a quiet statement that this world has too much to offer for me not to want to reach out with arms wide, that there is too much good music and good food and scenic beauty and I want to sample it all, that there is no place on earth where I can't go, where I don't belong, and nothing I can't do. Forget about taboos and accepted patterns and fears—even common sense. The only restrictions are the ones I (we all) put in place.

But for all my boldness and my reaching out to embrace the world, what would be waiting for me out there on the river? Kindness or evil? Beauty or savagery? Whatever, I didn't want to miss a thing. The up days would make up for the down, I knew; the beauty is worth the pain.

Itasca is worth every agony of getting here. For here, quite possibly, is the most beautiful place on earth.

The beauty surrounding Lake Itasca is so quiet. Other sites of sheer beauty—the Alps, the Himalayas, expansive seas and deserts—blare their splendor and overwhelm the beholder. But so pristine and serene in its beauty is this place, it can hardly be called majestic or imposing, overpowering or breathtaking. Instead, it whispers at you. It calls and sings sweetly, bathing you in melody that you finally notice and eventually feel and see, misting around you like a warm morning fog in spring, bathing you in delight and soothing you until you are at the same time both silent and on the edge of shouting with joy. It's not a Gothic cathedral, but a lovely little chapel whose absolute artistry you do not expect, and you're awestruck.

Itasca. From the Latin *verITAS CAput*, the true head, the real as opposed to any spurious source of the great river. The birth of a river, the calm before the rage.

Robinovich and I have stopped the car near the park ranger's office. We need to register and pick out a campsite before dark. I don't want to. I'm too anxious to get around to the outlet of the lake where the river begins, but Robinovich, the voice of reason, insists.

So okay. We'll go register, but the campsite can wait. I want to find the river. I'm like a kid who just can't deal with the vegetables for the nagging thoughts of dessert.

We manage to conclude the business quickly and rush back to the little road winding around the lake another mile or so to the north. After a few quick steps down the path and through the trees, there it is. Gurgling, cooing gently, the great river is just a baby.

Around here the lake is a still sheet of blue. As blue as the sky. (Minisota: a Dakota Indian word which means water painted blue like the sky.) Tall trees border the water and shield it from the wind. The trees rise up high but also lie upside down across the water. The lake is a mirror. I see everything twice.

A cloud of loons skirts low over the surface of the lake then lifts high and banks around the bend out of sight. Their cries are loud and wild.

The sun is going down, shadows are long, everything is swathed in hues of yellow and gold. Along the edge where the lake is shallow, marsh grass grows the color of ripening wheat and creates a fake shoreline extending out ten yards or so. It looks solid and thick enough to walk on, but it's not.

And just south of those golden reeds, the bank of the lake turns in, receding like an old man's hairline. Big rocks stretch across the opening almost as if to stop the flow, but there is no stopping this spill. The little flow of water which babbles playfully over these rocks is the start of something. Like a snowball down a mountain. Like the storming of the Bastille. Like a great upheaval whose time has come.

My God! The greatest river in the world. The Ojibway Indians call this river Mesipi: the great river. Other tribes call it Father of Waters. The Volga has been called the Russian Mississippi, the Murray-Darling has been called the Mississippi of Australia. But the Mississippi is compared to none. It is the yardstick, the standard for greatness. And here, it's just a creek. I stand on the rocks, and feel mighty. My shoes don't even get wet. A child could walk safely across here.

Maybe ten feet wide, about twelve inches deep, clear and clean enough to be drinkable. The creek bed is pebbly. The river is not at all the muddy monster that rolls by St. Louis. It hardly seems even a distant relative.

I leave the river with a casual wave. "See you tomorrow."

It's nearly dark now and time to make camp.

6

Pitching camp is a breeze. Modern tents are so simple, especially the one I've brought, I could set it up in five minutes in the dark. And in fact I was so quick getting it up and done with, Robinovich and I had time for a leisurely stroll in the woods before dark.

The shimmering refections darkening on the lake faded into the dusk. The wind fell to a breeze. The evening stilled to the quiet time that's perfect for strolls hand in hand and for silent thinking.

Suddenly, a pounding. The earth trembled. It sounded like a heavy fist slamming quickly against a punching bag, then stopped. It startled us. I looked but saw nothing. Then the pounding came again and a huge buck bounded out of nowhere, emerging from the trees to stop and eye us. His antlers stuck up from his head like a TV antenna. He lowered them and charged straight at us, his hooves thumping the cold hard ground and creating that frightening sound of thunder. Neither Robinovich nor I budged a muscle. Threatening as he was, he was still too wonderful to take our eyes from. Better to be gored to death by a TV antenna than to miss such effortless athletics.

His running turned to leaping and just at the very last second, he sprang to his left and darted out of sight. Triumphant.

The pounding came from inside my chest now. I was breathing hard. *Life in the woods,* I thought.

Lying in the tent later on, reality and its questions grab hold. *What the hell am I doing?* Sure, the thing that awaits me is a creek. In three days' journey, though, it turns into a series of lakes, one of which stretches more than ten miles across. After that I'm facing a real river, with current, wind and waves, and traffic. And animals and no phones and no easy way out.

I was very nearly ready to call it quits.

It's gotten very cold out by now. I've put on my long underwear, tops and bottoms, and tried to get a good blaze going for warmth, but it's been raining up here lately and the wood is all wet. I'd always heard that birch makes such wonderful firewood. The bark does burn easily, but when the wood itself gets wet, it turns into soggy pulp. And the pine needles and cones lying around which would usually make good kindling are wet as well. It's a miracle that we can get any fire started at all, and even then it's only enough to cook by, not a blaze that throws off heat.

And to think, the ranger's office had bundles of wood for sale. They're closed by now and anyway, I had said to Robinovich:

"That's too easy, not like really roughing it. And if I can't find wood enough and can't get a fire started, I'm going to be in a world of trouble."

After a quick dinner of soup and cheese and crackers, the cold opened to us like a freezer door and we hurried to get inside the tent and stay there for the night. Anything we'd left out could just stay there until morning.

We broke out the tequila and made funny noises after every sip. It's strong and burning, just the way it's supposed to be.

Deep in the night I was awakened by growling and snorting. I couldn't tell where it was coming from. I looked over at Robinovich. I couldn't really see her but, by her stillness and by the deep heavy breathing I knew she was sleeping soundly.

I sat up straight in the darkness to listen. Each time I would try to hear, the sounds died away. When I lay back down, they came again. Animal sniffing noises. Spooky sounds in the night.

Soon I heard clankings of pots and cans, tearings of paper and plastic and cardboard. What did we leave out for it to get into? I wonder what kind of beast it is and hope it doesn't decide to slash its way inside for more treats.

Later on, after the sounds have once again moved around to the rear of the tent and I've unzipped the back flap for the nth time, I catch a glimpse of the beast by the soft white light of the risen moon. It's a bear. A small one, rising up on its hind legs stretching up against a tree. I know bears, even these small ones, can be lethal, but my fears go away and the vacuum fills with amazement.

I poke at Robinovich, but she is too far into sleep and dreams. And quickly the bear is gone anyway.

I settle back in my sleeping bag and I'm excited. I'm wishing I could see the bear again, more clearly, and the moon and stars too. I can hardly sleep, but I do. In the morning I'm raring to go.

A quick scan of the area just at sunrise reveals the bear's activity. The metal pots and plates and cups have been investigated and discarded. The empty soup cans have also been tossed aside; too hard for a bear to get into. But there had been a box of crackers and it's clear the bear enjoyed them. The plastic has been ripped to pieces and the cardboard box torn apart and dragged to the edge of the woods. There was nothing else for the bear to get its paws on and I'm glad. Feeding the wild animals is as bad a habit as it is for the animals to eat man's garbage. So I vow never to leave food out for the animals to get into, and to leave no trash behind. Whatever I bring in comes out with me and no one will know by such trashy signs that I've ever been along this river. It's a promise I end up breaking only twice.

I am ready then for what turns out to be a beautiful morning and a glorious afternoon and, until a few weeks later, the roughest night of my life.

7

We were up before the sun. The air was soft and fine, but cold. The morning seemed brittle. When the sun finally rose it looked like it would have taken any excuse at all and gone back to bed. The same for me, so it was quickly tea and soup, break camp and head on down to the lake.

Without much ado we unloosed the canoe from its perch atop the car and set it in the water. I tied an extra paddle to one of the cross struts in the canoe, slipped a line through the stern, and I was ready.

Nothing else needed to be stowed in the canoe because Robinovich had agreed to stay on for the day and meet me periodically along this early portion of the river. Just to make sure I got the hang of it and to put both our minds at ease.

I took a long hug and a kiss, donned my yellow life jacket, and I was away.

The lake invites me with its stillness. Any turbulence might have discouraged me, but the water is so calm and pretty and the morning so quiet and finally beginning to take on some color that I shove off easily and paddle straight out to where the water is deep and cold and scariest. I suddenly have no fear of falling in and if not for the river calling me I could easily stay here and paddle up and down this lake all day.

But the river does call. I turn my canoe north and glide toward it.

Right away I discover that canoeing is an art, one which I will eventually have to learn. On the quiet lake my zigzagging poses no problem, but I will need to learn to control this thing or I might find trouble later on. I don't want that.

I settle in quickly amid the cushioning quiet of this near-wilderness. The lake reflects the dark green trees and the sky striped white and blue. The trail I lay behind me in the water is a soft S-curve of bubbles and swirls. I make so little noise. Only the light swishing of my paddle, the drips of water tapping the lake when I cross the paddle from my left side to my right, a little plop when each time I dig the paddle into the water, and a slight suction sound when I pull it out for the next stroke. And all about me is fine and silent until a handful of ducks skims across the water. Their noise is the flapping of heavy wings and the dragging of duck feet across the lake.

I lengthen my stroking. I'm coming faster and faster across the water now. It's almost effortless, a feeling much like gliding across calm seas in a sail boat. I feel the spirit of this water rising up from the morning's mist and I hear it whispering to me that I have nothing to worry about.

As I carve my path across the water, I see ahead the river falling away as though spilling into a drain. I'm caught in the current. Still paddling, of course; the current isn't *that* strong. It must be a psychological pull that makes me feel I could stop paddling and still not keep from aiming for those rocks and that river.

A father and mother are showing the baby river to their two children. They wave and call to me as I slow to negotiate the rocks that cross the river.

"Where are you headed?"

"New Orleans." I feel like an expert now, an old pro at this. I try to look cool, like I know what I'm doing, but I add, "I hope." They laugh and wish me luck.

It's a transaction I will undergo a hundred times before I reach the end, each one very much like this one. Some will wish they could go along, others will think I'm a little on the loony side, but each one will encourage me and no one will wish me bad luck or ill. Well, almost no one.

When the river finally falls into the gulf, it will have reached a depth of about two hundred feet, but just beyond these big rocks the Mississippi's bottom lies only inches below the surface. My canoe and its 185-pound paddler have a draft of about six inches and when the creek bed rises to its shallowest point, the canoe touches bottom and I'm stuck. Not ten yards from the beginning and I'm stuck. I hope no one is looking. Is this an omen?

There! I dig my paddle hard into the pebbly bottom and lean against it and just shove until the canoe slides free, dragging bottom at first but finally getting loose and afloat again. This will happen many more times before the river has found a few more inches to accommodate me, but a little strength is all I need. I manage.

Shortly on I come to a little bridge. Lying flat in the canoe I slide under the bridge, scraping bottom again and having to shove my way free while almost lying down. With higher water I could have floated under more easily but my head would have been taken off by the low bridge.

The creek bends left, it bends right. Another footbridge lies across my path and blocks my way. No way can I get under this one, not even if I lie flat and try to slide by again. Easy solution. Get out, set the canoe adrift and let it float under the bridge by itself, then grab it as it comes through the other side. Good idea, but when I get out of the canoe and take the weight of my body with me, the canoe rises in the water and sits too high to squeeze under. The bow of the canoe knocks into the bottom of the bridge. I can stand in the canoe until the front end is under the bridge, climb up onto the bridge myself and then push the canoe through, but the canoe still won't go. It gets stuck in the rafters that support the bridge. I pull it back out and think again.

The bridge is just too low. The embankments are too high to drag the canoe up, but I've no choice. Unless I want to go back and go home. That remains a possible solution to every difficulty I encounter along the way, but I don't take the consideration seriously here. I'm simply forced to get out of the canoe and try to drag this thing up the embankment and across the bridge to the other side.

The canoe is not mine. It's on loan to me from a youth organization in St. Louis, run by a friend of Robinovich's. I hope I don't bend it or beak it or put holes in it, but it feels like all of these will happen. In the meantime I'm pulling this boat inch by inch, slipping into the mud and getting my feet wet. At times I go to the back end and lift and shove and finally I get the cursed canoe up and over and back down into the water. No damage to the canoe, only to me and my already weak back.

But soon I'm on my way again along the sparkling waters. I'm in a canyon of trees, two-hundred-year-old pines. The river cuts left, it cuts right.

Up ahead another bridge. This time the river has been funneled through what looks like a huge metal sewer pipe and the water builds up there and shoots through to the other side with a rushing noise that sounds like Niagara Falls. I can only go through if I lie down. I do and I'm at the mercy of the river. I hold my breath and go for it. Gathering speed I shoot through the tunnel and out the other side and I feel like I've shot the rapids or done a ride at Disneyland.

For a few minutes I sit in a large, quiet pool at the other end of the tunnel. The river is coming hard and noisily at me. But here it widens and quickly quiets once more and becomes clear and slow again. I move on.

A beaver dam blocks my way. The beavers will create many problems for me before this day is done, and this first dam is the least of them. It stops up the river and a tree has been thrown across half the creek to make getting around it difficult. I wonder if these dams serve a purpose, if beavers really live in them, or if beavers are just great big jokers who like to slow down people in small boats. I'm certainly slowed down. I'm not an expert yet and I struggle to get the canoe going sideways at the right times. Too often I get going backwards. I hit a branch. I'm caught in a snarl of limbs. I get stuck.

The river here is so gentle. A heron rises up out of nowhere. It squawks: follow me. I do. It drifts downstream to hide, be flushed again, and hide again. It's playing games with me. Eagles in the sky above soar over me and probably laugh at me. Critters scurry through the brush on the banks and never let me see them. The air is crisp and cool but sunny enough and I'm paddling enough to stay warm. Further on I find baby fishes flickering as they dart for cover when I disturb their water. I feel I've got a continuum here, that fish will be with me unlike any other creature all the way to the end and I'll not be so alone. When the river deepens and I encounter the bigger fish loitering in the shade, I know it for certain. But I'm wrong. At the highway bridge just this side of the marsh the river deepens considerably and a school of fish live here, but they are the last fish I see. The river shallows very quickly again and the fish are gone.

I'm totally alone. This is wilderness.

Now the river really meanders. Soft curves become zigzags and I must cover a lot of ground to gain such a short crow-fly distance. I find myself enmeshed in a maze of meanderings and marsh. The trees stand a long way off now but are still all around, and I'm floating in a plain of rice grass. Tall blades of dense pale yellow, the color of ripened wheat, surround me and the river branches infinitely through. I do not know which branch to take.

Advice from an old man in Wallace, Idaho: When you come to a fork in the road, always take the right road.

The route left looks just as good. The right might be the wrong. Maybe they all come out at the same place. Maybe this way is shorter than that. If I only had a helicopter. Or if I had a motorboat and could just plow through the rice fields. Or a pole instead of a paddle.

The sun is behind me and to my left, high in the sky. I'm okay for time, and the branch to the right seems to go the most north. I take it.

Ducks quack up around me, breaking the quiet. A hawk hovers overhead. The rifle shots of deer hunters echo way off in the distance. Other than that I am so totally alone and the day is so serene and noiseless, I can hear the whooshing of the wind through the tall grass. I feel like singing. Even if I take the wrong way and have to double back, I'm doing fine. The weather is fine, I've got my Nature Valley granola bars to eat, and a canteen filled with tasty spring water. As long as I don't get lost in this maze, I'm okay.

These three miles—by park ranger estimation—take forever. Later in the journey I will expect to do three miles in no time, but these three take so long that by the time I reach Wanagan Landing to stop for lunch, I'm actually considering staying here for the night.

Already my legs are stiff, my hands are sore and my back is tense and tired. I pull the canoe up and lie in the grass. I drink from my canteen.

In a moment, Robinovich arrives. She's been out admiring the area on her own, driving dozens of miles in the time it's taken me to make three. And she's laughing at how tired I am.

We get a small fire going and have a simple lunch. I get warm. Robinovich opens up the treats sent along to me by friends. Trail mix, peanuts, cashews, cookies, and a mountain of granola bars, which I never liked before but which by the time this trip ends will be among my favorite snacks.

Never before could I understand why bicycle racers are surrounded by cars carrying extra bikes, food, and drink. I always thought a racer should be out there doing his job, on his own, and if he has a breakdown he just pulls out. I look at Robinovich, my support team—preparing lunch, encouraging me, prodding me with her presence so I'd be too ashamed to quit—and I understand.

I'm back on my way and we've agreed to meet twelve miles further on at the campsite called Coffee Pot. The Minnesota Parks and Recreation Department has carved into the wilderness along this first sixty-mile stretch of river a series of landings and campsites. They are beautifully done and clean. Some have fire rings and pit toilets and water pumps, others picnic tables. Others are primitive. But they all blend in well with the green surroundings and don't intrude much.

Three miles took forever. Twelve more should take four times as long. But no! The next twelve will take much longer. But how can this be? I was rested. The sun was still high. I had just eaten. And the river straightened. On top of that I was gaining experience as a canoeist with every stroke. How could I not make the next twelve miles in a hurry?

I'm feeling really fine. The river deepens and the rice marsh lines only one bank. The other bank is woodsy for now.

Too quickly the marsh and the meanderings are back, but only for a short time. Still, the going is not swift. Soon the sun is slipping down beyond the pines. When the sun goes, the cold comes. And now I'm deeper in the woods where the air is naturally fresher and cooler. I put on my gloves and don a sweatshirt with a hood. Robinovich has my warm jacket. I was thinking she would need it more than I. After all, all this paddling so far has kept me warm. In the sun.

I come to a low wooden dam that threatens to force me out of the canoe. But I'm feeling expert. I can ride this. I do, but the riding is tricky and I get wet. The wet makes me colder. The beaver dams take time. Time takes away my light. There is another obstruction and I'm forced out of my canoe to portage around it. More time. More effort. More cold coming fast into the valley. Whose idea *was* this?

Rapids. They are loud and swift and the rocks are boulders and I'm scared. I may be expert, but I'm not *that* expert. But what choice have I? I've got to shoot them, and shoot them I do. A long series of rapids after rapids—probably because of the shallow water in autumn—and with each one I gain more and more confidence. After each one I shout with triumph and glee. But with each one I get wetter. And as the darkness descends, each one gets more difficult to see and thus trickier to negotiate.

One time the river spins me into a rock and I nearly fly from my seat. The rock spins me around sideways and soon I'm going swiftly downstream backwards. I can't turn around. The river narrows and the canoe won't fit. I'm stuck.

Another time I'm thrown into the side of the river. Low branches force me into the bank and I can't turn around. The water from the side is too fast and strong for me. I have to get out and push the boat around. My shoes get soaked and my feet get cold and my gloves get wet.

To dry the gloves I lay them on the struts. The next set of rapids tosses up the front end of the canoe. Only a keen sense of balance— no canoeing skill—keeps me from falling into the icy water.

I look. My gloves are gone.

The river has become an adversary. I see deer munching leaves on the shore. They know better than to do what I'm doing and they feel safe from me. How can I get at them even if I want to? They watch me and I feel stupid.

Finally it's dark. Then it's night. I'm freezing right through to the bone and my hands and feet are numb. I'm worried about frostbite. I'm worried about being lost. I'm worried about how to find Robinovich out there in the night. I don't know how far I've come or how far I've got to go. I'm scared. So I sing. I worry about running across more rapids. falling in, freezing to death.

That rushing sound, the sound of rapids, terrifies me each time I hear it. The river has begun to meander again and the bank has hidden deep behind the marsh that has popped up again. I can't get out of the river because I can't get out of the canoe. I don't know if I'll find solid ground or if I'll sink to my waist. I'm forced on.

The sound of rapids is the same sound of water falling over those huge beaver dams that threaten my progress. I hate the dams but I fear the rapids even more. The dams I can go around—when I can see them. The ones that completely cross the river I can plow over. The ones that are too thick I can approach and step out on and slide the canoe over. I'm hoping beavers don't bite.

Finally the moon rises and throws down its light. I breathe easier. I can see a bit. But it's still very dark and mostly what I must do is listen. Hearing, smelling: other senses take over when you can't see and right now (despite the moonlight) my eyesight is fairly useless. I rely on a sense I didn't even know I had and it somehow keeps me in the water, upright, away from the marsh and out of too much trouble. I carry on and I sing.

I'm wondering how long before the search party comes looking for me. Off in the distant night sky a signal flare shoots a bright arc and falls. Someone, I'm sure, is looking for me. Pretty soon a helicopter will thump through the air overhead and shine down an intense spotlight on the river. A voice in a loudspeaker will ask me if I'm all right and will light my path on the water. I'm sure of it.

But no. I'm still all alone and still miserable. My toes are dead numb and my fingers are swollen. They're locked around the paddle and cannot unbend. Frostbite.

Off in the distance, high on a hill, a light. I aim straight for it and tell myself when I get close, I'll get out and hike. It's a good mile straight up a hill, but at least I know there's a house. I can phone from there or get a ride to Coffee Pot. But dogs are howling up there on the hillside. I keep going.

Beaver dams. Each time I step from the canoe to go over them my feet get wetter. I'm just freezing. In my pocket I do have a box of waterproof matches. If I could find a place to pull out I could at least build a fire and dry off and warm up a little.

Up on a rise, not far from the river, a shed. Old and rickety, but made of wood. I can burn that thing if I need to, burn it to the ground for warmth, and yes I need to. My life or the life of this old shack.

But then I smell smoke. Someone else has built a fire. Hunters maybe, or Robinovich. I keep going.

A big mistake. I find no fire, no hunters, no Robinovich. My spirit is sinking fast. I sing to keep from losing it completely. Between songs I call out to Robinovich. No reply. Just my own voice echoing hollowly back to me from the walls of the night.

I can give up, get out right now and just die. It'll be easier.

I find every scrap of energy that's in me and push on. I can't see any better now and I don't need too much speed to make me crash into something or send me into the weeds. I pick my way carefully.

And then I see the light from a fire. I smell smoke. I see the lights from a car. I'm yelling my head off but no sound comes back to me. How far away am I?

Finally I arrive. Coffee Pot. The fire, a big smoky blaze, is ours. Robinovich has built it. She's gone, though, when I pull out from the river, gone to search for me. Not knowing where or how to search she quickly returns. The car lights I saw were hers.

I'm by the fire trying to warm myself when she comes back over the hill. She runs down the hill from her car and throws herself at me. We hold onto each other, but that's not warming enough. I'm back at the fire shedding wet clothes for dry ones.

I pitch the tent. I open cans. Robinovich gets the dinner going. Pork and beans from a can with bits of chopped up Polish sausage mixed in. A little sugar on top and slices of bread. Cups of tea and swigs of tequila.

It's glorious. I moan with delight and satisfaction. I spoon the beans and sausage into me. It's hot and delicious and thick and sticky. I'm slopping food all over. Beans drip down my chin and hang from my beard. It's messy but it feels so nice. I can't get enough. I'm going faster and faster until my legs tremble and I'm shaking all over and finally I drop exhausted and satisfied to my knees. Breathing hard I moan pain and pleasure at the same time. This is the most passionate meal I've ever had.

Until now my best meal ever had been *Lapin à Pantillaise*, a rabbit dish I had one night in Montreal in a restaurant owned by a Cuban who thought I was Haitian and so brought out his best. My eyes lit up like rockets in the night when I took the first bite, just as they did tonight. I thought that no other food would sting me through and through with good flavor the way that dish had done, but that meal has been surpassed by beans and weenies in the wilds of Minnesota. Never have I been so happy to be living.

8

In the night the mind voices what was only a creepy suspicion during the day. *What in the world am I doing out here?*

I'm a city fellow, urbane and civilized. I always use the correct fork. I keep my napkin in my lap. And like a good little boy who does what his mommy tells him, I chew my food fifty-six times before swallowing. My idea of travel and good fun is shooting craps in Las Vegas or playing roulette in the Grand Casino at Monte Carlo, fishing for marlin off Bimini, scuba diving the reefs of the Caribbean, hiking the Swiss Alps and skiing the Austrian, dining and wining in Paris, bicycling through Scotland. I see myself wearing tuxedoes and drinking champagne, not eating beans and weenies and wearing the same smelly clothes for weeks.

And I'm no expert in a canoe. That much is evident now. I think I'd been in a canoe maybe five times before. Floating the Black River a couple of times—mostly just an easy stream but I still managed to tip over and fall in. One time canoeing leisurely in the summer sun on the Thames not far from London. Once on a lake just drifting lazily with a fishing rod in hand but not even a nibble to worry about, only the weeds and the marsh and the water lilies snagging the canoe and forcing me to work. And once on the Severån, a lazy little river in the north of Sweden. Not exactly training for the proving ground of the Mississippi.

Nor was I any more experienced as a camper. Not an outdoorsman at all. Cleaning fish is not one of my favorite things. I don't like snakes, can't stand mosquitoes, and creatures that growl in the night scare me.

And yet . . .

I'm haunted by the ghost of Ernest Hemingway. All writers— American male—probably are. His style of writing, sure, but mostly his zesty style of living—big-game hunter, deep-sea fisher, hard drinker. Lover of man and women and good times and travel to exotic locales. A courter of danger.

It was a different world then, though. Everything wasn't taken so much for granted. A punch in the nose risked a return punch in the nose, a few moments' sweat and adrenaline, not a lawsuit. Air travel was an adventure. Getting there—anywhere—was as thrilling as being there. Skiing was not chic, the thing to do, but rather hard work down the mountain, harder work back up, an exhilaration, an exotic adventure. Your tales had zing in those days because everyone you knew hadn't already been to Europe. Living was an adventure. And Paris was really Paris.

It was a different world all right.

Now life is a media event. Well publicized, well signposted, the paths well worn and all the right things to do and places to go marked out. And absolutely everyone has a ticket to watch.

Is that what we've become? Mere spectators at a zoo? With real living removed from us and kept safely behind bars?

I hope to God I'm not out here because I miss the Good Old Days.

The River of Returning

John A. Murray

> That it will never come again
> Is what makes life so sweet.
> —Emily Dickinson

The river was green. Not just green, but bright green. Even with the eastern clouds turning red as the eggs of the sea-run salmon, you could see that. I asked Brian, the guide, about it and he said the Kenai was glacially fed.

"How fast is this thing running anyway?"

Brian strained on the oars, rowing the twelve-foot drift boat toward the middle of the river.

"Between five and six miles an hour."

The water was moving fast. No doubt about that. I had first noticed the current from the bank as we climbed over the gunwales. Now we were out on the flood of yesterday's rain, being swiftly pulled downstream. The speed was noticeable, even exhilarating. At this rate the boat could reach the north Pacific by evening. We were in the middle of the river before long, thanks to Brian's efforts, and I picked up the spin-cast rod and cast the hook with the imitation salmon egg into the nearest slow water. Three lead sinkers carried it to the bottom. The idea was to drift the morsel along the cobblestone, where everything in the universe was feeding on them. I got a bite right away, a two-pound Dolly Varden trout that flashed vibrantly like a piece of polished metal, and I quickly released it. I looked back and Brain was smiling. And why not? I was another happy client making a payment on his new four-thousand-dollar drift boat.

But the cheerful spirit was more than that.

It was a privilege to be out on one of the world's finest streams in September. To smell the wet-fish scent of the river and to watch the cold Alaskan sky coming to life. To have everyone back in the cities and the campgrounds empty and the restaurants and bars uncrowded, to enter a time machine, as it were, and visit the mountains of Colorado around Aspen or those of Montana around Livingston in the 1940s. Fifty years from now, when Anchorage is the size of Denver, and Denver is the size of Los Angeles, the Kenai will no doubt resemble the western Colorado of today. Fifty years after that, God help us. Most of what remains of America's Wild West will probably appear about as pristine as the chalet and pasture, condo and chairlift country of Grenoble, France.

Truly, we live in those long-ago times people will talk fondly of.

Brian rowed the boat from one slow stretch to the next, each one better than the last, and the Dolly Vardens were ravenous. I was glad we had started early, even if it meant no breakfast. The mature char was striking, with their emerald-green flanks and brilliant pink and orange spots. It was hard to believe the state once paid a bounty, per tail, simply because they scavenged a few salmon eggs.

Moose season was in progress and every now and then we heard a distant thump as the winter meat was either felled or sent off like a freight train through the birches.

A king salmon as heavy as a young wolf jumped beside the boat.

"Why do they jump like that, Brian?"

"Nobody knows."

I liked that. The mystery, I mean. The inexhaustible ability of nature to exhaust our capacity to understand it.

We floated around the shoulder of a mountain and a dozen sandhill cranes flew by, only a few hundred feet above the river, their wings beating loudly and their voices calling back and forth.

We watched until they could not be heard.

Brian said they were local birds that summered in the black spruce muskeg of nearby Kenai National Wildlife Refuge. The cranes had been grounded by the rainy weather and were only today moving again. They would follow the Pacific coastline south to Oregon and California.

Another group flew by, this time so low I could see the ashen gray feathers of the outstretched wings and the red caps on the heads and the short dark bills and the loose webbing between the toes at the end of the long slender legs. Their voices were as insistent as the creak of a rusty handle on an old-fashioned water pump.

On either side of the river the cottonwoods and alders still held their summer green. Only a few willows and alders had begun to change to gold and they stood out like prematurely grayed people at a ten-year high school reunion. Skinny white spruce, the trademark of the auroral country, were everywhere and I felt right at home among them, living as I do up north near the Arctic Circle. They are not much of a tree, but they are all we have around Fairbanks and so you grow to love them. The mist was lifting from the water now and the ancient weathered peaks on either side of the Kenai River were catching the first light. The autumn colors on the heights were fired from the early frost, the orange swales of dwarf birch, and the rust-colored bilbery patches on the tundra ridges; and even without the binoculars I could see the white dots that were Dall sheep moving in a line across the black shale below the first dusting of snow. Above it all was the sky, painted a blue like one of those Winslow Homer watercolors from the Bahamas, a blue which says the sea is near.

The boat drifted around a wide bend, past a cow moose and her calf drinking in a quiet backwater. They seemed to realize we were not hunters and that they were not legal game, and so they ignored us in the dignified way of wild animals.

Their eyes were the color of the forest, and they possessed the same calm.

On the fourth cast into the pool past the moose I caught my first rainbow trout of the day. Brian said they would go much larger. Coming originally from Colorado, the land of sixteen-inch stocked fish, I had never seen one as large. The rainbow is a native to southern Alaska, and so I carefully returned him, flashing silver and purple like something from a William Butler Yeats poem, to his element.

Brian was smiling. Always smiling. I liked that about him. He reminded me of myself in my early twenties, those idyllic days long ago (everything is idyllic in retrospect), working summers as a wrangler near Yellowstone and autumns as a hunting guide in the

Colorado Flattops. He had the mountains in him, and the rivers too, and so was doubly blessed.

We drifted on, and I lost count of the Dolly Vardens and Rainbows. I told Brian this and he chuckled, "There are worse things."

There was a narrow band of deep water near a bank thick with Devil's Club and bracken fern. The rainbows lived here, and the Dollies, and so we lingered in an eddy.

Brian rested with the oars under his armpits and, as I fished, told me his life story.

He lived across the river in a cabin he built himself. He had grown up here, in Cooper Landing, had gone to school with fourteen other kids. The sweet elderly lady I had talked to in the log house by the state road, the one with the hand-painted fishing sign out front, had been his schoolteacher. She was also his mother. His father had once owned a local moose- and caribou-outfitting business but sold it to work on an oil rig in Cook Inlet, a lucrative job the hard-working patriarch loathed. Both of Brian's brothers were state troopers and one was lucky enough to be a Game and Fish officer and flew his own Piper Supercub. I decided not to tell Brian about my friends up north who had been cremated on impact: about good-natured Joe Firmin from Fort Yukon, with whom I'd hunted caribou in the Arctic Refuge, who popped a control cable and crashed upside down into Mount Schwatka; or hardworking Lynn Castle from Denali Lodge, who dipped an alder on takeoff and cartwheeled into the Wood River; or my former student Billy Campbell, who lost manifold pressure on final approach to the Fairbanks airport and nose-dived into the mosquito bog at the end of the runway.

I asked Brian about winters and he said that in the snowy months he worked as an independent logger in the Chugach National Forest (a forest larger than New Hampshire) and also dove for sea urchins in Kachemak Bay near Homer. I asked him if he was married yet and he said his girlfriend had just left for the fall semester at U.N.L.V., and his voice tensed as he talked about that subject.

Up ahead were rapids and Brian told me to put the rod down and hold on.

"By the way, John," Brian said, "that life preserver is to find your body. Your arms and legs will freeze in thirty seconds."

"Thanks, man."

So much for the water survival course I barely passed in the Marines about twenty years ago.

Brian was proud of his boat and rowed us directly for the most massive wave, a standing monument of four or five feet, and we went right over the top, then down into the trough below, and up and over a couple of more waves. We were backwards now, and Brian rowed us around in the right direction. Brian yelped and pointed to an immature bald eagle with a dirty white hood, staring at us from the top of a dead cottonwood. The eagle never blinked in the time I watched him.

In the long stretch below the rapids, some more cranes passed overhead. They beat their wings a little more vigorously once they noticed the eagle.

We were around the bend before long and Brian rowed the boat toward a broad expanse of still water. As we came in, there were countless salmon of three different species in the clear shallows below. Some were as red as a really bad sunburn, and others were the silver of well-used half dollars. A few were dead, heavy with fungus, their fins rotted away. Most were alive, hovering in the twilight between life and death, struggling to keep themselves afloat. One was enormous, about four and a half feet long, and in his flat eyes was the knowledge of the grim joke. For this he had grown big, evaded the salmon sharks and Taiwanese drift nets, battled thirty-five miles up from the sea, attacked the other males so that he alone would orgasm with the female, all for the immortality of fertilized eggs the trout were eating for breakfast.

There were red-fox tracks on the bank, and brown-bear tracks, and the stray markings of seagulls. Salmon heads and well-scavenged fish vertebrae littered the sand.

Brian beached the boat and threw out the anchor. He asked if he could fish a special place upstream by himself, and I said sure. He gave me a pair of pliers to remove the hook, and told me to be certain to release all king salmon, which are protected during their spawning season.

"Watch their teeth, John. They are like barracudas. They are evil, nasty-tempered things. Especially the males. They are mad at the world. They can take your finger off like that."

He snapped his fingers.

Brian disappeared down a bear trail into the yellow alders, a magnum revolver on his cartridge belt, and I was alone with the beautiful green river. With the sun fully on it now, the brilliant green reminded me of the turtle-grass lagoons fringing the Yucatán coast north of Belize, those warm tropical waters and peaceful coconut groves where I spent a wild honeymoon with my first wife, Linda, in another lifetime.

I waded out into the river among the dead and dying salmon, the cold water pressing against the hip waders. I quickly caught and released two rainbows, and then I saw something jump out of the corner of my right eye and cast in that direction. The line immediately snagged on a sunken log. I was about to cut the line and retrieve some more leader and a new hook from the tackle box when the line started to move toward deep water, and I realized I had hooked some sort of fish. This was a size of fish unlike anything in my experience, and I felt the same stab of adrenaline I did as a six-year-old boy back in Ohio, when my father let me catch my first bluegill at Mr. Archibald's backyard pond. This was a Kenai River salmon that lived on everything smaller than it, from herring and crabs to Dollies and rainbows. Although his stomach had atrophied in freshwater, he still would snap at anything that irritated him. I tried to reel the salmon in but the reel turned in the other direction. The salmon was pulling me into the river, and I was staggering behind him. I was up to my thighs and the water would soon pour over the hip waders and so I planted my feet among the bottom rock and began the fight. It would not be good to tell my old college fishing friend Greg over the phone that the rod had been pulled from my hands. The salmon sounded in a pool and then the line went slack as he came clear of the water, thrashing his tail in the sun, the size of a freshwater marlin if there were such a thing, snapping his ugly jaws; and then he hit the water on his side with a resonant splash. It was a king salmon alright, a giant salmon borne of these ancient green waters, who had returned to spawn and die, and whose temper reflected his fate. He headed upstream for a fallen spruce and I kept pulling and reeling, pulling and reeling, sweating now under the three layers. After a while I had him close to the shore and my arms were tired from fighting him. He was ten feet from me now and I could see he would measure over four feet. His weight was anybody's guess. Brian said that a spawned-out king can weigh in the neighborhood of ninety pounds. I was wondering what I was going to do with him, how I could possibly get that hook out of his mouth without losing part of my hand, when he spit the hook out and disappeared over the flats toward the middle of the river and left me there, the muscles knotted in my arms and shoulders, my heart pounding.

Half an hour later Brian returned to tell me of the nice rainbow he had caught and released, and we pushed back into the river. It was good to be in the boat again, moving through new water.

There was another boat in the next stretch and the other guide rowed near to us.

"Having any luck?" the other guide called out, a paunchy man with the mottled face and swollen nose of a morning drinker.

"Just like in the brochure," said Brian with a smile.

"Ahh, everybody knows the brochures are full of shit."

The last word, in the surroundings, sounded about like the f-word would in a presidential state of the union address.

The two anglers in the other boat stared at me dejectedly. They wore blue and gold Lufthansa baseball hats and looked to be cargo pilots on layover from the international airport in Anchorage.

I waved hello and good-bye to the poor captives.

The river went under a bridge and I cast toward the bank and immediately caught a four- or five-pound Dolly with the enameled emerald body and Salvador Dali pink spots of a mature fish. I held him from the water for a moment.

"What do you think?"

"Naa. You'll catch a lunker yet."

I released the fish.

I'd seen a picture of Harry Gaines, the recently deceased Kenai River guide, on the cover of the 1993 Alaska fishing regulations, and asked Brian if he'd ever met him.

Brian said Harry visited his grade-school class once and told them funny stories about the various celebrities he had guided.

"Is that what you'd like to do, Brian, run your own guide service on the Kenai like Harry?"

"Not here. It takes twelve years to get a license. No, I'll start my business up north on the Gulkana. Salmon are smaller, of course, thirty to fifty pounds, but nobody has discovered it yet. It's like the Kenai was twenty years ago when Harry started."

It occurred to me that one day there would be no more new rivers in Alaska, even in the Russian Far East, that they would all be as well-known as the Kenai, and I counted my blessings that I lived before that dismal century. I suppose that John Smith in Massachusetts and Meriwether Lewis in Montana and Aldo Leopold in Mexico had all made that revelation, that they were seeing a world that would never be again.

A mile further on we approached a large forested island that split the river into sperate channels and Brian chose the left channel and beached the boat. He went downstream and I walked upstream to the head of the channel, where he said the salmon would be stacked like cordwood. On the fifth or sixth cast I caught a much larger Dolly than the one at the bridge, but lost him in seconds. It was my fault. I began to reel before I set the hook. I decided to cast in another area and then return to the place where I'd hooked the Dolly. While I let the egg drift I ate part of a chocolate bar, the first food all day. After a while I cast to the same spot, and the fish immediately hit the egg and I snapped the rod back and began to work on him. The Dolly was a heavy fish with a strong tail and put up a courageous fight, exploding from the depths and thrashing over the surface before making a run upstream and then a run downstream and then back again, trying to get behind or to the side of the hook and work it out. The rod was nearly doubled over, and each time I glimpsed the fish I grew more excited. I wanted to look downstream to see where Brian was, to see if he could get the net from the boat, but instead I concentrated on the fish, holding the rod at an angle, making certain he didn't free himself. I did not want to lose this fish a second time. When he was in the shallows I wished for a net. I had no choice and so I risked breaking the line and heaved him over my shoulder onto the shore and grabbed him there in the grass, a thirty-inch monster surging in my hands.

"Brian," I yelled, "I think I caught a big one."

I felt like I was ten years old again.

That's the whole point, isn't it?

We pushed off and Brian rowed us toward the center of the river. Once we were in the main stream, he anchored the oars under his feet and rubbed the back of his neck with his hand. His neck muscles were cramped from rowing the better part of seven miles and he tilted his head back to relax them.

"Hey, look at that."

He pointed upwards.

Far above a flock of cranes was forming up. They had circled on the rising heat of the earth. There were perhaps five or six hundred of them. As we watched, the leaders guided the others into an arrowhead-like formation. Every once in a while, the air stilled and we could hear them calling. Hundreds of voices, as from a distant county fair. After a while the flock angled south, toward the bright blue of the sea.

ℐOTES ON ℭONTRIBUTORS

John James Audubon • John James Audubon was almost sixty years old when he made his final wilderness trip in 1843, in a fur-company boat bound for the Missouri headwaters. Born in the Caribbean and educated in France, Audubon had taken up drawing and painting at an early age and eventually completed over one thousand life-size paintings of native American birds (published in four volumes during his lifetime). In his *Missouri River Journals*, he describes the Far West as it was two generations after the historic expedition of Lewis and Clark. Much had changed along the river since 1806—the Mandan Indians were by 1843 extinct—but much more change was destined to come, especially in the years following the Civil War.

William Bartram • William Bartram, the son of famed colonial botanist John Bartram, was born and raised in Philadelphia, where his father had established one of the first public gardens in the American colonies. At the urging of his father, William Bartram undertook a series of historic natural-history surveys of eastern America, including the legendary walkabout that covered most of the southeast and which is memorialized in his book *Travels* (1791). It was *Travels* that so influenced the English romantic writers, particularly Samuel T. Coleridge in the composition of his lyric poem "Xanadu."

Rick Bass • Over the past decade Rick Bass has quietly established himself as one of America's major prose writers. His many books include works of fiction (*The Watch*, 1989) and of non-fiction (*Wild to the Heart*, 1987; *Ninemile Wolves*, 1992; *The Book of Yaak*, 1997). Bass makes his home in northwestern Montana with his wife, Elizabeth, who is an artist, and their two daughters. For years he has worked tirelessly to bring wilderness protection to parts of the Yaak River valley where he lives. In 1997 Bass was awarded a Guggenheim Fellowship.

Joseph Conrad • Joseph Conrad was one of the most accomplished British novelists of the early twentieth century. His books include *Lord Jim*, *An Outcast of the Islands*, and *Almayer's Folly*. Prior to his career as a novelist, Conrad (who was born in Poland), worked for over twenty years as a sailor on the high seas, advancing in rank to first mate. *Heart of Darkness* is based on a trip he made to the Belgian Congo in the late 1890s, after Africa had been partitioned by the European powers and the colonial age was at its peak (or nadir, depending on one's point of view). The Congo River, then and now, led into the heart of a region that is both a literal wilderness and a metaphor for all that is unknown in human nature and wild nature.

Lisa Couturier • Lisa Couturier holds an M.A. degree from New York University. Her essays and articles have been widely published in national journals and periodicals. She is at work on a book about urban nature. She lives in New York City with her husband and daughter.

Annie Dillard • has been one of America's most distinguished authors for over two decades. Her first book of prose, *Pilgrim at Tinker Creek*, was awarded the Pulitzer Prize. Later works have included poetry, literary criticism, personal essays, a memoir, and most recently a novel entitled *The Living*.

Roderick Haig-Brown • Roderick Haig-Brown was born in England but lived most of his life in British Columbia. His books include such classics as *Fisherman's Summer*, *Fisherman's Fall*, *Fisherman's Winter* and *Fisherman's Spring*. Haig-Brown was also a judge of the Provincial Court of British Columbia and chancellor of the University of Victoria. He died in 1976.

Eddy Harris • A 1977 graduate of Stanford University, Eddy Harris has traveled throughout Europe and Central America as a journalist. His books include the best-selling *Still Life in Harlem* and *Mississippi Solo*.

Ernest Hemingway • Ernest Hemingway was born in Oak Park, Illinois, in 1899, the son of a prominent local physician and his wife, who was active in the arts. After distinguished service in World War I (he earned the Italian version of the congressional medal of honor), Hemingway settled in Paris with his first wife, Hadley, and began writing short stories. His first novel, *The Sun Also Rises*, was published in 1925 and the rest, as they say, is history. His unique minimalist writing style revolutionized literature, and authors as diverse as Solzhenitsyn, Kawabata, and Camus, later acknowledged his influence. One of his great loves was fishing, and Hemingway often paid tribute to his favorite rivers in his essays, articles, stories, and novels.

John Hildebrand • John Hildebrand owns the distinction of having been one of the few people who have floated completely down the Yukon River, from its origins in northwestern Canada to the delta on the Bering Sea. Hildebrand accomplished this feat while a graduate student in creative writing at the University of Alaska, Fairbanks, in the 1980s. He now teaches English literature and writing at the University of Wisconsin, Eau Claire. His books include *Reading the River*, which chronicles his trip down the Yukon River.

Dean Krakel • Dean Krakel worked for many years as editor-in-chief of the *Pinedale Roundup*, the weekly newspaper of Pinedale, Wyoming, and has since worked as a photographer and writer for *The Denver Post*. His articles and photographs have been published in *National Geographic*, *Audubon*, *National Wildlife*, and other publications. His works include *Season of the Elk*, a photo/essay book on the elk of the Jackson Hole region, and *Downriver*, which chronicles his long float down the Yellowstone River in Montana.

Meriwether Lewis • After serving as private secretary to President Jefferson from 1801 to 1803, Meriwether Lewis was appointed to lead an expedition into the area recently acquired through the Louisiana Purchase. He chose his good friend and former commanding officer William Clark to be his co-captain. The two men, over a two-year period, followed the Missouri to its source, crossed the Continental Divide, descended the Columbia River to the Pacific Ocean, and returned with a voluminous report on the geology, fauna, flora, and Indian tribes of the region. Lewis later served as governor of the Louisiana Territory from 1807 to 1809.

Barry Lopez • Barry Lopez grew up in southern California and New York City and later graduated from the University of Notre Dame in Indiana. He has authored such influential works as *Of Wolves and Men*, *Arctic Dreams* (winner of the National Book Award), *Winter Notes*, *Desert Notes*, and *River Notes*. He lives with his wife, Sandra, an artist, in a home along the McKenzie River in the Cascade Mountains of Oregon. The selection on his trip down the Colorado River is taken from his 1985 collection of essays, *Crossing Open Ground*.

Harry Middleton • The untimely death of Harry Middleton in 1993 was a profound loss to contemporary nature writing. In his short life he authored such memorable books as *On the Spine of Time*, *The Earth Is Enough*, *The Starlight Creek Angling Society*, and *Rivers of Memory*. His articles appeared in such publications as *Sports Illustrated*, *Country Journal*, *Sports Afield*, *Fly Fisherman* and *Reader's Digest*. No one has ever written more lyrically or beautifully of rivers or of river fishing.

Kathleen Dean Moore • Kathleen Dean Moore is the chair of the philosophy department at Oregon State University. Her essays and articles have appeared in *North American Review*, *The New York Times*, *Willow Springs*, and *Northwest Review*. In 1995 she published her first collection of essays, *Riverwalking: Reflections on Moving Water*, which tell of her favorite rivers in the American West.

John Wesley Powell • The life of Powell is one of the most fascinating in American biography. Born in New York in 1834, Powell later lost an arm during the battle of Shiloh, Tennessee, in 1862, served as an aide to General Grant, and left military service in 1865 to take a professorship in geology in Illinois. Following the completion of the Union-Pacific railroad in 1869, Powell journeyed west and began his historic explorations of the inter-mountain region, including his descent of the Green and Colorado Rivers. His book, *Explorations of the Colorado River and its Tributaries* is now one of the classics of exploration literature.

Theodore Roosevelt • Born an invalid in an old-line plutocratic New York family in 1858, Roosevelt dedicated himself early on to a disciplined program of physical and mental improvement. After graduating from Harvard in 1878, he became active in politics, studied law for a time, and lived in the Far West following the death of his first wife in 1884. No president has been closer to nature—toward the end of his life he wrote that he wished he had devoted himself to natural science. Roosevelt's many nature books include *African Game Trails, Ranch Life and the Hunting Trail*, and *Through the Brazilian Wilderness*. From the Little Missouri River in the Dakota Territory to the Mara River in British East Africa, Roosevelt knew and loved rivers as perhaps no other president has.

Henry David Thoreau • Henry David Thoreau is generally credited with having created the nature essay as a modern literary form. Born in Concord, Massachusetts, in 1819, he later graduated from Harvard and worked as a village schoolmaster and as a country surveyor. His friends and associates included such luminaries as Ralph Waldo Emerson and Nathaniel Hawthorne. Thoreau published two books in his short lifetime: *A Week on the Concord and Merrimack Rivers* (1849) and *Walden* (1954). His most influential piece of writing was a short essay entitled "Civil Disobedience," which inspired a variety of twentieth-century philosopher-activists, including Mahatma Gandhi, Martin Luther King, Jr., and Nelson Mandela, in their search for political justice.

Mark Twain • Samuel Langhorne Clemens, popularly known as Mark Twain, was born in 1835 and died in 1910. Those seventy-five years spanned a time of unprecedented change in American culture, and Twain's many books provide a detailed and often hilarious history of a nation lurching through its frequently turbulent adolescence. His books include *The Adventures of Tom Sawyer, Huckleberry Finn, The Prince and the Pauper, A Connecticut Yankee at King Arthur's Court*, and *Joan of Arc*. From

1857 through 1861 Twain worked as a river pilot on the Mississippi River, a period later recalled in his popular 1883 book *Life on the Mississippi*.

Louise Wagenknecht • Louise Wagenknecht was born and raised in Idaho, where she has worked as a seasonal firefighter for the National Forest Service and the Bureau of Land Management for twenty years. She and her husband maintain a small sheep ranch in Idaho. She has a bachelor's degree in English literature and writes periodically on topics of interest—such as firefighting, logging, and country life—for *High Country News*. She is working on a book about the environmental and economic upheavals that have transformed the Pacific Northwest in her lifetime. Her essays were published several times in the Sierra Club's *American Nature Writing* series during the mid-1990s.

Ann Haymond Zwinger • Ann Haymond Zwinger, who lives in Colorado Springs, Colorado, with her husband, Herman, a retired air force colonel, is the author of a dozen major works of natural history, including *The Aspen Grove*; *Run, River, Run* (about the Green River); *Wind in the Rocks*; and *Land Above the Trees*. Her work *Downcanyon*, from which the selection was taken for this anthology, focuses on the unique geology and biology of the Grand Canyon in northern Arizona. Zwinger is also an accomplished artist and often illustrates her books with her own pen and ink drawings. Her daughter Susan Zwinger is also very familiar to readers as a gifted nature writer and artist.

CKNOWLEDGMENTS

Rick Bass: "This Savage Land," from *The Book of Yaak*. Copyright 1997 by Rick Bass. Reprinted with permission of the author.

Lisa Couturier: "Reversing the Tides." Copyright 1997 by Lisa Couturier. Reprinted with permission of the author.

Annie Dillard: "Flood," from *Pilgrim at Tinker Creek*. Copyright 1974 by Annie Dillard. Reprinted with permission of the author.

Roderick Haig-Brown: "The Sachem River," from *A River Never Sleeps*. Copyright 1926 by Roderick Haig-Brown. Reprinted with permission of the Lyons Press.

Eddy Harris: Selection from *Mississippi Solo*. Copyright 1988 by Eddy Harris. Reprinted with permission of the Lyons Press.

John Hildebrand: "Along the Delta," from *Reading the River*. Copyright 1988 by John Hildebrand. Reprinted with permission of the author.

Dean Krakel: "Downriver," from *Downriver, a Yellowstone Journey*. Copyright 1987 by Dean Krakel. Reprinted with permission of Sierra Club Books.

Barry Lopez: "Gone Back into the Earth," from *Crossing Open Ground*. Copyright 1987 by Barry Lopez. Reprinted with permission of the author.

Harry Middleton: "Midnight Rivers," from *Rivers of Memory*. Copyright 1993 by Harry Middleton. Reprinted with permission of Pruett Publishing.

Kathleen Dean Moore: "The Willamette," from *Riverwalking*. Copyright 1995 by Kathleen Dean Moore. Reprinted with permission of the Lyons Press.

Louise Wagenknecht: "And the Salmon Sing." Copyright 1998 by Louise Wagenknecht. Reprinted with permission of the author.

Ann Haymond Zwinger: "Tanner Trail and Mesquite Thickets," from *Downcanyon: A Naturalist Explores the Colorado River through the Grand Canyon*. Copyright 1996 by Ann Haymond Zwinger. Reprinted with permission of the author.

Flow gently, sweet Afton, among thy green braes,
Flow gently, I'll sing thee a song in thy praise;
My Mary's asleep by the murmuring stream,
Flow gently, sweet Afton, disturb not her dream.

Thou stock-dove whose echo resounds through the glen,
Ye wild whistling blackbirds in yon thorny den,
Thou green-crested lapwing, thy screaming forbear,
I charge you disturb not my slumbering fair.

How lofty, sweet Afton, thy neighboring hills,
Far marked with the courses of clear winding rills;
There daily I wander as noon rises high,
My flocks and my Mary's sweet cot in my eye.

How pleasant thy banks and green valleys below,
Where wild in the woodlands the primroses blow;
There oft as mild evening weeps over the lea,
Thy sweet-scented birch shades my Mary and me.

Thy crystal stream, Afton, how lovely it glides,
And winds by the cot where my Mary resides;
How wanton thy waters her snowy feet lave,
As gathering sweet flowerets she stems thy clear wave.

Flow gently, sweet Afton, among thy green braes,
Flow gently, sweet river, the theme of my lays;
My Mary's asleep by the murmuring stream,
Flow gently, sweet Afton, disturb not her dream.

—Robert Burns, "Afton Water"

About The Nature Conservancy and The Freshwater Initiative

Founded in 1951, The Nature Conservancy is a private organization widely recognized as one of the most successful in the field of conservation. Its mission is to preserve plants, animals, and natural communities that represent the diversity of life on Earth, by protecting the lands and waters they need to survive. The Conservancy's staff of twenty-two hundred, a national volunteer force of more than twenty thousand, and a membership of more than nine hundred thousand have together protected more than 10 million acres in the United States and Canada and helped like-minded partner organizations protect millions more in Latin America and the Pacific.

Historically, the Conservancy has focused on land conservation and currently owns and maintains the largest private system of nature sanctuaries in the world. But recognizing that one cannot preserve both the terrestrial and aquatic life of a place without protecting the waters that run through it, the Conservancy developed The Freshwater Initiative as a blueprint for advancing freshwater conservation in the United States, Latin America, and the Caribbean.

The Freshwater Initiative targets dozens of biologically rich and threatened rivers and freshwater systems. This science-based initiative will identify critical watersheds, establish demonstration projects, and promote community-based conservation. The Conservancy will work at thirteen freshwater priority "demonstration sites" over the next five years to achieve measurable biological improvement, and will also take important steps to conserve twenty-five additional sites.

Demonstration Sites:

Altamaha River, Georgia
Apalachicola River, Florida
Big Darby Creek, Ohio
French Creek, New York
Green River, Kentucky
Illinois River, Illinois
Mackinaw River, Illinois

Maya Mountain Marine Transect,
  Belize
Neversink River, New York
Upper Klamath Basin, Oregon
Roanoke River, North Carolina
Silver Creek, Idaho
Truckee River, Nevada

Additional Sites:

Acopian Ecosystem, Pennsylvania
Blue River, Indiana
Bocas del Polochic, Guatemala
Cache River/Bayou DeView,
  Arkansas
Clinch River, Tennessee and
  Virginia
Conasauga River, Georgia and
  Tennessee
Condor Bioreserve, Ecuador
Cuatro Cienegas, Mexico
Fish Creek, Indiana
Gila River, New Mexico
La Encrucijada, Mexico
Madre de las Aguas,
  Dominican Republic

Mattaponi/Pamunkey Rivers,
  Virginia
Mt. Bethel Fens, Pennsylvania
Paint Rock River, Alabama
Pantanal, Brazil
Platte River, Nebraska
Poultney River, Vermont
Upper Mimbres River, New Mexico
Sacramento/San Joaquin Bay Delta,
  California
Sandia Springs, Texas
San Luis Valley, Colorado
San Pedro River, Arizona
Santa Margarita River, California
Upper Colorado River Basin,
  Colorado

For information about the Conservancy and its work, contact:

The Nature Conservancy
International Headquarters
1815 North Lynn Street
Arlington, VA 22209
(800) 628-6860
www.tnc.org